Praise for *A Homemade Life*

"Wizenberg's delightful first book will undoubtedly be gobbled up like a tin of Christmas cookies. Sometimes touching, sometimes humorous, often both, this collection of essays is as much about growing up and family as it is about food. The tantalizing recipes interspersed throughout cover all bases."

—Courtney Greene, *Library Journal*

"Wizenberg's book is one of the most enjoyable food memoirs I have ever read. Self-deprecating, intelligent, wise and witty . . . Wizenberg never bores with overt sentimentality or verges into sappy food territory. . . . Her personality is so endearing and the writing is so clever that you'll savour every page. . . . Good stuff."

—Lesley Chesterman, *The Gazette* (Montreal)

"You will sit down to read it and you will fall under a spell. Her stories will take you deeper into her world—trips to Paris, first love found and lost, a family of food-lovers, holidays and summer evenings around a table, unspeakable loss, and unexpected love coming from a surprising quarter. The stories will sweep you away, as Molly's writing is wont to. . . . The English artist William Morris once said, 'Have nothing in your houses that you do not know to be useful, or believe to be beautiful.' Molly's book, I can honestly say, is both. I know I'll be savoring my copy for years to come."

—Tara Austen Weaver, author of *The Butcher and the Vegetarian*

"The arrival of review copies of cookbooks always gives me a little thrill, but ripping open a thick envelope to find *A Homemade Life* was like opening a long-anticipated birthday present. . . . In the tradition of some of our very best food writers, Ms. Wizenberg's subject is life; food is part medium, part metaphor. She tackles some extraordinarily challenging subjects. . . . Reading a great memoir can make you feel like you know someone, but cooking through Ms. Wizenberg's recipes allows a particular kind of access that is especially fulfilling."

— China Millman, *Pittsburgh Post-Gazette*

"In *A Homemade Life: Stories and Recipes from My Kitchen Table*, every story tells a recipe."

— Christine Muhlke, *The New York Times Book Review*

"With flair and great enthusiasm, Wizenberg tells the story of her life in terms of the foods she's relished over the years. Especially vivid and gently affecting is her detailed recollection of her father's death from cancer."

—Mark Knoblauch, *Booklist*

"Molly Wizenberg offers us a book filled with personal, beautifully written essays that, like an excellent box of chocolate truffles, can be enjoyed individually, or, as is my preference, all in one evening. And the recipes aren't just a literary coda—they're truly delicious."

—David Leite, publisher of leitesculinaria.com and author of *The New Portuguese Table*

Also by Molly Wizenberg

Delancey

A HOMEMADE LIFE

stories and recipes from my kitchen table

MOLLY WIZENBERG

illustrations by Camilla Engman

SIMON & SCHUSTER PAPERBACKS ■ NEW YORK LONDON TORONTO SYDNEY

Simon & Schuster Paperbacks
A Divison of Simon & Schuster
1230 Avenue of the Americas
New York, NY 10020

First Simon & Schuster trade paperback edition March 2010

SIMON & SCHUSTER PAPERBACKS and colophon are registered trademarks
of Simon & Schuster, Inc.

For information about special discounts for bulk purchases,
please contact Simon & Schuster Special Sales at
1-800-456-6798 or business@simonandschuster.com.

Portions of this book have been adapted from the author's blog *Orangette*.

The recipe for Pickled Grapes with Cinnamon and Black Pepper was first published in the
Kitchen Window column at NPR's Web site, www.npr.org.

Designed by Jaime Putorti

Manufactured in the United States of America

10   9

Library of Congress Cataloging-in-Publication Data

Wizenberg, Molly.
A homemade life / by Molly Wizenberg.
    p. cm.
    1. Wizenberg, Molly. 2. Women food writers—United States—Biography. 3. Cookery.
I. Title.
    TX649.W588 A3 2009
    641.5092B—dc22   2008036430

ISBN 978-1-4165-5105-8
ISBN 978-1-4165-5106-5 (pbk)
ISBN 978-1-4165-9445-1 (ebook)

ACKNOWLEDGMENTS

Whenever this book gave me trouble, I worked instead on the acknowledgments. It was the easiest part to write. Without the following people, this book would be a shadow of itself—or nothing at all. I owe them an enormous, sung-from-the-rooftops *Thank You*.

To Gigi Lamm, for cheering from the beginning.

To my former colleagues at the University of Washington Press, for encouraging me to write.

To Ashley and Chris Saleeba, for being willing eaters, recipe testers, and good neighbors.

To Luisa Weiss, for inspiring me with her effortless prose.

To Hannah Huffman, for sending me vanilla beans, hand-sewn potholders, and constant inspiration, and for testing recipes.

To Maria A. Vettese, or "mav," for showing me that everyday life is art.

To Bill Farrell, for being my A+ #1 recipe tester, even though we have never met.

To Aria Baker, whom I have also never met, but who had the incredible kindness to offer her skills as a recipe tester; she is a gem.

To Rachael Mann, for her help in testing recipes.

To Kirsten Anderson and her family, for cheerfully eating everything I sent.

To David Lebovitz, for making very fine ice cream.

To Austin Walters, who doesn't complain when I talk for hours, and who offered priceless feedback on the manuscript in its early stages.

To Tara Austen Weaver, for her wise counsel and many delicious dinners.

To Anne Buchanan, whose sharp eye and fine palate made her a valuable tester.

To Amy Leo, for being my first "blog friend," and for cheers, squeals, and recipe testing.

To Andrea Akita, a fantastic cook and recipe tester.

To Matthew Amster-Burton, for his keen ear and dry humor.

To Laurie Amster-Burton, for her thoughtful comments.

To Carla Leonardi, for her belief in me, and for her abundant skills at cooking and photography.

To Elizabeth Reeds and Doron Beeri, for the summer of 2004.

To Rebecca Leone and Jimmy Chorley, for Sunday breakfasts and so much love.

To Lucas Oswalt, for having a huge heart.

To Jessica and Mataio Gillis and Doug Doolittle of Ciaò Thyme Catering, genius cooks and lovely human beings.

To Susan Kaplan and Renee Erickson of Boat Street Café and Kitchen, for pickles and precious encouragement.

To Keaton Hubbert, for a decade of friendship, quiet grace, and good food.

To Kate Knight, for countless nights at the table, planning cocktail parties and our entire lives.

To the late Dr. Stephen M. Gens, my high school history teacher and friend, who made me work harder than anyone else, who gave me my first C, and whom I miss terribly.

To Michael Davilman, one of my father's dearest friends, an effortless cook and a brilliant mind, for believing in me from day one.

To Ben Smith and Bonnie Whiting-Smith, for many happy evenings of beer, steak, and ice cream.

To Olaiya Land, a gifted cook and invaluable recipe tester, for friendship and cauliflower.

To Chris Oakes and Martine Curtis-Oakes, for suggesting that I start Orangette in the first place.

To Camilla Engman, artist, illustrator, and all-around sensation, who took my words and brought them to life.

To Michael Bourret, my agent, for his smarts, his patience, and his tireless support.

To Stacey Glick, who introduced me to Michael.

To Sydny Miner, my editor, for her belief in this project, her trust, her confidence, and her uncanny understanding of my voice.

To Shauna James Ahern, for being a friend and mentor, sister and champion, in every single step of this process.

To Sam T. Schick, also known as Our Man Sam, for friendship, fierce intelligence, and all those summer nights around our little white table.

To Arnold Weisenberg, my uncle, for being so generous with his recipe collection.

To Lisa Chalif, my sister, for her companionship in the kitchen, her fine-tuned palate, and love.

To my family members and friends not named here, every one of whom helped to see me through.

To the readers of Orangette, for cheering and believing.

To Burg, for reading to me from *When the Sky Is Like Lace*, for believing in the magic of words and poems, and for everything he was, down to the last second.

To Mom, the strongest woman I know, my guide in this life.

To Brandon, the man who whistles wherever he goes, my first reader, my husband, my love. He is my partner, in every sense of the word. He was with me all the way.

FOR MORRIS J. WIZENBERG,
ALSO KNOWN AS BURG

We know we are shining, / Though we cannot see one another.
–JAMES WRIGHT

CONTENTS

Acknowledgments   v

Introduction   1

How to Use the Recipes in This Book   7

A Place to Start   11

The Baker in the Family   17

In Need of Calming   23

The Whole Messy Decade   29

An Uncalculating Science   35

Better with Chocolate   41

The Dark Horse   47

A Brood of Seven   51

La Boule Miche   59

A Strange Sort of Coming of Age   65

The Hardball Stage   71

A Personal Chronology in Christmas Cookies   77

The Right Answer to Everything   85

Quite that Magnificent   91

What France Would Taste Like   97

The Best of All Possible Worlds   103

High Points   111

Heaven   119

9:00 A.M. Sunday   127

Italian Grotto Eggs   135

The Mottling   141

Whatever You Love, You Are   153

Summer of Change   161

Pretty Perfect   171

Promise to Share   177

With Cream on Top   183

Happiness   189

Baby Steps   195

Like Wildflowers   207

Delicious in Its Way   213

Rough Going   219

Bonus Points   223

Herbivores Only   229

Special Game   235

The Diamonds   241

Sugarhouse   249

The Change Thing   253

Bonne Femme   259

So Much Better   267

A Big Deal   275

Freeze Frame   281

Pickling Plant   287

So Easy   293

I Have Learned Not to Worry   299

Winning Hearts and Minds   309

Recipe Index   315

INTRODUCTION

I t started when I was a freshman in high school. We'd be sitting at the kitchen table, the three of us, eating dinner, when my father would lift his head from his plate and say it: "You know, we eat better at home than most people do in restaurants." Sometimes, for good measure, he'd slap the table and let loose a long *ooooh* of contentment. It didn't seem to matter what we were eating. It could have been some sliced tomatoes, or a bowl of mashed potatoes, or some fish that he'd fried in a pat of butter. At least every couple of weeks, he said it. To me, it sounded like tacky bragging, the kind of proud exaggeration that fathers specialize in. It's the suburban man's equivalent of ripping open his shirt and beating his chest with his fists. I would shrink into my chair, blushing hotly, the moment it crossed the threshold of his lips. I was mortified by the weird pleasure he took in our family meal. After a while, I could even sense it coming. I'd mouth the words before he could say them: *You know, we eat better at home than most people do in restaurants!*

But now I'm old enough to admit that he was right. It's not that we knew how to cook especially well, or that we always ate food that was particularly good. There were hot dogs sometimes, and cans of baked beans. Our garlic came in a jar, minced and ready, and our butter was known to go rancid. What was so satisfying, I think, was something else. It was the steady rhythm of meeting in the kitchen every night, sitting down at the table, and sharing a meal. Dinner didn't come through a swinging door, balanced on the arm of an anonymous waiter: it was something that we made together. We built our family that way—in the kitchen, seven nights a week. We built a life for ourselves, together around that table. And although I couldn't admit it then, my father was showing me, in his pleasure and in his pride, how to live it: wholly, hungrily, loudly.

When I walk into my kitchen today, I am not alone. Whether we know it or not, none of us is. We bring fathers and mothers and kitchen tables, and every meal we have ever eaten. Food is never just food. It's also a way of getting at something else: who we are, who we have been, and who we want to be. When my father sat down at the dinner table, he saw more than what was on his plate. He saw his childhood as the son of two Polish immigrants; his youth in a working-class neighborhood in 1930s Toronto; his immigration to the U.S. after medical school; his troubled first marriage; his first three children; the beautiful woman in a brown faux-fur mini-dress who danced with him at a Christmas party; their move to Oklahoma; his successful private practice; his big house in the suburbs; and me, his fourth child, born when he was just shy of fifty. No wonder he was proud. He made a good life for himself. He might as well have won the lottery, for all his glee over those tomatoes or potatoes or fried fish.

When I walk into my kitchen today, I bring all of this with me.

Like most people who love to cook, I like the tangible things. I like the way the knife claps when it meets the cutting board. I like the haze of sweet air that hovers over a hot cake as it sits, cooling, on the counter. I like the way a strip of orange peel looks on an empty plate. But what I like even more are the intangible things: the familiar voices that fall out of the folds of an old cookbook, or the scenes that replay like a film reel across my kitchen wall. When we fall in love with a certain dish, I think that's what we're often responding to: that something else behind the fork or the spoon, the familiar story that food tells.

I grew up in the kitchen. When I was a baby, my mother would put me on a blanket on the kitchen floor, where I would bang around with pots and pans and spoons. I crashed my first dinner party at the age of three, and I still remember it—mainly because my grand entrance consisted of falling, half asleep and holding a unicorn hand puppet, into a family friend's swimming pool. When I was old enough to reach the kitchen counter, my mother let me make what I called "mixtures": weird, what-would-this-taste-like concoctions made from such winning combinations as Diet Coke and cake flour, or sugar, garlic salt, and food coloring. As a kid, I loved to play the card game Old Maid, but I didn't call it by that name: I called it Homemade, a word that made much more sense to me. Everything interesting, everything good, seemed to happen when food was around.

My family believes in cooking. It's what we do, where we put our money and our free time. I may have grown up in landlocked Oklahoma, but I ate my first lobster at age six, when my father came home from an East Coast business trip with a cooler full of them. He upended it on the kitchen floor, spilling them onto the linoleum like giant spiders, and while they clattered around on their spindly legs, I stood on a chair and screamed. Then, of course, I had a taste of their sweet meat. That shut me right up.

This is my family. My sister Lisa keeps a plot in a community garden, where she grows her own asparagus, lettuce, and snap peas. She also makes a near-perfect scone and, for a while, wanted to open a chocolate shop. My brother Adam can whip up a terrific impromptu tomato sauce and, with only the slightest prompting, will tell you where to find the finest gelato from Italy to the Eastern Seaboard. My brother David has a degree from the Culinary Institute of America and owns a handful of restaurants in Washington, D.C. He can also roast a mean piece of beef. A recent Christmas in our clan consisted of forty-eight hours in the kitchen, a twenty-five-pound turkey, five quarts of soup, four dozen scones, three gallons of boozed-up eggnog, two dozen biscuits, and a bushel of spinach, creamed.

I learned to cook because it was a given. But I didn't learn in any sweet, at-the-apron-strings way. Neither of my grandmothers ever stood me on a chair and showed me how to make biscuits or beef stew. To tell you the truth, I hardly remember my grandmothers' cooking. My father's mother, Dora, used to send us Jewish holiday cookies from her kitchen in Toronto, but she packed them in a cardboard shoebox, so by the time they arrived, they were only crumbs.

I learned to cook because the kitchen was where things happened. No one told me to, but I hung around, and I was comfortable there. I learned how to handle a knife. I learned how to cook a string bean by eye, until its color turned bright green. It was no big deal. I hardly even thought about it. By a sort of osmosis, I picked up a sense of comfort in the kitchen, and a hunger that lasted long past breakfast, lunch, and dinner.

For a long time, I thought that this meant that I should be a chef. Interests came and interests went, but at the end of the day, I always wound up at the stove. It was the only place I really wanted to be. It seemed only natural, then, to try to make something of it. *I can cook,* I thought, *and I like to cook, so maybe I should* be *a cook.* I should try working in a restaurant kitchen, I decided.

So one summer, the summer after my sophomore year of college, a friend set me up with an internship at a well-known vegetarian restaurant in San Francisco. I was a vegetarian at the time; it was one of those interests that came and went. I was assigned to the pantry station, prepping salads and plating desserts. I got to eat a lot of day-old ginger cake, which was pretty fun, and with the exception of the time the chef handed me an onion and asked me breezily, as though it were as obvious as brushing my teeth, to slice it "as fine as an angel's eyelash," it went all right. But I didn't love it. I wasn't even sure I liked it. I never saw the faces of the people who ate what I had prepared. I never saw anything but my corner of the counter, actually. I didn't like the discontinuity between the kitchen and the dining room, between the procedure of cooking and the pleasure of eating.

I didn't last long. I didn't leave college for cooking school. I got a degree in human biology and another in French, and then another in anthropology. If I had stayed my course, I'd probably be standing in front of a class somewhere, talking about the concept of *solidarité* and social security in France. But then, you wouldn't be reading this.

All along, something kept calling me back to the table. Every time I opened my mouth, a story about food came out. In July of 2004, I decided that I had to listen. I left my PhD program with a master's degree instead. In an effort to make something of my madness, I started a blog called *Orangette,* a space where I could store all my recipes and the long-winded tales that spun from them. I named it for one of my favorite chocolate confections—a strip of candied orange peel dipped in dark chocolate—and started to fill it with my favorite people, places, and meals.

I wanted a space to write about food. That's all, really. But what I got was something much better. I got an excuse for long afternoons at the stove, and for tearing through bags of flour and sugar faster than should be allowed by state law. I got a place to tell my stories and a crowd of people who, much to my surprise, seemed eager to listen and share. What started as a lonely endeavor came to feel like a conversation: a place where like-minded people could swap recipes and dinner plans, a kind of trading post where cakes and chickpeas are perfectly valid currency. I'm not the only one, I learned, who believes that the kitchen, and the food that comes from it, is where everything begins. What started as a simple love for food grew to have a life of its own— and a life that, in turn, has changed mine.

———

Now, of course, all this is not to say that my kitchen is full of sunshine and puppies and sweet-smelling flowers that never wilt. When I cook, there's often a lot of cursing. I've made soups that tasted like absolutely nothing, as though the flavors had miraculously united to form a perfect zero sum. I once charred a pork loin so thoroughly that it looked like a tree stump after a forest fire. I have eaten my fair share of peanut butter and jelly and two-dollar beans and rice from the taqueria down the street. But I still believe in paying attention to those meals, no matter how fast or frustrating. I believe in what they can show me about the place where I live, about the people around me, and about who I want to be. That, to me, is the "meat" of food. That's what feeds me—why I cook and why I write.

That's why this book is called *A Homemade Life*. Because, in a sense, that's what we're building—you, me, all of us who like to stir and whisk—in the kitchen and at the table. In the simple acts of cooking and eating, we are creating and continuing the stories that are our lives.

HOW TO USE THE RECIPES IN THIS BOOK

I don't like being told what to do. In fact, when I see this page in a cookbook, I usually skip right over it. Of course, as a result, I've messed up quite a number of recipes.

So before we get this show on the road, as my mother says, I'd like to give you a few pointers. That way, you can make the recipes in this book without a hitch, right from start. *Oh, the irony,* I know.

■ Before you so much as lift a finger toward the stove or oven, read through the entire recipe, ingredients *and* instructions. That way, you'll know exactly what lies ahead of you.

■ Buy an oven thermometer. You can get one at any grocery store, and it'll be the best five bucks you've ever spent. Most ovens do not run true to the temperature on the dial, but with an oven thermometer inside, it doesn't matter. You can just peek in, see what the temperature reads, and adjust the dial as needed. My oven, for instance, always runs about 10 degrees too cool. When I want it at 350°F, I've learned, I have to set it for 360°F instead. (I could also, I suppose, have the oven guy come out and calibrate it, but even then, I would still keep the thermometer around.)

■ Buy a kitchen scale. Many common ingredients—chocolate, for one—cannot be measured reliably by volume. A cup of chopped chocolate is not the same around the world: we all chop our chocolate to different sizes, so no cupful is identical. But one pound of chocolate is always one pound of chocolate, no matter how you chop it. So in most cases, when I call for chocolate, I call for a quantity by weight. (Except where chocolate chips are concerned; those are pretty well standardized.)

■ When I measure flour, I use the spoon-and-level method. Short of switching over entirely to weight measurements, that's what I recommend. Whenever I open a sack of flour, I stir well with a spoon to aerate it, then I spoon it lightly into my measuring cup until it heaps above the rim. Then I sweep the straight edge of a knife across the top to level it, letting the excess flour fall back into the bag.

■ Last but not least, clean up as you go. My father taught me that, and I thank him for it almost every day. When you're cooking, if you have time—any time at all—to stop and wash a few dishes or wipe the counter, do it. It'll mean less mess in the end, which means more time to enjoy your food, your company, your day, all of it.

A PLACE TO START

I had meant to start with something more glamorous than potato salad. I always thought it would be good to begin with hors d'œuvres, something appetizing and sexy, or maybe dessert, to cut right to the chase. A bowl of chunked potatoes in creamy dressing isn't any of those things. But when you grow up under the wing of someone who felt as strongly about potato salad as my father did, your priorities are special.

Plus, you can tell a lot about someone by their potato salad. I like to think of it as the Rorschach test of foods. Potato salad means many things to many people. For some, it means mostly mayonnaise and starch; for others, it means oil and vinegar and fresh herbs. Some people add eggs; others swear by pickles. For Burg, as we called my father—a nickname my mother made up, a shortened version (and inexplicable misspelling) of our last name—it was something in between. Like his potato salad, he was hard to pin down.

I guess the first thing to point out about his recipe is the presence of Ranch dressing. I'm not sure how to make much sense of it, since Burg was, in all other cases, against bottled salad dressing. He was a staunch advocate for homemade—the house vinaigrette maker, in fact, with a dedicated jar and a complex system for creating his signature slurry of oil, vinegar, mustard, and herbs. But he was also full of contradictions.

He was a doctor who never went to the doctor, a Republican on fiscal issues and a Democrat on social ones. He had a fat belly and pencil legs. He was, by the calendar, an old man, but he had an almost full head of black hair. He was a Francophile with terrible French. He liked foie gras on the one hand and Ranch dressing on the other. And I can't really blame him. It tastes good.

Then, of course, there were the caraway seeds. His recipe calls for one to two teaspoons' worth. He liked them in almost everything. Whenever he bought sandwich bread, it was Jewish rye, flecked with those tiny, canoe-shaped seeds. He was the son of Polish Jews, so they were in his blood, I imagine, along with bagels and beet soup. But much to his mother's chagrin, that was about as Jewish as he got. He married two *shiksas* (one a Catholic, even) and raised nonreligious children. I remember once, as a kid during the Gulf War, hearing one of my father's cousins in Toronto say something about Tel Aviv, worrying that it might come under missile attack. I'd never heard of Tel Aviv. I thought she had mispronounced "TV," and that our television was some sort of military target. I would hear scarcely more about Israel until I was in high school and took a world history class, and it would take my going away to college to learn what Passover was, when I read parts of the Bible in a Western civilization course. I've always known, however, what a caraway seed was.

Then there's mayonnaise. My father did not mess around when it came to mayonnaise. His potato salad called for 1¾ pounds of baby red potatoes and, to bind them, a ballsy ¾ cup of mayonnaise (mixed, of course, with Ranch dressing). If my math is correct, that works out to approximately one tablespoon of mayonnaise per small potato. You can't be timid when you're dealing with ratios like that. You have to be the type to go after life with your arms open and your teeth bared. That's the type Burg was.

He could be pouty, of course, and a real huffer-and-puffer. His favorite weapon was the silent treatment, and he wielded it with impressive skill. But he had more love, and more passion, and more enthusiasm for pretty much everything than you and me combined. He loved being a doctor. He loved Dixieland jazz. He loved the old Alfa Romeo Spider that sat in the driveway and never ran. He loved crossword puzzles, Dylan Thomas, and Gene Krupa banging on a drum kit on the stereo upstairs. He loved omelets and olives; murder mysteries and short stories; and a hideously ugly ceramic wild boar that sat on his bathroom counter. He loved his children, even while he forgot our birthdays; loved a cold beer on Saturday at noon; loved lamb shanks, smelly cheese, and my mother in high heels; loved mayonnaise, and me.

He was the kind of person who could teach you a lot of important things, such as how to ride a bicycle or drive a stick shift, or that dill and potatoes were made for each other. He always put dill in his potato salad. We had a kitchen garden out back that he and my mother planted, thick with tomatoes and herbs. He would rub rosemary under the skin of roasting chickens and stir thyme into his corn chowder. He got such a kick out of that garden. He taught me to make pesto from the basil we grew there, using a recipe by James Beard, who I'm sure, would have gotten a kick out of it, too.

When your father dies, especially if he is older, people like to say things such as, "He was so lucky. He lived a long, full life." It's hard to know what to say to that. What often comes to mind is, "Yes, you're right. He was seventy-three, so I guess it was his time. But did you know him? Did you see how he was? He bought wine futures seven months before he died. He saw patients the afternoon he was diagnosed. He *wasn't finished*."

My father woke up each morning wanting that day. You could see it on his face. He was the one at the end of the table, laughing so hard that his round face split open like an overripe watermelon and his fillings shone darkly like seeds. He laughed so hard that he gagged a little and pulled out his handkerchief to wipe his mouth. He knew what he had, and he loved it.

He could have taught me a lot of things. We'd hardly begun. But I have his recipe for potato salad, and when all else fails, it's a place to start.

I am biased, no doubt, but I love this potato salad. The key is to prepare it the day before you want to eat it. It needs to sit overnight in the refrigerator, so that the flavors can mix and mingle, so to speak.

Also, you'll note that I've made the caraway seeds optional. Not everyone loves caraway seeds as much as Burg did, and I'm sure he wouldn't mind if you left them out. (I usually do.)

FOR THE SALAD

1¾ pounds red waxy potatoes, scrubbed
4 large eggs
8 scallions (white and pale green parts only), thinly sliced
¼ teaspoon salt, plus more to taste

FOR THE DRESSING

¾ cup mayonnaise, preferably Hellmann's/Best Foods or homemade
4 tablespoons bottled Ranch dressing, preferably Hidden Valley
2 tablespoons finely chopped fresh dill
1 to 2 teaspoons caraway seeds (optional)

Put the potatoes in a Dutch oven or large saucepan and add cold water to cover by 1 inch. Add a generous dash of salt, and bring to a boil over medium-high heat. Reduce the heat to maintain a gentle simmer and cook, uncovered, until the potatoes are tender when pierced with a small, thin knife, about 15 minutes. Drain them into a colander, rinse with cold water, and set them aside to cool. (If you're in a hurry, put them in the refrigerator to speed the process along. You want the potatoes to be completely cool when you dress them.) When the potatoes are cool, cut them into rough 1-inch chunks. For the smaller potatoes, I halve them; for the bigger ones, I cut them into quarters or eighths. Put them in a large bowl.

Meanwhile, cook the eggs. Place them in a small saucepan, and add cold water to cover. Bring to a boil over medium-high heat. When the water begins to boil, remove the pan from the heat, cover it, and let it sit for exactly 12 minutes. Immediately pour off the hot water and run plenty of cold water over the eggs. When the eggs are cool, peel them, chop them coarsely, and add them to the bowl of potatoes. Add the scallions, sprinkle with ¼ teaspoon salt, and toss to mix.

In a small bowl, stir together the mayonnaise, Ranch dressing, dill, and caraway seeds, if using. Pour the dressing over the potato mixture, and stir to evenly coat. Taste, and adjust the salt as needed. Cover and refrigerate overnight before serving.

Yield: about 6 servings

THE BAKER IN THE FAMILY

While we're in the business of getting started, I'd like you to meet my mother, too. I think you'll like her. It's hard not to.

For one thing, she's quite petite; barely over five feet tall. "Five feet and three-quarter inches," actually, is what she would tell you. When someone hugs her, she almost disappears, swallowed up in arms and fabric. Like those impossibly tiny lamps and teacups you find in doll-houses, she inspires a lot of cooing, and though she's very assertive, people often want to pat her on the head. Luckily, she has a special trick for times like these, when a little height would come in handy: she can trot around in a pair of high heels as though they were bedroom slippers. Legend has it that she wore them straight through her pregnancy with me, with nary a swollen ankle to be seen. She may be eligible for the senior discount at the movie theater, but she's very much a fox. She also, incidentally, makes a fine pound cake, and between you and me, that's the clincher.

My mother is the baker in the family. It's always been that way. She can make all manner of things, but in most cases, my father was the savory cook and my mother, the sweet. He was the mad scientist, the Benjamin Franklin type, flying his kite in the proverbial lightning storm, while my mother is more of the pastry chef ilk: methodical and precise, with measuring cups and measuring spoons and much less mess. She loves recipes, and she executes them exactly. That's a trait she passed down to me, along with a load of others for which I am very grateful. It's from my mother that I learned how to plan a menu, how to throw a dinner party, how to keep a check register, and how to spit cherry pits from the window of a moving car. She also taught me that, when in San Francisco and in need of a bathroom, all you have to do is walk commandingly into the stately Campton Place Hotel, as though you had legitimate business there, and cut through the lobby to the bathroom on the left. That's a skill that has come in handy more often than you might think.

We weren't the type of family to have dessert every night, but when the occasion demanded it, my mother shook out her apron and got to work. She made Katharine Hepburn's famous brownies for my school bake sale and, for my birthday, a pink layer cake from a Junior League cookbook, slathered with raspberry frosting. For dinner parties, she made apple crisp with walnuts and brown sugar or nectarine cobbler with blueberries. I've never had her chocolate cheesecake, but I've heard about it: namely, that she once, on a whim, set it atop the scale, and it weighed in at a terrifying five pounds. That's why I've never had it. She rarely made it again.

My mother's annual holiday baking bonanza was, until it petered out a few years ago, the highlight of the season for a sizable fraction of Oklahoma City. The Saturday before Christmas, she and I would load up the backseat with cookie tins, each lined with red or green cellophane and filled with sweets, and we'd drive around town, delivering them to the doorsteps of family friends. It's the closest I ever came to having a paper route.

Then, of course, there was her blueberry-raspberry pound cake, a perennial classic. It lay dormant for the bulk of each year but awoke without fail in July to accompany us to picnics and barbecues. It's scented with kirsch and shot through with berries, and it is *delicious*. To me, it's what summer tastes like. My mother found the recipe in a magazine article about food processors, and it's been in her repertoire ever since.

Most years, the cake made its seasonal debut at one of the outdoor jazz concerts at the Oklahoma City Museum of Art. This was back when my mother used to volunteer there, and when the museum was housed in the old Buttram Mansion. In the summers, the museum would host jazz concerts on its back lawn on Saturday nights, on the wide strip of grass that ran down to the rectangular reflecting pool and a marble statue of the Three Graces. Admission was free, and the better part of the neighborhood would come, toting blankets and picnic baskets. My parents had a wicker picnic basket that opened at the top like a present, and they'd fill it with cold roasted chicken, Burg's potato salad, and blanched green beans with vinaigrette, along with some sort of dessert, which, at least a couple of times each summer, was my mother's pound cake. While it was still light outside, we would unfold the blanket and eat dinner, and then, before dessert, I would be allowed to run around the grounds until dark. I usually got to invite a friend along, and we would torment the toads in the grass near the reflecting pool or, when I was brave enough, climb trees. (I hate splinters.) Once, during the summer after first grade, my friend Jessica and I invited our mutual crush Lucas to come to a concert with us, and she tortured me by saying that she planned to take him up into one of the trees and kiss him. Much to my relief, she didn't, and anyway, we all drifted out of touch not long after. But fifteen years later, when we were twenty-two, I ran into Lucas while shopping with my mother in a grocery store in Tulsa and spent the next three years as his girlfriend. I am very proud of that, especially because I didn't have to get any splinters to make it happen.

I know there are a million recipes out there for pound cake, and probably berry versions, too, but as you can see, I consider this one to be very important. It accompanied me through some crucial times. It's also delicious, and it's my mother's, and more than any of that, it has the lightest, most delicate crumb I've ever seen on a pound cake. In fact, I'm tempted to call it a butter cake instead, because the word *pound* is too heavy for what is actually going on here. It's rich, yes, but not too much so, and its crumb is fine and tender. The batter is very smooth, and folded gently around fragile berries and scented with fruity liqueur, it bakes up into the kind of cake that you can't help but want to eat outdoors. Preferably on a picnic blanket, with your mother.

i love this cake as is, of course, but because I happen to live near a thicket of blackberry bushes, I've discovered that they are also lovely here, in place of the usual blueberries and raspberries. For that variation, I recommend omitting the kirsch (it's a bit too fruity for the dark flavor of blackberries) and instead adding 1 teaspoon each of grated orange and lemon zest with the flour.

2 cups plus 8 tablespoons cake flour	*2½ sticks (10 ounces) unsalted butter,*
1 teaspoon baking powder	*diced, at room temperature*
½ teaspoon salt	*2 tablespoons kirsch*
5 large eggs	*1 cup blueberries, rinsed and dried well*
1⅔ cups sugar	*1 cup raspberries, rinsed and dried well*

Set an oven rack to the middle position, and preheat the oven to 300°F. Butter a standard-sized 9-cup Bundt pan and dust it with flour, shaking out any excess. (If your pan is nonstick, you can get away with a simple coating of cooking spray, no flour needed.)

In a medium bowl, whisk together 2 cups plus 6 tablespoons flour, the baking powder, and salt.

In the bowl of a food processor, blend the eggs and sugar until thick and pale yellow, about 1 minute. Add the butter and kirsch, and blend until the mixture is fluffy, about 1 minute, stopping once to scrape down the sides of the bowl. If the mixture looks curdled, don't worry. Add the dry ingredients and process to just combine. Do not overmix. The batter should be thick and very smooth.

In a large bowl, toss the berries with the remaining 2 tablespoons flour. Pour the batter over the berries, and, using a rubber spatula, gently fold to combine, taking care that all the flour is absorbed. Pour the batter into the prepared pan, spreading it evenly across the top. Bake until a toothpick inserted in the cake's center comes out clean, 1 hour to 1¼ hours.

Transfer the cake to a rack, and cool in the pan for 5 minutes. Carefully invert the cake out of the pan onto the rack, and cool for at least 20 minutes before slicing. Serve slightly warm or at room temperature.

NOTE: Sealed in plastic wrap and stored at room temperature, this cake will keep nicely for 2 or 3 days. And it also freezes well. Once, when my parents went to visit a friend in Aspen, my mother baked one of these cakes the week before, froze it, and then packed it in her suitcase. It defrosted en route, and they ate half for dessert that night. Then, the next morning, their friend warmed leftover slices on the grill for breakfast. My mother highly recommends that.

Yield: 10 to 12 servings

IN NEED OF CALMING

I was not an easy child. I guess you could say that I was fearful, but that alone doesn't adequately capture it. I was born with my hands over my ears, and I don't mean that metaphorically. Any sort of loud noise—thunder, vacuum cleaners, backfire from cars—made me cry as though on cue. But it wasn't only noise. I was also morbidly afraid of blood, needles, and people with any type of visible injury. Also, my head was enormous. I wound up in tears every time my mother tried to wedge it through a turtleneck. I was not a fun, happy-go-lucky kid, the kind who sticks her hand in the birthday cake and smears frosting all over her smocked dress. My parents, as you can imagine, were quite disappointed by this. On my first birthday, my mother carefully set the whole scene: me in my high chair, enormous cake on the tray in front of me, camera poised and ready. But I wouldn't touch the frosting, not even with a fingertip. And, on top of all that, I also hated bananas. Kids are supposed to *love* bananas. When all else fails, that, at least, is supposed to be easy.

My parents did their best. To ease her mind, my mother once consulted a psychic. The psychic said that I was a "new soul," that this was my first time on earth, so quite naturally I was fearful. This didn't explain the turtleneck problem, but still, it was something.

But new soul, old soul, if the me of twenty-five years ago could see what's in my freezer right now, she would scream. Lurking within its icy depths are no fewer than six ripe bananas, hard and frosty-skinned, lying in wait like small, shriveled snakes. It's like a stockpile of tropical fruit terror. And what's more, I *love* it. Growing up really is great.

I'm not exactly sure of the chain of events that led to my conversion, but I do know that it started with a banana nut bread made by Linda Paschal, the mother of my childhood friend Jennifer. The Paschals lived in the house diagonally behind ours, and our families became friendly when Jennifer and I, then five and three, heard each other playing in our respective backyards. Not long after, our fathers built a gate through the fence, and we spent the next several years running back and forth from one house to the other, playing with my plastic toy ponies, staging elaborate lip-synch performances to Juice Newton's "Angel of the Morning," and eating, as it would happen, her mother's banana bread. Such is Linda's talent with quick breads that not even I could resist. Her banana bread was a model of the species: moist, tender, and spotted with walnuts. It was soulful and persuasive, familiar and softly scented, like the nape of a baby's neck. I have thought of it often in the years since, wondering if it shouldn't be produced *en masse*, sold in drugstores, and fed to anyone in need of calming.

Of course, it would take many doses of Linda's bread before I was solidly on board with bananas, and even today, I am no great fan of eating them plain. But I find it very easy to tuck away baked goods made from them. Sometimes I buy bunches of bananas just to bring them home and let them go brown. There's something profoundly reassuring about having a bunch at the ready, ripe and speckled and on the verge of stink. It's like hoarding gold bullion, only this type of gold needs to be kept in the freezer or else it will start to rot. I love to bake with bananas. They make baked goods miraculously moist, with a sort of sweet, wholesome perfume that, I sometimes imagine, Betty Crocker herself might have worn.

If I didn't watch myself, I would probably dump mashed bananas into anything that held still long enough to let me. I cannot have too much banana cake with chocolate ganache spread over the top, or too many banana-scented bran muffins. But my standby banana vehicle is the one that started me down the road in the first place: the tried-and-true, the humble loaf called banana bread.

I love the classic banana-nut combination, just like Linda Paschal used to make. But I also like my banana bread with more exotic additions, like shredded coconut or dark rum, and my all-time favorite is a plucky variation involving chocolate and crystallized ginger. It's a formula I stumbled upon a few years ago, with the help of my friend Kate.

One Saturday morning, when Kate met up with her usual running buddy Glenn, he handed her a present. It was heavy and rectangular and wrapped in foil, and when she tore into it, she found a loaf of homemade banana bread flecked with chocolate chips and chewy ginger. Had I been Kate, I probably would have hidden it away and hoarded it, but lucky for us all, she is a better person. That night, she invited me to dinner, and after big bowls of mussels and a baguette, she whipped a carton of cream and served me a thick slice of the cakelike bread with a dollop on top. And then, bless her heart, she didn't even bat an eyelash when I ate three slices. In fact, she nearly matched me at two and a half and may have outdone me in cream consumption.

These days, I bake banana bread all the time, and I usually do it as Glenn did, with chocolate and ginger. It's homey but a little sophisticated, and it's almost impossible to stop eating. The flavors of banana and chocolate get along so well, and ginger makes them even better, cutting through their richness with its spicy heat. It's the kind of thing that begs to be cut into big, melty slices while the loaf is still hot.

I am still not sure how I feel about turtlenecks and thunder, but I'm willing to bet that, with enough banana bread, I could find a way to warm to them, too.

BANANA BREAD WITH CHOCOLATE
AND CRYSTALLIZED GINGER

*t*his recipe is my take on Glenn's. If you don't have any chocolate chips lying around, try chopping up a bar of chocolate instead. I like the look of the irregular chunks and shards that result.

6 tablespoons (3 ounces) unsalted butter	1/3 cup finely chopped crystallized ginger
2 cups unbleached all-purpose flour	2 large eggs
3/4 cup sugar	1 1/2 cups mashed banana (from about 3 large ripe bananas)
3/4 teaspoon baking soda	
1/2 teaspoon salt	1/4 cup well-stirred whole-milk plain yogurt (not low fat or nonfat)
3/4 cup semisweet chocolate chips	1 teaspoon vanilla extract

Set a rack in the center of the oven, and preheat the oven to 350°F. Grease a standard-sized (about 9 by 5 inches) loaf pan with cooking spray or butter.

In a small bowl, microwave the butter until just melted. (Take care to do this on medium power and in short bursts; if the heat is too high, butter will sometimes splatter or explode. Or, alternatively, put the butter in a heatproof bowl and melt in the preheated oven.) Set aside to cool slightly.

In a large bowl, whisk together the flour, sugar, baking soda, and salt. Add the chocolate chips and crystallized ginger and whisk well to combine. Set aside.

In a medium bowl, lightly beat the eggs with a fork. Add the mashed banana, yogurt, melted butter, and vanilla and stir to mix well. (The same fork works fine for this.) Pour the banana mixture into the dry ingredients, and stir gently with a rubber spatula, scraping down the sides as needed, until just combined. Do not overmix. The batter will be thick and somewhat lumpy, but there should be no unincorporated flour. Scrape the batter into the prepared pan, and smooth the top.

Bake until the loaf is a deep shade of golden brown and a toothpick inserted into the center comes out clean, 50 minutes to 1 hour. If the loaf seems to be browning too quickly, tent with aluminum foil.

Cool the loaf in the pan on a wire rack for 5 minutes. Then tip it out onto the rack, and let it cool completely before slicing—unless you absolutely can't help yourself, in which case, dig in.

NOTE: Fully cooled, this bread freezes beautifully. And it tastes delicious cold, straight from the freezer. To protect it from frost, wrap it in plastic wrap and then again in aluminum foil.

Yield: about 8 servings

THE WHOLE MESSY DECADE

I was born in 1978. That means that I lived a good portion of my formative years in the presence of mullets, crimped hair, and shoulder pads, hallmarks of that rollicking decade now known plainly as the eighties. I'm not sure it's good to admit that I was in any way present for such an era, but I'm willing to go out on a limb.

Anyway, it's hard not to feel nostalgic about the eighties. If you think about it, mullets really *were* a smart, well-meaning invention. Anyone with long hair can tell you that it gets in your face sometimes. Mullets handily took care of this by cropping the front short while leaving the back alone. With a mullet, you got the best of both worlds: long hair without having to choke on it. I don't expect to convince anyone of the truth of this anytime soon, but I am content to try.

My mother did the eighties very well. She could work a pair of shoulder pads like no one else. You should have seen her in the periwinkle dress she wore to my sister Lisa's wedding, the one with the shoulder pads, the open back, and the enormous bow. She looked stunning—a little like royalty, really, like Princess Diana with braided brown hair and a better-looking husband. She was the fashion beacon of Oklahoma City. Our town may not have been Milan or Paris, but if you doubt me, you probably never met my mother.

Like many other beacons of generations past, my mother dove head-first into the trends of her time. Luckily, I do not mean cocaine, or hair crimping, or MTV. In my mother's case, I mean aerobics, with its perky wardrobe of pastel tights and leotards with matching belts, leg warmers, and terrycloth sweatbands. For a large part of my early childhood, my second home was a place called The Workout, an aerobics studio in a strip shopping center about ten blocks from our house. My mother would suit up, pack me a bag of books and other diversions, and off we'd go for entire afternoons. Today, people often ask about the origins of my ability to remember 1980s dance songs, and I tell them that I owe it all to The Workout, to the thud of Reeboks reverberating off the studio mirrors.

My mother was a natural at aerobics. She quickly came to be friendly with the instructors and even considered teaching her own classes. For my part, though I was only four or five, I used my time at The Workout to do some serious thinking about my life. I decided that I wanted to be someone else. Namely, I wanted to be Sherry. She was one of the aerobics instructors. She had a soft voice and leotards in all sorts of bright colors, and her shiny brown hair was something out of a VO5 Hot Oil ad. First, I reasoned, I would have to change my name. Then we would have to spend lots of time together, so that I could learn to be just like her. This could be difficult, I knew, but I had a plan. It happened that around the same time, I had been informed—probably on the playground at preschool, although I can't really remember—that in order to get a driver's license, I would someday have to pass a test requiring me to take a car apart and put it back together. It sounded like an insurmountable task. Clearly, I would never get a driver's license. Instead, I privately decided, I would get Sherry to drive me everywhere. Then we would be together always, forever.

But I did not change my name, and Sherry never drove me anywhere. My mother, however, was invited by the instructors to appear on local television, which struck me as a nice consolation prize. She, along with a team of other Spandex-clad women, did an aerobics demonstration on the morning television show hosted by brothers Butch and Ben McCain. We were both very excited. She later went on to become a personal fitness trainer and is now a Pilates instructor.

But my mother's glory in the 1980s wasn't limited to fashion or exercise fads. She was also very skilled in the realm of white chocolate.

I'm sure you remember white chocolate, that sweet, melty substance made from cocoa butter, milk solids, and sugar. It was first popularized in the mid-eighties, when Nestlé released its Alpine White bar, and it went on to take the country by storm. For a while, it was everywhere, stuffed into brownies and cheesecakes and squiggled on top of biscotti. It even showed up in chip form, invading cookies across the land with its comrade-in-arms, the macadamia nut. White chocolate *was* the eighties, right up there with blackened redfish.

Of course, in the intervening years, white chocolate has fallen out of favor. In some circles, I understand, it ranks up there with mullets among the most vilified relics of the era. But I would like to argue in its favor. I would like to argue that white chocolate made the whole messy decade worthwhile, if only because of one dessert. It is called a white chocolate *cœur à la crème*, a creamy mousse of sorts spooned into a heart-shaped mold and served with a berry sauce, and it appeared on my personal horizon in February of 1987, when *Bon Appétit* ran a recipe for it. My mother, a regular subscriber, had the good sense to clip the recipe, and I had the good fortune of eating it on many occasions.

Cœur à la crème is a delicious, delicious thing. For a good part of my childhood, it was my favorite dessert. It was made mainly from cream cheese and heavy cream, with a smooth texture that sat somewhere between cheesecake and mousse. It was also very pretty: a velvety, ivory-colored heart whose surface was quilted daintily from the cheesecloth that lined its mold, with a deep red puddle of puréed raspberries on the side. It was beautiful in a precious, bed-and-breakfast kind of way, but it went down like a New York cheesecake, in lusty, sauce-slinging gulps.

My mother made it mainly for dinner parties, but once, when I was in the fourth grade, I begged her to let me bring it to a special lunch with my French class. My teacher, a frail, black-haired Frenchwoman named Madame Boutin, had been teaching us basic food vocabulary— *baguette* and *fromage*, *pomme* and *poire*, *poulet* and *viande*—and now we were to celebrate with a small, brown-bag feast. When I came to class with my mother's *cœur à la crème,* she *ooooooooh*ed approvingly.

"*Magnifique,*" she breathed. It most certainly was.

It's sad, really, that with the end of the 1980s, white chocolate went the way of crimping irons and Boy George. Because *cœur à la crème* is really something. That's why, on the eve of a barbecue last summer, I decided to trot it out for an encore. It's cool and unfussy—a little like ice cream, but better—and perfect for a warm, sticky night. We stood at the kitchen counter and ate it straight from the serving platter, eight of us with eager spoons, talking with our mouths full. I highly recommend it, even the straight-from-the-platter part.

CŒUR À LA CRÈME WITH RASPBERRY PURÉE

*T*hough this dessert is traditionally served in the shape of a heart, I can't, in good conscience, ask you to run out and buy a special mold for this one recipe. I can't even make *myself* go out and buy one. I don't believe in kitchen equipment that serves only one purpose, even if that purpose is creamy and delicious.

Instead, I use a small colander, the kind you might keep around for rinsing cherry tomatoes or a handful of herbs. Mine has a capacity of 1½ quarts, and it makes for a small, handsome dome. If your colander is larger, that's fine, too; your dome will just be wider and flatter. This dome-shaped version—*dôme à la crème,* as I call it—isn't quite as glamorous as the traditional *cœur,* but it tastes just as good.

Last, use the best white chocolate you can find. I like Valrhona.

FOR THE CŒUR/DÔME
3 ounces white chocolate, finely chopped
One 8-ounce package cream cheese
* (not low fat), at room temperature*
1¼ cups heavy cream
¾ cup powdered sugar, sifted

FOR THE PURÉE
One 10-ounce bag frozen
* unsweetened raspberries, thawed*
3 tablespoons sugar

First, prepare the mold or colander (see headnote). Cut two sheets of cheesecloth large enough to line its interior and extend beyond its edges enough to enclose the filling completely. Wet the sheets of cheesecloth under the tap, wring them out well, and line them up together, so that they form a double layer. Lay the cheesecloth atop the mold or colander, pressing it smooth along the base and walls and letting the overhang fall over the sides. Set aside.

In a microwavable bowl, microwave the white chocolate on high for 20 seconds at a time, stirring well after each go, until just smooth. Set aside to cool slightly.

Combine the cream cheese, ¼ cup of the cream, and the powdered sugar in a medium bowl. Using an electric mixer set to medium speed, beat until light and fluffy, scraping down the sides of the bowl with a rubber spatula as needed. Add the white chocolate, and beat until very smooth, about 2 minutes. Set aside.

In another medium bowl, beat the remaining 1 cup cream to stiff peaks. Gently fold the cream into the cream cheese mixture. Spoon the finished batter into the prepared mold, smoothing the top with a spatula. Fold the cheesecloth over to enclose it completely. Place the mold on a rimmed sheet pan or another rimmed dish. Refrigerate for at least 8 hours or overnight.

Meanwhile, prepare the raspberry purée. In a blender or food processor, combine the thawed raspberries with their juice and the sugar. Blend until smooth. Press the purée through a sieve into a small bowl to remove the seeds. Cover and chill for up to 4 hours.

When you're ready to serve, remove the mold from the refrigerator, and discard the liquid, if any, that has collected beneath it. Pull back the cheesecloth, and carefully invert onto a serving platter. Gently pull away and discard the cheesecloth. Serve in generous dollops in shallow bowls, topped with a spoonful of raspberry sauce.

Yield: 6 to 8 servings

AN UNCALCULATING SCIENCE

Every night, when he came home from work, my father went to the kitchen. First, to set the mood, he'd take off his suit jacket and pour himself a Scotch. Then he'd while away a few minutes at the counter, his belly pressed against the drawer pulls, leafing through the day's mail. Then, fully readied, he'd open the refrigerator and, easing into action, begin the final stage of the day, dinner. That was where he relaxed: in the kitchen, in the space between the refrigerator and the stove. Sometimes he would scour the cookbook shelf, looking for ideas, but mainly he would move by feel and by taste—stewing, sautéing, melding this and that, and much to my consternation, hardly ever keeping note of what he'd done. I can only think of a handful of recipes that he ever wrote down in their entirety, his potato salad being one of them. (I'm pretty sure he knew it was his best shot at immortality.) His experiments were many, and most of them were fruitful, but his was an uncalculating science. His cooking was personal, improvised, and maddeningly ephemeral.

Burg was never a late sleeper. Most weekend mornings, he would get up early to cruise the garage sales in his khakis and topsiders. He had a good eye for secondhand shopping, and with few exceptions (like the kitchen scale that zeroed at 700 grams and still sits, unused, in my closet) he usually did us proud. Over the years, he brought home old leather suitcases embossed with loopy initials, oil paintings in gilt frames, coffee grinders, and silver candy dishes. He even found a few vintage lapel pins shaped like ladybugs or flowers or delicate little spiders, which always made my mother swoon. Then, at mid-morning, he sat down with me, and we ate breakfast.

Sometimes he made omelets, and sometimes he scrambled eggs. But most of the time, our breakfasts tended toward the sort of thing that could be doused in maple syrup, such as pancakes or French toast. From an early age, I was schooled in the doctrine of pure maple syrup. As a native Canadian and former East Coaster, my father would have nothing else. His chosen brand came in a round-bellied plastic jug the color of Silly Putty and had a permanent home in the door of our refrigerator, right next to the jar of horseradish. It would loll from side to side whenever we opened the door, dropping crusty bits of dried syrup onto the shelf. I loved unscrewing the cap, the way the crystallized sugar made a raspy crackle under the grooved plastic lid.

My father's pancakes were very good, and I'll tell you more about them in a minute, but as is the case for most things cooked in lots of hot fat, it was his French toast that I couldn't get enough of. He would put a cast-iron skillet on the stove and, just to its left, on the tiled counter, a Pyrex brownie pan. Then he'd take up his station in front of them, cracking the eggs into the Pyrex pan and whisking them lightly with milk. Working methodically, he would drag slices of stale bread through the square, pale yellow puddle, soaking them like fat sponges, and then he'd slide them, bubbling and hissing, into the pan. I could smell it from my bedroom at the other end of the house, the smell of custard meeting hot fat. At the table, I'd douse them in syrup and swallow in gulps, almost burning my tongue. His French toast was exceptional, and I'll tell you why: it was cooked in oil, not butter.

It sounds strange, I know. Most people make a face when I tell them, so don't feel bad. I'm used to it. But really, it was tremendous. My father had done his share of comparisons, and for a stellar outcome, he swore by oil. Even in the last weeks of his life, lying in a hospital bed and hooked up to a morphine drip, he was counseling me and my sister

on the merits of oil over butter. The hot oil, he explained, seals the surface of the bread, forming a thin, crisp, outer crust. Meanwhile, the
center melts into a soft, creamy custard, not unlike the texture of a
proper bread pudding. The man was clearly onto something, because
I've never had a better French toast. *Never.* I don't throw those words
around lightly.

For a long time, I wasn't sure I could replicate it. But I figured it
was worth a shot. Going the rest of my life without it wasn't a palatable
option. So I consulted a few recipes, bought myself a bottle of neutral-
tasting oil, and set to work.

The key, and I learned this the hard way, is that you can't pussyfoot
around when it comes to the amount of oil. This is no time to worry
about calories. It's time to upend the bottle and *pour*. A glug will not do.
I don't understand those French toast recipes that call for only a tablespoon or two of fat. How on earth can you get a nice, crispy crust if you
don't have lots of hot, bubbling oil? You cannot. Let's not argue about
this.

The second point to note is that you need somewhat squishy bread,
and it needs to be slightly stale. When it comes to bread for my dinner
table, I like rustic, chewy types with thick, craggy crusts, but for French
toast, you want something a little softer and more mundane. That way,
it easily soaks up the custard, giving you a lovely, moist center.

I can say this all now, but it wasn't easy, I'll tell you that much. I
had to eat my way through some pretty crappy French toast to get back
to my father's. But I'm happy to report that I finally got it. Or as close
as I can get, anyway, given that he never had a recipe to start with.

It was an April morning, I think, when I finally got it right. My
father was born in April, so it felt auspicious. It was unseasonably cool
that morning, but the sun was out—a rarity in Seattle so early in the
season—and I remember thinking that its yellowy light made the new
leaves look like tiny stained-glass windows. It reminded me of a poem
that my father once wrote on the back of an index card. I found it in his
bathroom drawer about a year after he died, when we were going
through his old clothes and cufflinks. I think it was intended for my

mother, although she let me keep it. I don't think Burg would mind my sharing it, but if he does, I trust he'll find some way to let me know. Or then again, since I've said awfully nice things about his cooking, maybe he'll let me enjoy my French toast in peace.

SUNRISE (A TOO-LONG HAIKU)

The sun bursts
Out of the eastern night
And flames the sky
With joy—
Your smile.

I had to make a lot of phone calls to get this French toast right. My mother, my sister, and my uncle Arnie all had a hand in helping me to develop this recipe. What follows is a result of our pooled memories and my own trial and error.

My mother swears that Burg always made his French toast with day-old "French bread," or its Oklahoma City grocery store equivalent, an oblong loaf of squishy bread with a thin, crisp crust. You're welcome to use any bread you like, so long as it has a soft, light crumb and isn't too dense. Some baguettes work well. I've also used challah, and I think it's nice, although my sister doesn't like it. Whatever you use, make sure that it's a day or two old.

As for the oil, when I say to "coat the bottom of the skillet," I mean to *completely* coat it. Don't just pour in a little bit and let it run around until it covers the pan. You want a good amount of oil here. You won't be sorry. As my sister says, oil is a "converting force" in French toast cookery. Once you've tried it, you won't go back.

3 large eggs	*Canola or other flavorless oil, for*
1 cup whole milk	*frying*
1 tablespoon sugar	*6 to 8 slices day-old bread (see*
1 teaspoon vanilla extract	*headnote), cut on the diagonal,*
¼ teaspoon salt	*about ¾ inch thick*
Pinch of freshly ground nutmeg	*Pure maple syrup, for serving*

Break the eggs into a wide, shallow bowl or, as my dad did, an 8-inch square Pyrex dish. Whisk the eggs to break up the yolks. Add the milk, sugar, vanilla, salt, and nutmeg and whisk to blend.

Place a heavy large skillet—preferably cast iron—over medium-high heat, and pour in enough oil to completely coat the bottom of the skillet. Let the oil heat until you can feel warmth radiating from it when you hold your hand close over the pan. To test the heat, dip the tip of a finger into the egg mixture—*not* the oil!—and flick a drop into the oil. If it sizzles, it's ready.

Meanwhile, when the oil is almost hot enough, put 2 to 3 slices of bread into the egg mixture, allowing them to rest for 30 seconds to 1 minute per side. They should feel heavy and thoroughly saturated, but they shouldn't be falling apart. Carefully, using tongs, place the slices in the skillet. They should sizzle upon contact, and the oil should bubble busily around the edges. Watch carefully: with hot oil like this, the slices can burn more quickly than you would think. Cook until the underside of each slice is golden brown, 1 to 2 minutes. Carefully flip and cook until the second side is golden, another 1 to 2 minutes. Remove to a plate lined with a paper towel, and allow to sit for a minute or two before serving.

Repeat with the remaining bread. If, at any point, the bread starts to burn before it has a chance to brown nicely, turn the heat back a little. You want to keep it nice and hot, but not smoking.

Serve hot with maple syrup.

Yield: 6 to 8 slices, serves 2 to 3

BETTER WITH CHOCOLATE

I'm not sure if many parents today belong to the cult of milk, but when I was growing up, my mother was a carton-carrying member. (Sorry.) She made me drink a glass every night with dinner. I'm not talking about a little juice tumbler, either. Picture a highball glass—tall and seemingly bottomless, the kind best reserved for a gin and tonic with lots of ice cubes and lime—and you've got the right idea.

As it also happened, I hated the taste of milk. Given this information, I'm pretty sure that the right course of action would have been to cease and desist, but my mother paid no heed.

"Milk is *good for you*," she assured me. And every single night, that glass showed up next to my plate, filled almost to the brim. I don't know where parents get these sorts of ideas. Probably from the same school of thought that teaches them to tell their little girls that boys are mean to them because, deep down, they have a crush. If I had a nickel for every time an adult told me that, I would build a new school of thought and teach more accurate things, like that little kids are mean to other little kids because being a little kid is very hard and confusing. I am still trying to work through the fact that a boy named his dog after me in the third grade.

Milk, however, was a little easier to cope with. It didn't take me long to learn that milk tastes marginally better and less milklike when it's icy cold, so I tried to drink it the moment we sat down, before it could warm up even a little bit. I also got good at gulping as quickly as possible, in big, open-throated glugs, so as to minimize the duration of my torture. I was also very skilled at begging for the bottle of Hershey's chocolate syrup. I'd squeeze a slow, fat ribbon of syrup from the upended bottle and stir until the milk looked like melted chocolate ice cream. Then, and only then, was it pleasantly potable.

Those nightly glasses of milk didn't create much in the way of happy memories, but they did do one thing. They taught me that anything, *anything*, can be made better with chocolate. It's a lesson that has served me well. And I suppose that, in an indirect way, I owe my mother, and the cult of milk, for that.

Take banana bread, for starters. It's a lovely thing on its own, plain or with walnuts, but with a palmful of chocolate chips, as my friend Kate taught me, it's much more than that. It's no longer an after-school snack; it's a full-on dessert, preferably served with loosely whipped cream.

Even savory foods taste better with chocolate. My friend Shauna swears by cauliflower roasted with a sprinkling of cocoa powder and smoked paprika, and my husband has taken to sprinkling bittersweet chocolate into our arugula salads. (It's a lot better, I swear, than it sounds. I'll tell you more about it later.) And in some parts of Mexico, they even sauce their meats with chocolate. They combine it with chiles, nuts, and spices and turn it into *mole,* a smooth, rich sauce for poultry, beef, and pork.

You know, I'd be willing to go out on a limb and say that chocolate even makes *chocolate* taste better. Take, for example, a basic chocolate cake. I've tried several recipes over the years and have finally settled on one in particular, a dark, fudgy one with yogurt for moisture, coffee for depth of flavor, and two types of chocolate. It's what I use when I want a traditional chocolate cake for birthdays, or for making into cupcakes, and it's delicious with any number of frostings or glazes. But it's pointless to deny the truth, which always leads back to chocolate. These cupcakes don't want ganache, or whipped cream, or buttercream. All they need is a simple, strictly chocolate finish: a smooth, firm cap of bittersweet spooned over the top, the sort of thing that melts the instant it meets your tongue.

They also need a cold glass of milk, but that's a whole other matter.

CHOCOLATE CUPCAKES WITH BITTERSWEET GLAZE

*T*his recipe is my standby chocolate cake formula. It makes a spectacularly moist, rich cake. I got the idea for the glaze from a local grocery store, where they used to sell chocolate cupcakes with a thin cap of chocolate instead of frosting. It was such a nice departure from the typical specimens you see these days, mounded high—almost obscenely, I think—with swirls of buttercream. Of course, much to my dismay, the market replaced "my" cupcake a couple of years ago with the usual, lots-o-frosting kind. I guess that's what people expect, but it was sad. Their cupcakes were never as good as homemade, though, so it was hard to complain for long.

If you're not the cupcake type, you can use this recipe to make a single cake instead. Follow the directions as written, but instead of a muffin tin, use an 8- or 9-inch cake pan, greased and lined with a round of parchment. (Be sure to grease the parchment, too, or else it could stick to the cake.) It will take 50 minutes to an hour to bake. The recipe also doubles easily to make a layer cake.

FOR THE CUPCAKES

1 ounce semisweet chocolate, finely chopped

½ cup hot brewed coffee

1 cup sugar

¾ cup plus 1 tablespoon unbleached all-purpose flour

½ cup unsweetened cocoa powder, sifted

½ teaspoon baking soda

¼ teaspoon baking powder

¼ teaspoon salt

1 large egg

¼ cup canola oil

½ cup well-stirred plain whole-milk yogurt (not low fat or nonfat)

¼ teaspoon vanilla extract

FOR THE GLAZE

8 ounces bittersweet chocolate, finely chopped

Preheat the oven to 300°F. Line the wells of a standard-sized muffin tin with paper liners.

Put the semisweet chocolate in a medium bowl with the hot coffee.

Let stand, stirring occasionally, until the chocolate is melted and the mixture is smooth and opaque.

Meanwhile, in another medium bowl, whisk together the sugar, flour, cocoa powder, baking soda, baking powder, and salt.

In the bowl of a stand mixer or, alternatively, a mixing bowl, if you plan to use handheld beaters, beat the egg on medium speed until it is pale yellow, about 1 minute. Add the oil, yogurt, and vanilla, beating well. Gradually pour in the melted chocolate mixture, and beat to thoroughly combine. Add the dry ingredients all at once, and beat on low speed until the batter is just combined. Using a rubber spatula, scrape down the sides of the bowl and briefly stir to make sure that all the dry ingredients are absorbed.

Spoon the batter into the wells of the muffin tin, making sure that it is evenly distributed. Bake for 20 to 25 minutes, or until a toothpick inserted in the center of one of the cupcakes comes out clean. Transfer the pan to a wire rack, and cool for 20 minutes before—carefully: they're tender!—removing the cupcakes. Allow them to cool completely before glazing.

To make the glaze, melt the bittersweet chocolate in a metal or glass bowl set over a pan of gently simmering water. Stir frequently to prevent scorching. When the chocolate is completely smooth, it's ready. Working with one cupcake at a time, spoon a heaping teaspoonful of melted chocolate on top. Tilt and rotate the cupcake to coax the chocolate out to the edge. Alternatively, use a knife or icing spatula to spread the chocolate. The top of the cupcake should be entirely covered with a thin layer of chocolate. Spoon on more chocolate as needed.

Set the cupcakes aside at room temperature until ready to serve, at least an hour. The chocolate glaze will firm up a bit and become matte. You can, of course, serve them with the chocolate still warm and soft, but I prefer the taste and appearance of the cooled chocolate.

NOTE: Stored in an airtight container at room temperature, these cupcakes are even better the second day.

Yield: 12 cupcakes

THE DARK HORSE

Where food was concerned, my father was an equal-opportunity guy. There was little that he wouldn't try and even less that he didn't like. He loved chicken livers and scrapple, fat and gristle and escargots, and sardines straight from the can, all manner of things questionable and daunting. He even loved prunes. No one loves prunes. In the English language, there are just a handful of words that come with their own built-in laugh track, and *prune* is one of them. He didn't care. I am most definitely his daughter, because I don't either.

In recent years, marketers have tried to spiff up the public image of the prune, calling it a "dried plum" and fitting it with cheery new packaging. I like plums, especially the green type that comes out in late summer, as fragile as water balloons, but in all honesty, I like prunes better. I think of them as plums that have been improved by hardship, made finer by old age and wizening. They're the dark horse of dried fruits. Their concentrated flavor has more depth than a dried apricot, but without the shrill tang of raisins or the sticky sweetness of dates. And unlike their precursor, the fresh plum, they're available year-round, always at the ready. They may not be pretty, but they make up for it in other ways.

Straight from the bag, prunes are very good, but with a little heat and moisture, they get very, *very* good. I consider myself lucky to have been schooled from an early age in the art of stewing them. In our house, it usually happened late at night, after Burg had changed out of his suit and into his blue polka-dotted bathrobe. He would load up a heavy saucepan with prunes, water, and thin slices of orange and lemon. Then he'd bring it to a boil, turn off the heat, snap on a lid, and let the pan sit until morning. By that point, the prunes hardly counted as dried fruits anymore; they were now soft, silky pockets of juice. When you scooped one up, it would slump wearily on the spoon, as though it had been woken up too early. Its skin would yield to the tooth with a gentle, dainty pop, and underneath, the flesh was lip-lickingly sweet, winey, and complex. The food safety people would have probably looked askance at Burg's overnight method, so I can't really advise it, but it did make ours a solidly pro-prune household.

Which is a good thing, no matter what people say.

i treat my prunes very simply, as my father did. I use a method that's a little more conventional than his, but it's every bit as easy. They're delicious warm, with oatmeal or ice cream or thick Greek yogurt, although I also like them cold. That's how I eat them most days, in fact, alongside my bowl of cereal.

1 small orange or tangerine, preferably seedless, or ½ small orange and ½ lemon

1 pound best-quality pitted prunes
1 cinnamon stick

Cut the orange in half from stem to tip, and then slice it very thinly, peel and all. If it has seeds, pick them out as you go. Put the orange slices in a medium saucepan with the prunes and the cinnamon stick, and add water to just cover. Place over medium heat. Bring to a gentle simmer and cook, adjusting the heat as needed so that the liquid barely trembles, for 30 to 45 minutes, or until the prunes are tender, the orange slices are soft and glassy, and the liquid in the pan is slightly syrupy. Remove the cinnamon stick, cool slightly, and serve. Or let the prunes cool to room temperature and then store them in a sealed container in the refrigerator for up to a week.

NOTE: Stewed prunes improve with rest, so I try to make mine a day or so before I want to eat them.

Yield: about 10 servings

A BROOD OF SEVEN

When I was little, I thought my mother came from the most perfect family. They were all petite and attractive, four sons and three daughters, raised in a little house in Towson, Maryland, with a flagstone path that led to the front steps, a kitchen the size of an airplane galley, and three small bedrooms tucked under the eaves. I always thought of *Stuart Little* when I thought of that house. He would have been right at home there. He could have tucked his matchbox bed into a corner of the kitchen and become the official family mascot.

My mother was the third child in the brood. First came Chris, then Jerry, then my mother and, a minute or two after, her identical twin sister Tina. Eleven months later came a second set of twins, Millicent and John, and then the last, a baby boy named Jody. (My grandmother, as you might guess, was a real champ in the pregnancy department.) For his part, my father had one brother, Arnold, but we didn't see him nearly as often as we saw my mother's brothers and sisters. Arnie lives on the East Coast, and he doesn't like to fly. But my mother's siblings were spread out all over the place, and when we weren't spending holidays or summer vacations with my half-siblings, who were all a good deal older than me and likewise spread out all over the place, we spent them with my mother's family.

My aunts and uncles were fascinating and exotic. When we sent mail to them, I got to write all sorts of strange names on the address label, like "Snowmass, Colorado," where winter, I imagined, lasts all year long, or "Santa Rosa, California," where my uncle Jerry once took me to a knick-knack store called Sweet Potato and bought me a pinky-sized set of bowling pins. I remember Jerry coming to visit us once in Oklahoma City, and how I couldn't sleep that night, waiting for him to arrive. I remember him flicking on the lamp beside my bed and leaning down to hug me. He was a horseman, and he wore flannel shirts all the time, mainly red and black checked ones, with blue jeans and boots. He had a boyish voice that could switch from serious to playful at the slightest instigation, one of those voices that sounds kind of crinkly, for lack of a better word, the way a person's voice sounds when he is smiling. When he spoke, his voice rustled in his throat like a bowl of potato chips does when you reach your hand in. Jerry was gay, and he lived with a man named Tom. My mother told me that they were "partners." So far as I could tell, they were just like any other couple in the family, except that when my cousins and I were playing in their house one Christmas, we found a book full of black-and-white pictures of naked men in weird positions. I had never heard of my parents doing anything that looked like that.

When I was nine, Jerry died of AIDS. It was March of 1988, fairly early on in things, as the disease went. They didn't have any of the medications they have now. When he died, he was on his way to New York to see a doctor about an experimental treatment. He had flown to Baltimore to meet up with my grandmother, who was going to accompany him to New York, when he had to be hospitalized with Pneumocystis pneumonia. I remember sitting on the edge of my parents' bed late one night, or maybe it was early in the morning, and watching my mother pack her suitcase for the memorial service. It was held in the Catholic church where they went every Sunday as kids, and afterward, the siblings went to see the movie *Hairspray* at the Senator Theater. John Waters, the director of *Hairspray*, is from Towson, and so was Divine, the enormous transvestite who played Edna; they went to high school with my mother and aunts and uncles. As it happens, Divine died on March 7, the day after Jerry, and was buried in the local cemetery. I always thought that was very cool, that my uncle and Divine might be putting on drag shows in the afterlife together.

After Jerry died, everything was different. It was like some seal had been broken, and whatever it was that was holding our family in place wasn't there anymore. My mother's sister Millicent was diagnosed with cancer only three weeks after Jerry's memorial service. Millicent was forty-one, with a baby who wasn't quite yet two. She'd been married only three years before, on a boat in Seattle, and I was a flower girl, along with my cousins Katie and Sarah, Tina's daughters. We wore poofy-sleeved dresses with smocking across the chest. My dad made mix tapes for the reception, and we danced to Lionel Richie and Whitney Houston. Mia, as we called her, was beautiful in her ivory lace dress, with a ripply laugh that reverberated through the room. Not long after, she got a sore throat that wouldn't go away, and the doctors said it was lung cancer. She died at home in June of 1989, asleep, in a nightgown dotted with pink flowers.

I knew that what was happening to my family was really bad, and I knew that my mother cried a lot, but I didn't know that all this early death wasn't normal. I guess whatever you grow up with seems normal. It's your life, no matter what it is. The year after Mia died, I found Gilda Radner's memoir on my mother's bookshelf. It's called *It's Always Something*, and it tells the story of her struggle with ovarian cancer. I thought it was fantastic, and I gave a book report on it for my fifth grade Language Arts class. My teacher, Mrs. Waldo, must have wrung her hands as I stood at the chalkboard and told my classmates about Gilda's meditation practice. Gilda loved to do laundry, especially towels, and when she was sick, she used to visualize her abdomen as a pink terrycloth towel. She envisioned the chemotherapy as a detergent swishing through, cleaning away all the specks of dirt (the dirt being cancer) which had embedded themselves in the little pink towel. I didn't know that eleven-year-old girls don't usually read books about ovarian cancer. In fact, until I started to write this paragraph, it didn't seem strange to me at all.

In my family, for many years, all the adults had "sad attacks." They cried at the holiday dinner table. It was uncomfortable sometimes, but I was also intrigued by it, by the way we live and then sometimes, all of a sudden, start to die. We did the best we could to make sense of it. I gave my book report. My cousin Katie made a panel in Jerry's name for the Names Project AIDS Memorial Quilt. My cousin Sarah, though, did the best thing of all. She made pie.

For most of her adult life, my aunt Mia made Hoosier Pie for Thanksgiving. No one knows where the recipe came from or how she found it, but in essence, it's a pecan pie with chocolate and bourbon. It is, however, an unusually good pecan pie, with just the right ratio of nuts to soft, not-too-sweet goo. When Katie and Sarah were growing up, Mia lived nearby, so they had prime access to Hoosier Pie. In fact, Sarah told me the other day that it's the only food she remembers from holidays when she was little. She never liked the traditional pumpkin pie, and apple pie didn't excite her, but she loved Hoosier Pie.

"Thanksgiving was all about that pie," she says, "because it meant I could have *chocolate.*" Sarah loves chocolate. I love that about her.

After Mia died, that first Thanksgiving, Sarah asked if she could make Hoosier Pie. From then on, she decided, she would make it every year in Mia's memory. Nearly two decades have passed, but she's yet to miss a year. Even the Thanksgiving when her parents had just divorced and no one wanted to cook, Hoosier Pie made the cut. With their father, Sarah and Katie ate Boston Market chicken, garlic mashed potatoes, and Mia's pie. With their mother, they ate chicken breasts from the grill, more of the same potatoes, and more pie. They also, incidentally, made a pumpkin pie, but it fell on the floor, a classic example of survival of the fittest.

Sarah is now married, and though her husband's family is more of an apple pie clan than a pecan one, she makes Mia's pie anyway.

"I don't care what other people want," she says. "There *will* be Hoosier Pie."

Her mother-in-law is courteous and cuts herself a slice, but Sarah always has leftovers. They're fantastic, she tells me, for breakfast the next morning. I hope to try that sometime, if I can actually get my Hoosier Pie to last past Thanksgiving dinner. This year, wherever she is, maybe Mia will pull some strings for me.

t his pie is incredibly easy, which is part of why it makes such a good tradition. Sarah has made it in several kitchens over the years, and she says that it's hard to mess up. Sometimes she forgets to bring the butter for the filling to room temperature, so she melts it instead. In her first apartment, on Boylston Street in Boston, she didn't have a mixer or electric beaters, so she stirred in the sugar with a spoon. She also tells me that she's thrown a handful of dried cranberries into the filling, and they were wonderful—"to die for," actually—with the pecans and chocolate.

Sarah uses a store-bought crust, but I like to make my own. Whatever you do, use the best bourbon you have, because its flavor will shine through. It should be the sort of thing you'd want to drink on its own. I like Woodford Reserve.

FOR THE CRUST
4 tablespoons ice water, plus more as
   needed
¾ teaspoon apple cider vinegar
1½ cups unbleached all-purpose flour
1 tablespoon sugar
¾ teaspoon salt
1 stick plus 1 tablespoon (4½ ounces)
   cold unsalted butter, cut into cubes

FOR THE FILLING
4 tablespoons (2 ounces) unsalted
   butter, at room temperature

1 cup sugar
3 large eggs
¾ cup light corn syrup
1 teaspoon vanilla extract
¼ teaspoon salt
2 tablespoons bourbon
½ cup chocolate chips, preferably
   bittersweet, such as Ghirardelli
   60%
1 cup pecan halves

FOR SERVING
Unsweetened whipped cream, optional

In a small bowl or measuring cup, combine the ice water and cider vinegar.

In the bowl of a food processor, combine the flour, sugar, and salt. Pulse to blend. Add the butter, and pulse until the mixture resembles a coarse meal; there should be no pieces of butter bigger than a large pea. With the motor running, slowly add the water-vinegar mixture, processing just until moist clumps form. If you pick up a handful of the dough and squeeze it in your fist, it should hold together. If the dough seems a bit dry, add more ice water by the teaspoon, pulsing to incorporate. I often find that 1 additional teaspoon is perfect.

Turn the dough out onto a wooden board or clean countertop, and gather it, massaging and pressing, until it just holds together. Shape into a ball, and press into a disk about 1½ inches thick. If the disk cracks a bit at the edges, don't worry; just pinch the cracks together as well as you can. Wrap the dough in plastic wrap, and then press it a bit more, massaging away any cracks around the edges, allowing the constraint of the plastic wrap to help you form it into a smooth disk. Refrigerate for at least 2 hours. (Dough can be kept in the refrigerator for up to 4 days or sealed in a heavy-duty plastic bag and frozen for up to 1 month. Thaw it in the refrigerator overnight before using.) Before rolling it out, allow the dough to soften slightly at room temperature.

TO ASSEMBLE

Set an oven rack to the middle position, and preheat the oven to 375°F. Roll the dough into a circle wide enough to fit a 9- or 9½-inch pie plate. Transfer the dough gently into the pie plate, and fold and crimp the edges to form a high fluted rim. Put the prepared pie plate in the refrigerator while you make the filling.

In a medium bowl, beat the butter on medium-low speed until soft and creamy. Gradually add the sugar, beating all the while. When the sugar is fully incorporated, add the eggs one at a time, beating well after each addition. Then add the corn syrup, vanilla, and salt. Beat well. Beat in the bourbon. The batter should be pale yellow and fairly thin.

Remove the prepared pie plate from the refrigerator. Scatter the chocolate chips and nuts evenly over the base of the crust; then pour in the batter. Bake for 35 to 45 minutes, checking every 5 minutes after the 30-minute mark. The filling will puff gently as it bakes. The pie is ready when the edges are firm, the top is deep brown, and the center seems set but jiggles ever so slightly. Transfer the pie to a wire rack to cool to room temperature. The filling will firm up as it cools.

Serve with whipped cream, if you like.

NOTE: Wrapped in plastic wrap, Hoosier Pie will keep at room temperature for up to 3 days, if it doesn't get eaten first.

Yield: 8 servings

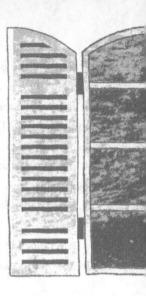
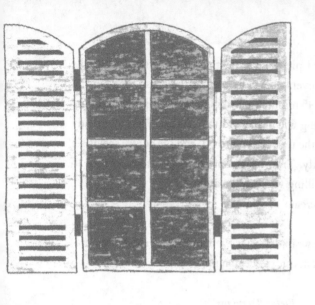

10 **BOULANGERIE**

LA BOULE MICHE

My parents took me to Paris for the first time when I was ten. It was spring break, and I was in the fourth grade. I told everyone in my class where we were going, and they *ooh*ed and *ahh*ed approvingly, although I don't think any of us knew what Paris really was. I certainly didn't. It was like going to the moon.

It strikes me now, in retrospect, that we took that trip barely a year after Jerry died, and that only three months later, Mia would die, too. My mother probably felt like she was *living* on the moon. She didn't need Paris for that. I guess that's why so much of what I remember from that trip is about my father. She's like a blur at the edge of a photograph.

I can't really tell you about that trip, or about Paris at all, without starting with him. It's funny. It's not so much because of something he showed me or taught me there. In fact, sometimes it's hard to remember anything more than a ghost of that first visit. And it's not that Burg knew Paris particularly well, either. I've come to know it much better now than he ever did. But he *loved* that city, and I guess that's it, really. He loved it so much. And in a sense, he gave it to me.

To properly set the scene, what you need to know first is that my father had a truly excessive coat collection. My father had coats the way old spinsters have cats. He had something like thirty of them. He wasn't a clotheshorse by any stretch of the imagination, but between his garage sale habit and his seemingly psychic attraction to half-price sale signs, it just sort of happened. The front hall closet was a minefield on hangers, a mishmash of wool, tweed, down, fleece, Gore-Tex, leather, and oilcloth, each so tightly packed against the next that it wouldn't have surprised me to find, upon opening the closet one day, that they had melded together into an enormous, all-weather quilt.

On the chilly, mid-March morning that we landed in Paris, it was a beige trench that he had chosen from amidst the rabble, one of those thin, starchy kinds that fold, for ease of packing, into a zippered travel pouch sewn into the lining. (There is something in the Code of Fatherhood, I believe, that dictates that all dads must own this kind of collapsible, suitcase-ready jacket. That, and collapsible sunshields for their cars, and hammers that transform into screwdrivers that transform into corkscrews.) It was right up his alley, if not particularly Parisian. He was ready for anything.

We had flown all night, from Oklahoma to Atlanta and on to Orly, where we deplaned into what looked to me more like a dingy warehouse, lit in dirty yellows and fluorescent whites, than any airport I'd ever seen. We dragged our bags out to the wet curb, and he flagged down a cab.

"The Latin Quarter," he yelled to the driver over the din of the highway. "The *Hôtel des Saints-Pères.*" I didn't know what Latin meant, but I knew it had something to do with E PLURIBUS UNUM, those words printed on dollar bills.

Our hotel was on a skinny street lined with tall stone buildings that seemed to sit too close to the curb. They reminded me of men in starched suits, puffing out their chests. Our room was a sparse, compact cube crammed between a spiral staircase and a central courtyard. It had the usual amenities, but each looked somehow askew, sort of muddled in the translation. The bedspreads were dusty brown, and I'd never seen a bathroom so small. You couldn't open the door without scraping the knees of the person sitting on the toilet or smacking the rear end of someone at the sink.

"Europe is *different*," my mother said. "This is a really nice hotel." But coming from Oklahoma, with its big trucks and strip malls, I wasn't sure. Paris seemed very small, as though its proper inhabitants were those prehistoric men in my social studies book, the ones who were only four feet tall.

My parents had been there before, and they loved the Latin Quarter. My father, especially. That was his Paris. He'd first seen the city in the early sixties, when he spent a month there on sabbatical with his first wife and their children. He was a young radiologist, and he'd come to visit the Institut Curie, which was tucked away in the fifth arrondissement, the old, still-beating heart of the quarter. The way he talked about it, you'd have thought he'd stayed for years. He'd eaten in this brasserie here and that bistro there. He remembered Métro stations and streets with the sort of awkwardly instinctive memory that made me wonder if he'd once sat down with a map and memorized them.

Of that trip, I really only remember one street: the next one over from our hotel, the rue du Dragon. It had a familiar name, but in French, it was hard to pronounce. When I tried to say it aloud, it snagged on my thick American tongue, making me sound, I thought, like I had a tiny dragon stuck in my throat. I liked the idea of that.

We stumbled upon the rue du Dragon that first afternoon. Like most of the other streets in that area, it was a narrow strip of pavement with buildings close in on both sides, but it was a little brighter and more lively, with a few small businesses, two or three restaurants, and a stationery store that sold Mrs. Grossman stickers. (I had a collection at home.) A couple of doors down from the stationery store was a glassy window with a sign above it, written in fat, squatty letters. *La Boule Miche*, it said.

"I think *boule* and *miche* are names," Burg said, leaning down to my ear, "for a type of bread. Like that round one over there." He pointed through the window to a shelf where flat, floury disks were propped side by side, like books on a shelf. "But *boule* might also be short for *boulangerie*. That's what they call a bakery."

We stepped inside. A gray-haired woman was standing behind the cash register, busily arranging a stack of long paper bags, the sleeves that clothe baguettes when they are sent out into the world.

"Remember," he said, nudging us closer to the pastry case, "the big street we crossed this morning, in the taxi? The *boulevard Saint-Michel?* They call it the *boul' Mich* for short." He stooped down to peer into the case. "I wonder if the name of this place is a play on that."

I have no idea how my father knew these things. Between you and me, his French was awful with a capital A—*affreux,* as the French would say. By the time I was old enough to know the difference, it was clear that his grasp of the language was most firm where food terms were concerned. Beyond that was shaky ground. One-month sabbatical in the sixties or no, when he spoke, Frenchmen winced. In his mouth, a poor, unsuspecting Loire Valley town called Cangey—pronounced *con-zhay*—became "Cainghee," a name better suited to a small town in central Texas. Neuilly (*nuoy-yee*), a well-to-do suburb west of Paris, was reduced to "Nigh-yule," which strikes me now as a quick, handy way of saying that Christmas is coming soon. But he always tried to speak, at least, and that got him far. It got us into the *boulangerie.* It even got a smile out of the lady at the cash register. If you've ever been to Paris, you know that's no easy feat.

He pulled a few coins out of his pocket. *"Deux croissants et un pain au chocolat, s'il vous plait,"* he said haltingly.

On the wall opposite the pastry case was a copper counter with a long mirror mounted above it. A row of black, velvet-topped stools squatted in front of the counter like spindly mushrooms. We sat down, watching ourselves in the mirror, and ate our pastries: the *croissants* for him and my mother, the *pain au chocolat* for me. It crackled when I bit into it, but underneath the shattery crust, it tore into dozens of stretchy layers and strands. The chocolate inside was still warm, and it oozed out the side until I caught it with my finger and brought it back to my mouth. I was sold.

Each morning after that, while my mother was getting dressed, my father and I would walk around the block to the bakery. It was always the same order for me: a *pain au chocolat* and a *chocolat chaud.* I'd perch myself atop one of the black mushroom caps, kicking my feet against its stem, and lean over the counter to sip the hot chocolate from its white ceramic cup. Sometimes, for an afternoon snack, he bought me one of the small, oblong breads—*pain passion*, they called them—from a basket by the register. Later in the day, if I got hungry before dinner, I would stuff a little square of chocolate, the kind they give you in cafés when you order coffee, into its doughy center. My father beamed.

For himself, he always bought a *croissant*. I never saw him turn one down, in Paris or anywhere. I can still see him now, sitting next to me on a stool with the street behind him. He'd bite into one pointy end, and then he'd reach for his cup and swallow noisily, wincing at the heat. He always did that with coffee, more of a slurp than a sip, a loud sucking sound that ricocheted around the room. He didn't want to miss a drop.

t his is a simple trick familiar to every French child. There's something surprisingly right about chocolate and bread together, all that dark, rich sweetness against the chewy, salty crumb. It's one of my favorite snacks.

French-style bread, preferably a baguette with a crust that's not too thick

Chocolate, preferably dark

Cut or tear off a hunk of bread. Slice or tear it partially across its middle, as though you were going to use it for a sandwich. Break off a piece of chocolate roughly the same length as the piece of bread. Insert the chocolate into the bread. Eat.

VARIATION: You can also warm the bread a little in the oven, either before or after inserting the chocolate. That way, the bread is soft and warm, and the chocolate gets a little oozy. Oozy chocolate is hard to beat.

A STRANGE SORT OF COMING OF AGE

I
n spite of the potato salad, pound cake, and *pains au chocolat*, I believed deep down that mine was a childhood of tragic deprivation.
My parents put a tight cap on processed foods, which meant no toaster
pastries, no grape-flavored bubble gum, no cinnamon toast–flavored
cereal, and none of those shiny, single-portion packets of fruit punch
with a tiny straw attached. Also not permitted were those stubby, twig-
like cheese puffs, which I wanted with a twisted desperation and, on
more than one occasion, stole from the lunch box of an unsuspecting
classmate. Save for a few packages of Oscar Meyer beef bologna, which
somehow crept in under the radar, and the Ranch dressing for my father's potato salad, we generally only ate things made from scratch. It
was a conscious decision that my parents made, a source of quiet pride.

None of this helps to explain, however, the fact that until well into
adolescence, I believed that pancakes came from a box. In the kitchen of
my childhood, pancakes had three ingredients: milk, eggs, and powdered mix. I can still feel the heft of that box in my hand. I can hear the
reassuring rustle and thump of the powder as it tumbles down the cardboard chute. It smelled like flour and fat and something faintly creamy,
and it made a very nice pancake. I loved Bisquick. I *believed* in Bisquick.
Bisquick was pancakes.

But then, sometime around age fifteen, I started reading the food magazines my parents kept stacked on the coffee table. Some nights, after my homework was finished, I would take one upstairs and thumb through it until I fell asleep. It wasn't long before I stumbled upon a recipe for pancakes. I was honestly miffed. The only box it called for was baking soda. Learning that pancakes could be made without a mix was a strange sort of coming of age. It was like learning that your favorite uncle, the one who could do a spot-on impression of Donald Duck, is a loyal subscriber to a skin magazine.

The box of pancake mix was an anomaly in our pantry. I don't know how to explain it. Maybe it sneaked in with the bologna. As these things go, it was pretty benign. But that anomaly meant that I spent the first two decades of my life eating one single, standardized pancake. I was so busy believing in that mix that a whole world of pancakes almost passed me by. Buttermilk pancakes. Whole wheat pancakes. Big fluffy ones splotched with blueberries! And buckwheat pancakes, the top of the stack.

I've worked hard to make up for lost time, as you can imagine. I've made a lot of pancakes. I've eaten a lot of pancakes. There are so many out there, and so many to love. But a few years ago, I found one in particular that still holds my attention.

The place was a kind of upscale greasy spoon, a funky storefront spot in Seattle called the Longshoreman's Daughter, where the waitresses all had gorgeous skin and messy hair. Everything they served was good, but the buckwheat pancakes were legendary: enormous, the size of salad plates, warm and toasty with a thin, lacy edge. Coming from such a hearty flour, they could have been heavy as bricks, but instead they were light—delicate, even. They were eminently satisfying, but not so much so that you'd want to sleep all afternoon. They came with a tiny pitcher of maple syrup and blueberries scattered around, and they were absolutely perfect pancakes.

Unfortunately, about two years after I first ate there, the Longshoreman's Daughter closed its doors. It was jammed with customers, so I'm not sure why. Maybe they decided to rest on their laurels. It could be hard to keep going, I guess, when you've made a pancake so good. It could be tempting to hole up and keep them all to yourself.

Which, frankly, is what I want to do whenever I make buckwheat pancakes. In the years since the Longshoreman's Daughter went defunct, I've been tinkering in my own kitchen, and though it took a lot of batches and botches—the recipe you see here took seven excruciating Sunday mornings—I've come very, very close. Mine are a little fluffier than theirs, which I like, and I make them smaller than salad plate size, but they're just as good as the ones that inspired them. There's no mix involved, so I'm not sure what my family would say. But I'm pretty sure that with a little nudge and some maple syrup, they'd come around.

*t*his recipe uses an unconventional mixing trick that I learned from *Cook's Illustrated*. Rather than adding the melted butter directly to the wet ingredients, you first mix it with the egg yolk. It does require an extra bowl—a Pyrex custard cup works nicely; you can microwave the butter in it and then just add the yolk—but it helps the butter to better incorporate into the batter, making for a more even-textured pancake. It's worth the extra bit of effort. Just be sure that you microwave the butter on medium power and in short bursts. If the heat is too high, butter will sometimes splatter or explode.

These pancakes are great on their own, but they're even better with some fruit. Slices of banana are always nice. Or you could try blueberries, raspberries, or blackberries, either fresh or frozen, 4 to 5 per pancake. In the summer, whenever I find myself with a surplus of berries, I arrange them in a single layer on a rimmed baking sheet, freeze them until they're hard, and then put them in a heavy-duty plastic bag and stash them in the freezer. They'll last that way for months, and freezing them on the pan means that they don't stick together, so you can pull out only as many as you need. You don't even have to thaw them before adding them to the pancakes; the heat of the pan takes care of that. Whatever you use, let the pancakes cook on their first side, undisturbed, for about 1 minute before you add any fruit. That gives them time to puff and begin to set.

Also, this recipe doubles easily.

⅔ cup unbleached all-purpose flour

⅓ cup buckwheat flour

2 teaspoons sugar

½ teaspoon salt

½ teaspoon baking powder

¼ teaspoon baking soda

¾ cup buttermilk

¼ cup plus 2 tablespoons milk
 (preferably not low fat or nonfat)

1 large egg, separated

2 tablespoons (1 ounce) unsalted
 butter, melted and cooled slightly

Vegetable oil, for brushing griddle

Pure maple syrup, for serving

In a large bowl, whisk together the flours, sugar, salt, baking powder, and baking soda.

Pour the buttermilk and milk into a medium bowl. (A 2-cup Pyrex measuring cup also works well; you can measure right into it.) Whisk the egg white into the milk mixture. In a small bowl, use a fork to beat the yolk with the melted butter. Whisk the yolk mixture into the milk mixture. Pour the wet ingredients into the dry ingredients all at once, and whisk until just combined. Do not overmix. The batter will be somewhat thick.

Meanwhile, heat a large nonstick skillet or griddle over medium-high heat. Brush the skillet with oil. To make sure it's hot enough, wet your fingers and sprinkle a few droplets of water onto the pan. If they sizzle, it's ready to go.

Ladle the batter in scant ¼ cupfuls into the skillet, taking care not to crowd them. When the underside of the pancakes is nicely browned and the top starts to bubble and look set around the edges, 2 to 3 minutes, flip them. Cook until the second side has browned, 1 to 2 minutes more.

Re-oil the skillet and repeat with more batter. If you find that the pancakes are browning too quickly in subsequent batches, dial the heat back to medium.

Serve warm, with maple syrup.

Yield: 8 to 10 pancakes

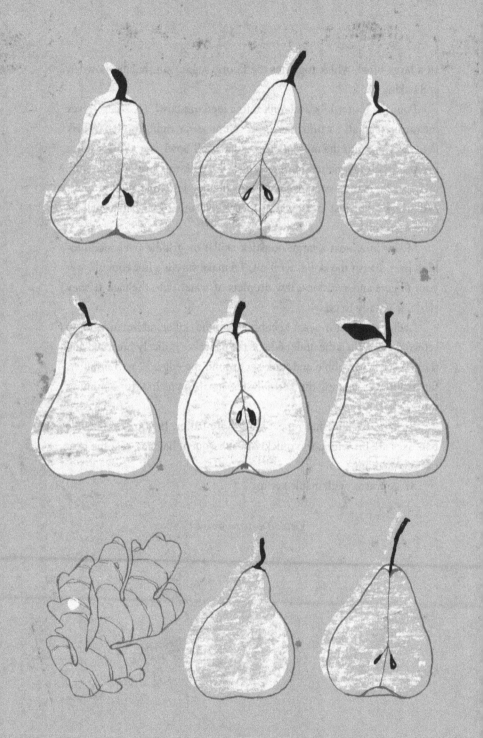

THE HARDBALL STAGE

I t wouldn't be right for me not to tell you about the fresh ginger cake. For one thing, it's wonderful: pale brown and spiced, sauced with warm, caramelly pears. It's a recipe I found in one of my mother's issues of *Gourmet* during my junior year of high school, and in the years since, I must have made it two dozen times, if not more. The first time I made it, it inspired a late night in the kitchen with my parents, all three of us stirring and tasting, working on different recipes. It was the beginning of something, I think. Coming from a family of avid cooks, the kitchen had always been a comfortable place. But it wasn't really *my* place until this cake came along.

I was seventeen then and writing a lot of poetry, wearing pink false eyelashes and vintage polyester shirts festooned with tiny flowers. My mother told me that my father's mother Dora used to wear shirts like that, and though I don't think she intended it as a compliment, it made me feel all the more sure of my choice. When I wrote the essay that follows, the story of the night in the kitchen with the ginger cake, I'd been pickling myself for quite some time in a potent mix of Flannery O'Connor, William Faulkner, and Armistead Maupin's *Tales of the City*. (Don't say I didn't warn you.) I wrote it for English class, for my teacher Perry Oldham, whose name always made me think of Old Hollywood, black-and-white movies, and marcelled waves. It was the first piece of writing I ever did that wasn't about a thwarted crush or the fact that I had yet to be kissed. I suppose I could retell the story today with the added wisdom of a decade or so, but I like it better the old way, the way I told it back then.

This is the story of how it all began, how one wordy teenager found her way to the kitchen. It comes straight from the sun-bleached yellow sketchbook that holds all my teenage writings—or the parts, at least, that aren't hidden in my parents' freezer. (I used to put all my poems in there, sealed in gallon-sized freezer bags, because I'd heard that was the only way to secure them against fire and vandalism.) It explains a lot.

It's midnight, and we converge upon the kitchen: Mom for poached pears, Burg for rice pudding, and me for fresh ginger cake with caramelized pears. Lately I've been really identifying with the kitchen, the way it's always warm in the pantry, its shelves lined with bottles or bags labeled Raspberry Apple Butter *or* Cranberry Beans *or* Quaker Barley, *the way there are cookbooks lying open on the butcher-block island, the way it smells good after dinner and in the afternoon when the refrigerator is cold and full. It's been this way since Christmas with me, always thumbing through magazines in search of recipes to read about, soak in, taste without tasting. But the recipe for fresh ginger cake with caramelized pears demands immediate attention. So we go to the store after dinner and come home with a backseat full of bags: gingerroot, a dozen eggs, a bottle of molasses with a granny on the label, a pint of heavy cream, a tub of sour cream, and two pears, firm-ripe.*

We all think alike. Burg is at the stove with the double boiler, then opening the pantry for rice. Mom is at the sink, peeling pears with her new swiveling vegetable peeler, leaning over the recipe for "Pears Noir" from her California Heritage Cookbook. *I am making the cake I can't stop thinking about. Me, I want fresh ginger cake with caramelized pears at midnight, with the kitchen warm and the cake and caramel and pears warm and the marble tabletop cold under my elbows.*

Rice pudding is fine, but it's not for me. It's Burg's once-a-week-or-so fun, later to be Tupperwared and tucked into the refrigerator for occasional spooning. The poached pears will tomorrow be coated in bittersweet chocolate and served to the guests who will sit and laugh in the dining room with my parents. But the cake is mine. Cake. I like it on my tongue, the word—not just the stuff itself—but even better in my throat, my stomach. Cake. It can only mean something good.

And anyway, I've never liked rice pudding all that much. Something about the dairy and the rice: they shouldn't be together. But lately I've started to change my mind. I wonder if it's my father's rice pudding that's done it, or maybe it's my uncle's rice. My father's brother Arnold—you can call him Arnie—sends the rice from Nanuet, New York. It's basmati rice, straight from India, still in the little burlap sack with the handles and the big red block letters spelling out the name of a town I can't pronounce. Arnie is great. He calls for Burg and speaks slowly, slowwwly, and it makes me crazy if I'm in the middle of something because it takes hours, it seems, to get him over to Burg. The word hello in and of itself takes a good minute. But Arnie is fun. He looks like Burg but with paler hair and a ponytail, and he has an Afghan hound that's almost as tall as he is. So I like rice pudding because of Arnie and the rice, and also, it is my own father's rice pudding. Though really, I don't think I'm biased at all.

And the poached pears. I like them, too. I mean, picture it: you're lying in an overstuffed bed in the upstairs bedroom of a bed-and-breakfast in Cape Neddick, Maine, just before Christmas, and there's snow piling high on the ground outside, but it's warm up there, under the canopy, in the bed. It's eight o'clock in the morning. There's a knock at the door. You roll out of bed. At your feet is a silver tray with one cup, a coffeepot, a cream pitcher, and a sugar bowl. You pick it up, close the door, rest the tray on your bedside table, pour yourself a cup of blacky-brown *coffee, and you sink back into bed under the comforter and return to the second volume of the* Tales of the City *series. It's a good morning because Mona is discovering her roots in a whorehouse in Nevada with Mother Mucca, and gynecologist Jon Fielding is wooing Michael again. And then, of course, there's breakfast at nine. First there will be pineapple scones, still warm from the baking sheet, and a cloth-lined tin of cinnamon muffins and spice bread. Then a poached pear, buoyed by a pool of Grand Marnier crème anglaise. Then a warm plate with a small poached egg on a bed of puréed spinach, with caramelized apples and a crispy phyllo purse filled with sausage, ricotta, and mushrooms and baked until flaky outside and melting inside. This is breakfast on this almost-Christmas day. You sigh and decide to stay seated right where you are until tea at 4:30 (cranberry linzer tart; ready?).*

So yes, I like poached pears. Because that was me in Maine last Christmas, and I ate everything and then another scone an hour after breakfast because I can never get enough, it seems. Because poached pears landed squarely in the middle of a breakfast to go down in history, a breakfast that set me on fire, afire with the love of the food! (Amen.) And hence this midnight meeting in the kitchen, this preoccupation with cake and caramel and pears.

To the kitchen I go. This cake will be incredible—mark my words—and I will grate this ginger even if the pale yellow milk that runs under the grater makes me feel a little queasy. It will be good. It will be delicious, yes. The kitchen smells full and alive, and the pears bubble with sugar and butter and cream.

It's midnight, and the kitchen is clicking and burbling and whirring. We lean into the soft, brown cake cooling on the island. We pour over pears and caramel all butterflow and melt onto the floor with it on our forks and in our mouths, even better than the word cake *itself on my tongue. Midnight, and we melt in the kitchen and check ourselves with the candy thermometer, declare that we've reached the hardball stage, and pour ourselves into bed.*

FRESH GINGER CAKE WITH CARAMELIZED PEARS

*t*his cake is lighter in flavor and less spicy than a typical gingerbread, with a subtle kick of warmth from the fresh ginger. Be sure to use a standard unsulfured molasses like Brer Rabbit Mild Flavor or Grandma's Original. Do not use blackstrap molasses. I happened to use it once, because I grabbed the wrong bottle in the pantry, and it made for a sad, sub-par cake, too dark tasting and dense.

FOR THE CAKE

1 cup unbleached all-purpose flour

½ teaspoon baking soda

¼ teaspoon salt

¼ cup unsulfured molasses

¼ cup sour cream (not low fat or nonfat)

4 tablespoons (2 ounces) unsalted butter, melted and cooled slightly

¼ cup firmly packed light brown sugar

1 large egg

2 teaspoons finely grated peeled fresh ginger

½ teaspoon grated lemon zest

FOR THE CARAMELIZED PEARS

2 medium firm-ripe pears

1 tablespoon fresh lemon juice

2 tablespoons (1 ounce) unsalted butter

¼ cup sugar

3 tablespoons water

3 tablespoons heavy cream

1½ teaspoons brandy or bourbon

Salt

Set an oven rack to the middle position, and preheat the oven to 350°F. Grease an 8-inch round baking pan with butter or cooking spray.

In a medium bowl, whisk together the flour, baking soda, and salt. Set aside.

In another medium bowl, combine the molasses, sour cream, butter, brown sugar, egg, ginger, and lemon zest and whisk until smooth. Add the flour mixture and stir until just combined. Pour the mixture into the prepared pan, and spread it evenly with a rubber spatula.

Bake until a tester comes out clean, 15 to 20 minutes. Cool the cake in its pan on a wire rack for 5 minutes, then turn it out onto the rack. Cool to room temperature.

When you're ready to serve the cake, prepare the caramelized pears. Carefully peel the pears, and cut each lengthwise into 8 wedges, discarding the cores. Place them in a medium bowl, and toss them with the lemon juice.

In a heavy skillet just large enough to hold the pears in one layer— a 10-inch is about right—melt the butter over medium heat. Add the pears and cook, shaking the skillet occasionally, for 3 minutes. Sprinkle them with sugar and continue to cook, shaking the skillet and gently turning the pears, until the sugar is melted and the pears are tender. (I like to keep mine on the firm side, so that they don't lose their shape or start to fall apart, but if you'd like them more meltingly soft, go right ahead.) Using a slotted spoon, transfer the pears back to their bowl. It's okay if there's still lemon juice in there—leave it.

Still over medium heat, boil the sugar-butter mixture remaining in the skillet, stirring occasionally, until it begins to turn a deep shade of caramel. While the mixture cooks, combine the water and cream in a small bowl or cup. When the caramel is the right color, remove the skillet from the heat and carefully—it could splatter—add the cream mixture. Then add the brandy and a pinch of salt. Return the skillet to the heat and simmer, stirring, until thickened slightly. (If your caramel seized when you added the liquids, don't worry; whisk briskly until it is smooth again.) Return the pears to the skillet, and cook until heated through.

Serve the cake in wedges, with a few pieces of pear alongside and caramel drizzled over the top.

Yield: 4 to 6 servings

A PERSONAL CHRONOLOGY
IN CHRISTMAS COOKIES

I t has a musical that bears its name and wheat that famously
waves, but what you might not know about Oklahoma is this:
that one of the best things it has produced is, or rather was, my
mother's holiday cookies. I say that as a loyal daughter and a native
Oklahoman, and I mean it as a compliment to both. Those cookies
were spectacular.

For nearly twenty years, December was no ordinary month on my
mother's calendar. It was a series of afternoons spent in the kitchen,
churning out cookies, candies, bars, balls, and toffees by the dozen. Her
partner in this onerous work was a woman by the name of Barbara
Fretwell, whom my mother met in an art class and whose name strikes
me now, suddenly, after all these years of saying it, as lovely and quaint,
the sort of name you might see in a child's storybook, the tale of an
overprotective British governess and her mischievous charges. Barbara
is a wonderful baker. Together, she and my mother were like a well-
oiled machine.

When the holiday baking tradition began, I had a pacifier and
played on a padded blanket by the sink. When it ended, I had earned
most of a college degree. Along the way, I had a sequence of fickle love
affairs with nearly every confection in the cookie tin. Some people mea-

sure maturity in birthdays, but I plot my personal chronology in Christmas cookies.

As is often the case, mine was a humble beginning. My mother's cookie tin was a gorgeous, glamorous thing, lined with colored cellophane that shimmered like a disco ball, but in the early days, I only had eyes for a modest, paper-bag brown candy called Aunt Bill's. No one seems to know the origin of its name, but it's an old tradition in the South and the Great Plains, all those places where pecan trees like to grow. It tastes like a praline but has a texture like fudge, and it's made from pecans, butter, browned sugar, half-and-half, and large amounts of muscular stirring. Barbara and my mother used to designate a special night for making Aunt Bill's, because they needed their husbands to help stir the pots. We'd get carryout Chinese from the place in Casady Square, where the maître d' wore deeply pleated khaki pants and greeted us by name, and then we'd retreat to the Fretwells' house to eat. Then the adults would roll up their sleeves and make candy. Meanwhile, their daughter Leslie and I would play hide-and-seek in the hallway closets or watch movies on Betamax. I loved it when our parents made Aunt Bill's. Especially because at the end of the night, we would go home with an entire pan of chewy, caramel-colored candy, just the thing for my preadolescent sweet tooth.

Then, of course, I tasted a Linzer cookie, classic and classy in its frilly powdered sugar coat, with raspberry jam for filling. It was the cookie that would accompany me into puberty. But before another holiday season had passed, I had already begun a slow turn toward the chocolate "rad," a cookie that climbed to previously unseen heights where chocolate was concerned. A single batch calls for a pound of bittersweet chocolate and two cups of chocolate chips, and it bakes up into something reminiscent of brownies, only tidier and round, with light, crackly shells. But then, at age eighteen, I found what I believed to be the final frontier: my mother's espresso-walnut toffee. It is absolutely stunning, its deep caramel flavor tinged with coffee, its topcoat marbled with white and dark chocolates. Candy lovers on coasts east and west, as well as in my own skillet-shaped home state, gush over it. My mother's friend Amalia, a gorgeous Spaniard who is also our eye doctor and makes a very fine toffee herself, can't resist it.

"I'm just going to have a leeettle sleeever," she says with a wink, reaching for the tin.

But I was mistaken about it being the final frontier. I had not yet tasted a chocolate-capped fruit-nut ball.

My mother has been making them since the late 1980s, but due to childhood prejudices and a phobia of all things bearing even a faint resemblance to fruitcake, the fruit-nut ball did not cross my lips until I was nineteen. And in the end, that first bite only took place because I was stuck in an airport somewhere between Oklahoma and California, in transit back to college after Christmas and cursed with a long layover. I was hungry, and I had a tin of my mother's cookies in my bag. They were intended for my adviser, a kind South Indian scientist who'd invited me into her home for countless dals and curries and was long overdue for a proper thank-you gift. But with a little rearranging of the tin's contents, I told myself, she might never know that something was missing. I studied the tin, deciding reluctantly that the fruit ball might be my best bet. It seemed at least sort of healthy (possibly more so than airport pizza) and since it was obviously the dud of the bunch, I wouldn't be depriving my friend of anything particularly tasty. So, taking care not to disturb its neighbors, I removed one from its ruffly paper cup and took a bite. The crisp chocolate cap buckled under my teeth, giving way to a rush of powdered sugar and, beneath it, a soft, dark, winey chew. The dried fruits and their accompanying walnuts, finely chopped and held together by a splash of liqueur, had morphed together into a third something, a flavor both floral and musky, familiar and complex, the sort of thing only an adult would like.

I stared at the empty wrapper. Then I reached for another. *This is delicious,* I said aloud, reaching for the third and fourth balls, which I handily tucked away shortly before boarding.

Needless to say, the tin never found its way out of my dorm room. I bought my adviser a book on cookie baking instead.

FRUIT-NUT BALLS

f or several years now, I've made an array of cookies and candies to give away at Christmastime, like my mother used to. The assortment changes a bit every year, but these fruit-nut balls are always on the list. They're ridiculously easy to prepare (you don't even need an oven) and they actually improve with age, which comes in handy. I try to make them at least a couple of days before I want to give them away, but they'll keep in the refrigerator for two to three weeks, easy.

One word of caution: be sure to check your prunes for pits, even if you bought them already pitted. One single pit in the food processor turns into billions of tiny, rock-hard shards. I know from experience.

1 cup walnuts	*1 to 2 tablespoons Grand Marnier,*
½ pound pitted dried cherries	*brandy, or apple cider*
½ pound dried figs	*½ cup powdered sugar*
½ pound pitted dried apricots	*10 ounces semisweet chocolate,*
½ pound pitted prunes	*coarsely chopped*

Put the walnuts in the bowl of a food processor fitted with a steel blade, and pulse to chop finely. Transfer to a large bowl.

Return the food processor bowl to its base (there's no need to wash it) and add half of the dried fruits. Pulse to chop finely. You don't want to turn the fruit into a gummy paste, but you want it to be chopped finely enough that there are no pieces larger than a pea. Add to the bowl with the walnuts. Repeat with the remaining dried fruit. When all the fruit is finely chopped, stir the fruit-nut mixture well. Add 1 tablespoon Grand Marnier and stir to incorporate. Pinch off a small wad of the mixture and squeeze it in your palm: does it hold together in a tight ball? If not, add another tablespoon of Grand Marnier.

Put the powdered sugar in a small, wide bowl or pie plate. Pinch off bits of the fruit-nut mixture and, squeezing and rolling them gently in your hands, shape them into 1- to 1½-inch balls. Roll each ball in powdered sugar to coat, shaking off any excess, and place them on a rimmed baking sheet. Set aside at room temperature, uncovered, for 24 hours.

To finish, line a second baking sheet with parchment paper or a silicone liner, and keep it close at hand. In a heatproof bowl set over a pan of simmering water, melt the chocolate, stirring occasionally, until smooth and loose. Remove it from the heat.

Working with one ball at a time, use a small spoon to dollop a bit of chocolate on top. Shake the ball lightly to coax the chocolate down its sides. (You may want to do this over the sink, rather than over the bowl of chocolate; otherwise, your chocolate will be contaminated by sprinkles of powdered sugar.) The chocolate will not coat it completely—only the top half or so, as though the ball were wearing a chocolate hat. Place the ball carefully, chocolate side up, on the lined baking sheet. Repeat with the remaining balls.

Slide the baking sheet, uncovered, into the refrigerator and chill until the chocolate has hardened, about 2 hours. Tuck each ball into a small paper candy cup. Store in an airtight container in the refrigerator for up to 3 weeks.

Yield: 45 to 50 balls

ESPRESSO-WALNUT TOFFEE

*A*nything that requires a candy thermometer can seem daunting, but don't let it get to you. This toffee, a riff on a recipe that my mother once found in *Bon Appétit*, is really very straightforward. Just be sure to have your ingredients measured and ready before you begin: once the process has started, you won't have time to stop and prepare them.

Also, on a precautionary note, do not double this recipe. Candy recipes do not tend to double well.

2 cups walnuts	1 tablespoon unsulfured molasses
1 cup sugar	4½ ounces bittersweet chocolate, very
⅓ cup packed light brown sugar	finely chopped
2 teaspoons instant espresso powder	4½ ounces white chocolate, very
½ teaspoon ground cinnamon	finely chopped
¼ teaspoon salt	2½ sticks (10 ounces) unsalted butter
⅓ cup water	

Preheat the oven to 325°F.

Put the walnuts on a baking sheet, arranging them in a single layer, and bake until they are fragrant, 5 to 10 minutes. Do not allow them to burn. Set them aside to cool, about 10 minutes, then coarsely chop them. Transfer 1½ cups to a small bowl. Then finely chop the remaining ½ cup, and put it in a separate bowl.

Prepare your ingredients and equipment. In a medium bowl, whisk together the sugars, espresso powder, cinnamon, and salt. In a small bowl or measuring cup, whisk together the water and molasses. Put the chopped chocolates in their own separate bowls. Grease a rimmed baking sheet with cooking spray or butter.

In a heavy, 2- to 3-quart saucepan, melt the butter over low heat. Add the sugars, espresso powder, cinnamon, salt, water, and molasses and stir until the sugar has dissolved. Attach a candy thermometer to the side of the pan. Raise the heat to medium and cook until the mixture registers 290°F (and no less), stirring frequently at first, and then slowly and constantly scraping the bottom of the pan with a wooden spoon or spatula, about 20 minutes.

When the mixture is up to temperature, remove the pan from the heat. Immediately stir in 1½ cups coarsely chopped walnuts. Quickly pour the mixture onto the prepared baking sheet; do not scrape the saucepan. Tilt and gently shake the baking sheet so that the toffee spreads to a ¼-inch thickness. Sprinkle the chocolates by generous tablespoonfuls onto the hot toffee, alternating rows of bittersweet and white. Allow them to melt for 1 minute. Using the back of a spoon, spread the melted chocolates, taking care not to mix them. Then drag the tip of a small knife or the tines of a fork across the chocolates, swirling them to create a marbled look. Sprinkle with ½ cup finely chopped walnuts. Slide the pan into the refrigerator, and chill until the toffee is firm, about 1 hour. Break it into pieces of whatever size you like.

NOTE: Stored in an airtight container in the refrigerator, toffee will keep for up to 2 weeks. Serve it cold or at room temperature.

Yield: about 2 pounds

THE RIGHT ANSWER TO EVERYTHING

Sometime around my nineteenth birthday, I had my tarot cards read by a woman named Marlene. Sadly, I don't recall the faintest bit of what the cards said. If I came seeking the answer to some juicy question, I have long since forgotten what it was. (Not that anything particularly juicy had happened to me yet, anyway.) I'm not even sure how I found Marlene, aside from the fact that some female members of my family have a weakness for such things, and they talk. I remember only two real tidbits of my meeting with her, and neither amounts to much.

First, there was the squirrel thing. When she closed her eyes, Marlene said, she saw an image of me as a squirrel, stuffing my cheeks with nuts. I'm not sure what she meant by that, but I think of it from time to time, especially when I find myself alone with a pan of brownies.

Second, there was the bit about delayed gratification.

"You want what you want, Molly, and you want it *now*," Marlene remarked solemnly. "You want instant gratification. You've got to work on that. You've got to get more comfortable with delayed gratification."

I have no idea what she was talking about. I was raised as an only child, so, yes, I guess I am accustomed to getting my way. But waiting for things is okay, too. I've never seen it as much of a stumbling block.

Or I hadn't, at least, until I got the idea to make a buttermilk cake scented with vanilla bean. I couldn't get it right. And I wanted that cake the way I wanted it, *right now.*

It started at the grocery store, as trouble so often does. It was early winter, high citrus season, and there were some especially lovely oranges in the produce section. They were heavy, smooth-skinned, and plump, the kind that might have, in another era, inspired Peter Paul Rubens. Unable to help myself, I bought a dozen. Then I lugged them home, cursing myself all the way. What is a single girl supposed to do with a dozen oranges? Eat them for breakfast, lunch, and dinner? That could quickly get old. Make a half-gallon of juice? I didn't own a juicer. Spike them with cloves and make a holiday centerpiece? Cloves and I keep our distance, especially since I had my wisdom teeth pulled and got dry sockets, which my oral surgeon packed with gauze dipped in oil of clove, *which,* after a week in my mouth, was NASTY, and I don't mean that in any Janet Jackson sort of way.

There was just one answer: cake. There is no problem that cannot be solved with cake. It's the right answer to everything.

So upon arriving home, I scoured the cupboards, mulling over what sort of cake this might be and, of course, where the oranges could come in. I vaguely remembered a cake that my sister had once made from an old Martha Stewart book, an almond cake served with glazed oranges. But I had no almonds or almond extract. Instead, I found a lone vanilla bean in the spice drawer and, in the refrigerator, a pint of buttermilk left over from pancakes. I could make a cake flavored with vanilla bean, I thought. Maybe a *buttermilk* cake, a moist one with a bit of tang. I'd seen a recipe recently somewhere on the Internet. I could do that. Then I could glaze some orange segments in a little sugar and juice and serve them with the cake. That would be *perfect.* I was so pleased with myself that I opened a bottle of wine.

It was in the execution, however, that things got a little sticky. It had nothing to do with the wine, unfortunately, although that would have probably been more fun and certainly easier to explain away. The cake was tasty enough, and the oranges were truly lovely, but something was missing. It was good enough for government work, as my mother likes to say, but in truth, the cake was sort of tough and rubbery. With a little time on the counter, I imagined, it might make a fine seat cushion in a diner somewhere. Also, when you slid a fork through it, it made the tiniest, strangest *squeeeeak*. It sounded like the creaking of a door in a haunted house, if said house were small enough to sit on a dime.

But still, I loved the idea. The oranges were delicious with the vanilla bean, a little like a Creamsicle in cake form. I really wanted it to work. I reread the recipe. It didn't call for much in the way of butter, and I began to suspect that was the problem. A cake needs fat for tenderness, the department in which this one was sorely lacking. I would have to try other recipes or fiddle with making my own.

So began a pursuit that took me through six different recipes, a gallon of buttermilk, more sticks of butter than I would like to say, and two years (with several months' hiatus, admittedly) of my young life. I will spare you the gruesome details and just say this: I laughed, I cried, and I ate a lot of cake. I made eight different versions before I found the right one. If you turn the number eight on its side, you have infinity. I could have been making cakes for *infinity*. Talk about delayed gratification.

Somewhere, Marlene is very proud.

The winning cake is one I adapted from Rose Levy Beranbaum, author of *The Cake Bible*. (I should have known that someone with that kind of title to her name would have the solution.) It's a tender, delicate cake with a hint of milky tang, just enough to give the sweet vanilla a good-natured elbow in the ribs, and with its fine crumb, it's perfectly suited to sopping up plump oranges and their warm syrup. It begs for a second helping.

VANILLA BEAN BUTTERMILK CAKE
WITH GLAZED ORANGES AND CRÈME FRAÎCHE

I may have stumbled upon this cake because of some oranges, but as it turns out, I like the cake itself so much that sometimes I don't even bother with the oranges. They *are* lovely with it, though, especially with a dollop of tangy crème fraîche.

Oh, and you might consider saving the egg whites left over from this recipe to make a batch of Coconut Macaroons (page 94).

FOR THE CAKE

4 large egg yolks
⅔ cup buttermilk
1 cup sugar
1 vanilla bean
2 cups cake flour
1 tablespoon baking powder

½ teaspoon salt
1 stick (4 ounces) unsalted butter,
  at room temperature

TO SERVE

Glazed oranges (optional), recipe
  follows
Crème fraîche (optional)

Set an oven rack to the middle position, and preheat the oven to 350°F. Grease a 9-inch springform pan with butter or cooking spray. Line the bottom of the pan with a round of parchment paper, and grease it, too.

In a small bowl, lightly whisk the egg yolks with about ¼ cup of the buttermilk. Set aside.

Put the sugar in the bowl of a stand mixer fitted with the paddle attachment. Alternatively, if you plan to use handheld beaters, put it into a medium mixing bowl. Using a sharp knife, split the vanilla bean in half from tip to tip. Run the back edge of the knife down each half of the pod, scraping out the tiny black seeds. Dump them into the bowl with the sugar. Using your fingers, rub the seeds into the sugar, taking care to break up any clumps. Discard the spent pod. (Or bury it in a container of sugar to make vanilla sugar.)

Add the flour, baking powder, and salt to the vanilla sugar. Beat on low speed for a few seconds, just to combine.

Cut the butter into pieces and add it to the dry ingredients, along with the remaining buttermilk. Beat on low speed until the ingredients are moist, then increase the speed to medium and beat until well combined, about 1 minute. Scrape down the sides of the bowl with a rubber spatula, then add the egg mixture in three doses, beating well after each addition. Scrape down the sides of the bowl, and beat for 30 seconds on medium speed. The batter should be thick but airy, very pale and smooth.

Scrape the batter into the prepared pan, and smooth the top with a rubber spatula. Bake for 30 to 40 minutes, or until a toothpick inserted in the center comes out clean.

Cool the cake in the pan on a rack for 15 minutes. Run a thin knife around the edge of the pan, then remove the sides. Position a wide, flat plate upside-down atop the cake, and invert the cake onto the plate. Remove the bottom of the pan and the parchment. Place a wire rack over the cake, and turn upright onto the rack. Cool completely.

NOTE: This cake is best on the day it's made. But if you have any leftovers, I find that they make for a nice "dessert" after breakfast.

Yield: 8 servings

GLAZED ORANGES

4 navel oranges, at room temperature
½ cup sugar

Using a small, sharp knife, supreme 3 of the oranges. To do this, slice off the top and bottom ¼ inch of each one, revealing the flesh at either end. Working with 1 orange at a time, stand the fruit on one end and cut closely down the sides, trimming away and discarding the peel and white pith. Holding the peeled orange over a medium bowl, carefully cut between the membranes to remove the individual wedges of flesh. Let the wedges, called "supremes," and their juice fall into the bowl. Discard the core.

Juice the fourth orange: it should yield about ½ cup juice. If it comes up a little short, add a bit of juice from the bowl of supremes to make up the difference. Pour the juice into a heavy 2-quart saucepan, and add the sugar. Place over medium heat, and cook, stirring frequently, until the sugar has dissolved and the mixture bubbles and reduces to deep orange–golden syrup, about 10 minutes. Add the supremes, stirring them gently in the syrup, and cook until warmed through, 1 to 2 minutes.

Serve immediately, with wedges of vanilla bean buttermilk cake and spoonfuls of crème fraîche.

Yield: 8 servings

QUITE THAT MAGNIFICENT

To most people, I guess, turning twenty-one is all about booze. To me, turning twenty-one was all about coconut. Booze is nice, but coconut is chewable, and when push comes to shove, I will always like eating better than drinking. Everyone has their priorities.

For the first two decades of my life, I absolutely hated coconut. I associated it primarily with the scent of cheap tanning oil, the kind that comes in brown plastic bottles at the drugstore, bottles the color that your skin is supposed to turn, apparently, upon application. I always hated those bottles. My mom occasionally had one kicking around in the cabinet under the bathroom sink, and after one trip to the pool, the whole thing would be slicked with a thin film of that pungent oil, a magnet for grit and dirt. I hated opening the cabinet, because it reeked of coconut. My aversion was especially pronounced because, as a red-head, my skin has only two settings: pale and burnt. Though my parents gave it their best, constantly slathering me with SPF 45, I had my share of sunburns as a child, and most were incurred at beaches and pools where the scent of tanning oil hung heavy in the air. Needless to say, coconut had a long row to hoe with me. Twenty years long.

But then along came Max's Café. The summer after my sophomore year of college, I was working at a grocery store in Mill Valley, California, and living with my aunt Tina, whose house is only a few minutes from an outpost of Max's Café, a California-based deli chain. Actually, the word *deli* isn't really strong enough; Max's is more like a deli-meets-pleasure dome. They serve cakes and pastrami sandwiches as big as your head. One night, after picking up a movie at the video store, we decided to stop by for something sweet. That was when I saw Max's enormous chocolate-covered coconut macaroon. It was conical and imposing, the size of a beehive hairdo, covered from head to toe in a rippling sheath of chocolate. There was coconut under there somewhere, I knew, but it certainly was skillfully hidden. I felt myself starting to succumb. We bought one and brought it home, and that night, I was converted to coconut worship. A one-pound macaroon will stand for nothing less.

There would be no turning back. That summer, I bought those macaroons more often than I'd like to admit, and I'm willing to admit to a lot. They were dense, toothachingly sweet, and rich enough to cause hot flashes. I'd usually cut one into quarters and savor it over a couple of days. Only once did I throw caution to the wind, tucking away three-quarters in a single evening. I barely lived to tell the tale, and with much, much regret.

But the near overdose only dampened my enthusiasm for a few weeks. By my birthday in mid-September, I had recovered enough to request a cake-sized macaroon as one of my birthday cakes. There would be two that year: the macaroon and a four-layer lemon cake with lemon curd. It was my twenty-first birthday, so excess was in order.

I called Max's central bakery in the South Bay. They had never taken an order like mine, so I really had to spell it out, and they questioned my resolve more than once. But in the end, they pulled through admirably, creating the biggest and most horrifyingly beautiful macaroon I have ever seen. It was made from four layers of macaroon batter, thick and sticky and piped into a spiral, and after baking, each layer was dipped in chocolate. Then they were stacked one upon the other, with the largest on the bottom and the smallest on top, so that, together, they looked like a jumbo version of a more standard-sized macaroon. Then the whole thing was doused in chocolate again. For all that, they charged me only thirty dollars, and they delivered it to the house. It was a coup. I haven't seen anything quite that magnificent since.

There's a picture of me taken that night, with the macaroon cake. In the photograph, I'm blowing out the candles on my other birthday cake, the lemon one, and I'm wearing some very aggressive purple eye shadow and a streak of lemon curd on my cheek, the latter coming courtesy of my cousin Sarah, who, even at the age of twenty-three, *had* to put her hand in the cake and then smear it across my face. The macaroon is sitting next to me on a glass cake stand, unfazed.

But then, a couple of years later, I would graduate from college and leave California. I would lose access to Max's macaroons. But that's okay, as it turned out, because I found a recipe that I like even better. (Max's always were a little too sweet.) They're incredibly easy to make—though I haven't attempted a cake version yet, so I make no claims there—and they're so moist and chewy that they're almost closer to candy than they are to cookies. Which, though it may sound strange, is a good thing, I assure you.

In fact, I once baked a batch of them for a friend's party, and I heard later that one of the guests actually hoarded some inside a plastic cup and sneaked them home in her purse. I don't blame her. I can't be left alone with these things, not even when they're hidden in the freezer. Each time I walk into the kitchen, I feel like Odysseus, during the part of the story when he is sailing past the Sirens. For my own good, I sometimes think that I should ask my husband to remove the macaroons from the house—to secure me to something solid and heavy, like the dishwasher, and to ignore my screams as he tosses them into the trash can outside. Coconut and I have come a long way.

*M*y favorite chocolate for this recipe is Valrhona Manjari 64%.

3 cups lightly packed sweetened
shredded coconut
¾ cup sugar
¾ cup egg whites (from about 5 large
eggs)

1½ teaspoons pure vanilla extract
4 ounces bittersweet chocolate, finely
chopped
½ cup heavy cream

Place the coconut, sugar, and egg whites in a heavy 2- to 3-quart sauce-pan and stir well. Cook over medium-low heat, stirring frequently, 10 to 15 minutes. The mixture will look very creamy as it heats, and then it will slowly get a bit drier, with individual flakes of coconut becoming discernable. Stop cooking when it no longer looks creamy but is still quite sticky and moist, not dry. Remove from the heat, and stir in the vanilla. Scrape the mixture into a pie plate or small baking sheet, spread it out a bit to allow it to cool quickly, and refrigerate until cold, about 30 minutes.

Preheat the oven to 300°F. Line a baking sheet with parchment paper or a silicone baking mat.

Using your hands or a small, spring-loaded ice cream scoop—I like to use one with a capacity of 2 tablespoons—scoop and firmly pack the coconut mixture into small domes. (If you're using an ice cream scoop, keep a bowl of warm water nearby. The scoop will need a quick swish every now and then to keep it from getting gummed up.) Space them evenly on the baking sheet.

Bake the macaroons until evenly golden, about 30 minutes. Cool completely on the pan on a wire rack. Then remove the macaroons from the baking sheet, and set them on the rack. Set the rack over the baking sheet.

Put the chopped chocolate in a medium bowl. Heat the cream in a small saucepan over medium heat, swirling the pan occasionally, until it is hot and steaming. Do not allow it to boil. Remove the pan from the heat, and pour the cream over the chocolate. Let sit for 1 minute, then stir until smooth. Spoon the warm ganache generously over the macaroons, shaking them gently, if needed, to coax the ganache down their sides.

Refrigerate the macaroons on the rack until the ganache sets, at least 2 hours. Transfer them to an airtight container, and refrigerate or freeze.

NOTE: Macaroons will keep in the refrigerator for up to 5 days. Frozen, they will keep for a month or two.

Yield: 14 to 18 macaroons

WHAT FRANCE WOULD TASTE LIKE

I am one of those people for whom college was just okay. I liked my classes and my professors and the people I met there, but I never felt completely at home. I always imagined college as a place where I would tumble, not unlike Alice falling down the rabbit hole, into some sort of lovely, wacky, self-contained world: a close-knit group of friends, a fully-formed post-teens family of sorts. Instead, I found myself living in on-campus theme houses with people who largely kept to themselves, and where the cook put a padlock on the freezer so we wouldn't eat the Otis Spunkmeyer cookie dough he kept there. I learned a few things, but it wasn't quite what I wanted it to be.

So when the opportunity arose to study abroad during my junior year, I pounced on it. I applied to my university's Paris program, writing a breathless essay about *le Quartier Latin* and that visit when I was ten. That fall, I packed an enormous suitcase, hugged my parents, and flew to Paris, where I was greeted by my host family.

My host mother was tall, trim, and proper, with a singsong voice and a name that, when properly pronounced, rang like chimes at Sunday mass. She moved through the house as though *en pointe*—softly, gracefully, decisively—and wore silver bangle bracelets that clicked sweetly against each other when she lifted her hand to secure the barrettes in her long brown hair. She was Catholic, very Catholic, in fact, as these things go. She had four children, ages nine to seventeen, a Labrador puppy, and a husband who'd lost his job and had gone to Canada to find work. Things were complicated. It must have been exhausting. She did an admirable job, but she often fell asleep in the bathtub after dinner.

Aside from her role at home, my host mother was also the French equivalent of a Tupperware saleswoman. She tested and sold silicone baking equipment, the bendy, nonstick baking pans, molds, and sheets that have become so popular in recent years. I was lucky enough to live under her roof, and within wonderfully close range of her kitchen, for six months. You can well imagine the glory that might have been, had I not taken down the crucifix she'd hung on my bedroom wall.

I was barely twenty-one, with a wardrobe that consisted largely of the color black, a long wool coat that made me look like Neo from *The Matrix*, and a short, spiky haircut. I was also mainly a vegetarian. (I never could give up my father's hamburgers, and I also liked the occasional piece of fish.) My host mother liked to tell me about her previous American student, a blond, all-American Mormon girl with whom she hit it off famously. She also liked to tell me, without the slightest wink of amusement, that she had specifically requested not to host a vegetarian. But she sensed that, under all the black eyeliner, I was very eager to please (still my greatest weakness, I'll freely admit) and so she took me on, gently correcting my French, delivering clean sheets to my door with admirable regularity, and teaching me about aged cheeses and soufflé.

As part of the hosting agreement, she was required to provide me with breakfast and dinner five days a week. Each weeknight at precisely eight o'clock, I'd climb the stairs from my bedroom to the second-floor kitchen, where my preteen host brothers and chatty teenage host sisters were waiting at the table. My host mother would have prepared something small and light for us to begin with: a simple salad of grated carrots or cubed beets in dressing, or half a grapefruit, its segments loosened with a thin, curving knife. Sometimes there would be a platter of warm steamed leeks with vinaigrette, everyone's favorite. The boys would argue over the white end nearest to the root, the sweetest, softest part. Then, depending on the season, we'd move on to a savory tart; pasta with a sauce of oil-packed tuna, chopped tomatoes, and sautéed onions; or *tartiflette*, a wintry casserole made from potatoes, *lardons* (graciously absent from my corner of the dish), and Reblochon cheese. Then came the cheese plate. It was at that table that I first learned of France's nightly cheese ritual, pungent and addictive, eaten with hunks of baguette from the *boulangerie* next door. And after that, there was always dessert: homemade applesauce topped with a sheet of crisp meringue, a butter cake with apples or pears, or, in January, a *galette des rois*, brought in from a nearby *pâtisserie*.

At least one night each week we'd have a "Flexipan dinner," a meal centered on a recipe that my host mother was testing in her silicone molds. Her individual tartlets of caramelized endive with goat cheese were staggeringly good, as was her flourless chocolate cake, which quickly became part of the regular dessert rotation. But my favorite were the *bouchons au thon* (literally, "tuna corks"), an odd, homely, and surprisingly delicious mixture of canned tuna, tomato paste, crème fraîche, Gruyère, and eggs, baked in muffin molds.

Canned tuna isn't usually something I go crazy for, but these *bouchons* were special. With a texture somewhere between the filling of a quiche and a freshly made country pâté, they tamed the flat pungency of canned fish with the sweetness of tomato and the rich butterfat of crème fraîche. We ate them warm with roasted potatoes, and, for lunch the next day, cold with a green salad. They were unlike anything I'd ever had. They tasted like what I imagined France itself would taste like, if it were small enough to fit in my mouth. I gave thanks almost daily for all that France and its Flexipans brought to my life, but mainly for those *bouchons au thon*.

As luck would have it, that winter, when my host mother went to visit her husband in Canada, she left me and my fifteen-year-old host sister alone with a freezer full of *bouchons*. I had just met a young Frenchman (more on him in a minute) and, seizing the opportunity, I invited him over for dinner. We ate *bouchons*, roasted vegetables and herbed potatoes, pricey cheeses, and baguette. For the grand finale, I baked oatmeal chocolate chip cookies. It was a pure, starry-eyed triumph all around, right on through to the next morning, when he went home, and though my skinny French cigarette pants might have helped things along, in all truth, I credit the *bouchons*. I also credit them with earning me, upon my host mother's return, my first and only *"Mo-lee, ce n'est pas un hôtel!"* (Molly, this is not a hotel!) speech. I was almost as stunned as she was. I didn't know I had it in me.

It was only the beginning, in all sorts of ways.

𝒴 ou can use either solid white or chunk light tuna.

One 6-ounce can tuna packed in
   water, drained well
1 cup lightly packed finely shredded
   Gruyère
⅓ cup crème fraîche
3 tablespoons tomato paste

3 large eggs
¼ cup finely chopped yellow onion
2 tablespoons finely chopped Italian
   parsley
¼ teaspoon salt

Set an oven rack to the middle position, and preheat the oven to 325°F. Grease 8 cups of a standard-sized muffin tin, and set aside.

Put the tuna in a medium bowl, and use a fork, mashing and poking, to break it up into small pieces. There should be no chunks larger than a dime. Add the remaining ingredients and stir well with the fork, mashing a bit as you go, until the mixture is thoroughly combined. It will be a soft orange-pink color.

Divide the mixture evenly among the 8 prepared muffin cups. Bake for 20 to 25 minutes, or until the *bouchons* look set on top and around the edges. Transfer the tin to a rack, and let cool for 5 minutes. Carefully run a small, thin knife around the edge of each *bouchon* to make sure it isn't stuck, then carefully remove them from the tin. They will collapse a bit as they cool.

Serve warm or at room temperature.

Yield: 8 bouchons, enough for 4 light eaters

THE BEST OF ALL POSSIBLE WORLDS

I promised to tell you about that young Frenchman, and it *is* kind of a good story, so I won't make you wait. I met Guillaume on a clear January night, in a club called Le Batofar. I am not much for clubs, but my friend Keaton had talked me into going. The two of us were in the same program in Paris that year, and she always knew what was hip. (I always knew where to find the best pastries.) Le Batofar was an old converted lighthouse boat docked on the south shore of the Seine, and it was the new hot thing, with an up-and-coming DJ spinning almost every night. So we went and danced a little, and I wore those same cigarette pants, and as we were getting ready to leave, about 10 minutes from the last subway of the night, I spotted him across the dance floor. He was tall and lanky, with olive skin and short, messy black hair. He was gorgeous.

We stared at each other. To be perfectly honest, I assumed that he was looking at Keaton, with her blond hair and pale, milky skin. Pretty much everyone, male or female, looks at Keaton. I gave him a hard stare—a close imitation, I hoped, of De Niro's "You lookin' at *me?*" from *Taxi Driver*—and he crossed the floor and stood in front of me. My hands were shaking. His name was Guillaume, he said shyly. He was gorgeous across the dance floor, but now he was *really* gorgeous. We talked awkwardly, yelling over the music. He was eighteen and in his second semester of college at Jussieu. He was studying some sort of physics in school, and he had a sweet, broad smile, and I was sweating through my coat. I had just missed the last subway of the night, and my host family's house was halfway across town, out of the question on foot.

Panicking, I tried to excuse myself to go find a cab, but he wanted to help. He gave it a good shot, too, even chasing one down the street, but none of them would stop. We walked back to the club, and he gestured to one of the cars outside. He could take me home, he suggested carefully. My mother would *kill* me, I thought, remembering her admonishment, back when I was in grade school, to never get into cars with strangers. In fact, as I write this, *I* want to kill me, just thinking of what could have happened. But I did it. I accepted. Guillaume had come to the club with his friend Sébastien in Sébastien's mother's tiny white hatchback, and the three of us piled in together. There was a reggae mix tape in the stereo, and the car smelled cold and clean. They lived in Drancy, a suburb to the northeast, and weaving through the dark, narrow streets of southern Paris, where my host family lived, they were instantly lost. I pulled out my Métro map and began to navigate, using the subway stations as landmarks. Half an hour and several miracles later, they delivered me to my doorstep. Guillaume gave me a kiss on each cheek, and in return, I gave him my phone number.

The next week, for our first date, we decided to meet outside my school. I was nervous, so I had my friend Clare wait with me on the bench by the gate, and Guillaume showed up with his friend Vincent. The two of them saw us off, and Guillaume steered me to a café around the corner, Café Charbon, where we ordered coffee and started to talk. Then we took a walk around the chilly city, and the afternoon faded into evening, and he bought me roasted chestnuts from a street vendor on the Place de la Bastille. They were warm and burnt at the edges, and we ate them from a newspaper cone as we walked. He was wearing one of those white cotton headbands that only a young Frenchman can get away with, and he'd written "JAH IS MY KING" down one strap of his back-pack. He told me that his birthday was December 30, and I decided not to think about how recently he had been seventeen. When he kissed me on a platform in the Concorde Métro station, I was so dizzy that I almost fell onto the tracks. The next day, Clare told me that after Guillaume and I left for the café, Vincent confided to her that Guillaume, feeling shy, had asked him to escort him to meet me. Clare laughed and admitted that she had done the same for me.

That was it. I was in love. First love is supposed to be misty and sweet, a slow-motion video set to a medley of meaningful songs, and mine was just that, except that our songs were a mix of reggae and the *click-click* of subway turnstiles. We would have two children, I decided, one with his black hair and the other with my red, and we'd walk them to the *école maternelle* each morning, listening to their perfectly bilingual voices ricochet down the city's ancient streets. I would live in France forever, but each summer we'd go to Oklahoma to see my family, where Guillaume would buy his first cowboy hat and help my father make French toast. All would be for the best in the best of all possible worlds.

We loved the foreignness in each other, the mispronunciations and bridged gaps. The first time I spent the night in his narrow bed under the eaves of his parents' house, he woke up early and went out for enormous croissants from the bakery around the corner. We sat sleepily next to the kitchen window, drinking hot chocolate from café au lait bowls. I invited him to my host family's house for the infamous *bouchon*-fueled sleepover, and the next morning, we ate oatmeal chocolate chip cookies for breakfast on my bedroom floor. He invited his friends to join us for a homemade dinner of *raclette*—buttery cow's milk cheese from Savoie, melted and poured over boiled potatoes, pearl onions, and lacy sheets of ham—and I invited my friends to meet us at La Belière, a tiny bistro with lots of smoke and a piano in the corner. It was there that, after a carafe of cheap red and a bowl of mussels in broth, he introduced me to tarte Tatin.

A classic among classic French desserts, tarte Tatin is essentially a sexed-up apple pie—a housewife in stilettos, you could say. It starts with wedges of apple caramelized to a deep amber, their juices mingling with butter and sugar to yield a complex flavor that verges on hard cider. Covered with a sheet of puff pastry, baked to golden, and then inverted, the apples sit coyly atop their many-layered blanket like Ingres's *Grande Odalisque* on her chaise. Dolloped with crème fraîche, tarte Tatin doesn't dally with small talk. It reaches for your leg under the table.

Guillaume and I both had school the next morning, and so we kissed good night on the street outside, him to his train and me to mine. His mouth tasted like baked apples and cigarette smoke, a combination more delicious than I should probably admit. He gave me a jar of chestnut cream that his mother had brought back for me from a vacation in the Ardèche, and he hugged me hard. Then he never called me again.

I cried for a week. I didn't say a word to my host mother. I was sure she would think I deserved it. A few more weeks passed, and spring break came, and my stay in Paris was over. I packed my suitcase and flew back to college.

Six months later, I found a letter from Guillaume in my post office box at school. He told me he was sorry, and that he had been afraid. I sobbed the whole way home. We wrote back and forth a couple of times, but it was hard for me, and eventually we stopped.

A year later, the fall after I graduated, I went back to Paris to take a job. I didn't tell him I was coming; we hadn't been in touch for months. But one afternoon, I was sitting on a café terrace on the Place de la Bastille and he walked by. In a city of almost 12 million people, he happened to walk by. He was with his friend Arnaud, who had been with us the night that we ate *raclette*, and he recognized me and pointed. Guillaume shook his head and looked at the ground, and I broke out in a cold sweat. Then he walked over and hugged me, both of us shaking.

Every now and then, we still e-mail. He usually finds me about once a year, and we swap letters for a week or so. It's always awkward, but still, I'm glad for it. Sometimes I can't help but wonder how things might have been if I hadn't had a return ticket, or if he hadn't been eighteen. For a long time, I dreamed about that bed under the eaves. Some nights, I even thought I could hear our perfectly bilingual children twittering like birds between the rafters. But most of the time, I just bake tarte Tatin.

t his recipe was inspired by Julia Child's classic method in *The Way to Cook*. Don't be intimidated by its length. It's surprisingly simple. And I'm pretty verbose.

Also, about the puff pastry: you can certainly make your own, if you're into that sort of thing, but I use store-bought, either Dufour brand or Trader Joe's. Thaw according to the directions on the package.

Juice of 1 lemon
1½ cups granulated sugar
5 to 6 large Golden Delicious apples

6 tablespoons (3 ounces) unsalted
   butter
About 14 ounces puff pastry

In a large bowl, stir together the lemon juice and ½ cup of the sugar.

Peel and quarter the apples, trimming away the cores such that each quarter has a flat inner side. Put the apples in the bowl with the lemon juice and sugar and toss well. Set aside for 30 minutes.

Meanwhile, in an 8- or 9-inch cast-iron skillet set over medium heat, melt 4 tablespoons of the butter. Add the remaining 1 cup sugar, along with 3 to 4 tablespoons of the lemon-sugar juices. Stir to mix. Cook the mixture over medium-low heat, stirring regularly with a wooden spoon, for about 15 minutes, or until the mixture is a smooth, bubbly, pale caramel color.

Remove the pan from the heat and carefully—hot caramel makes a nasty burn—add the apple pieces, arranging them rounded side down in a decorative pattern. Arrange a second layer of apples on top wherever they fit, closely packed. The second layer need not be terribly neat. Cut the remaining 2 tablespoons of butter into dice, and distribute them evenly over the apples.

Preheat the oven to 375°F.

Cook the apples over medium-low heat for about 20 minutes. Stay nearby while they cook, so that you can frequently spoon the bubbling caramel over them; this will help the uppermost layer of apples to cook. (This is, incidentally, a good time to make any phone calls you've been putting off. It'll help pass the time.) From time to time, press the apples gently with the back of the spoon. Don't worry if they shift a bit in the liquid: just move them back to where they were. The apples are ready when the liquid in the pan has thickened slightly and is amber in color. The apples should still be slightly firm. Do not allow them to get entirely soft or the liquid to turn dark brown. Remove the pan from the heat.

On a floured surface, roll out the puff pastry to a thickness of about ³⁄₁₆ inch. Using a sharp, thin knife, trace a circle in the pastry about 10 inches in diameter. (I often trace around the bottom of a 10-inch cake pan, or around a 9-inch one, leaving an extra ½-inch border all the way around.) Trim away any excess dough. Carefully lay the pastry circle over the apples in the skillet, tucking the overlap between the apples and the side of the pan.

Place the skillet on a rimmed baking sheet, and bake for 25 to 35 minutes, or until the pastry has risen and is dry and golden brown. Remove the skillet from the oven, and let it rest for a minute. Then tilt the pan slightly and look down the inside edge: there will be some juice down there. Pour as much of it as you can into the sink or trash can. Then place a serving platter upside-down over the skillet and, working quickly and carefully—*it's hot!*—invert the tart onto the platter. Rearrange any apple slices that may have slipped or stuck to the skillet.

Serve warm, preferably within an hour or two of baking. Puff pastry can't hold off sogginess for long.

Yield: 8 servings

HIGH POINTS

I guess this would be a good time to admit that despite all that Parisian drama, my dating history is a brief one. Compared to most people I know, I didn't date much. This was not intentional, I assure you. I certainly tried, but it didn't come easily. I have since been told that my tendency to sit in the front row in class and raise my hand at every question, not to mention the leather dog collar I took to wearing for a while, were possibly at fault, but I can't be sure.

No one asked me out in high school. The one person who professed a crush, my best friend Billy, who wore seersucker shorts and kept his blond hair in a handsome Ken doll cut, was too polite to do much about it. We went to our senior prom together, and he gamely took to the dance floor with me when I requested Michael Jackson's "Beat It," but that was as racy as our romance got. I think my four-pronged, Statue-of-Libertyesque updo was a bit much for him, although I have never asked. Sometimes I used to think about what it would be like to kiss him, but I had never kissed anyone before, and I didn't want to make the first move. I remember reading, around that time, a "Dear Abby" letter from a thirty-three-year-old woman who had never been touched by a man. I was terrified. I was certain that she was me, writing from the future.

You can well imagine my relief, then, when my first kiss came along, three months before my nineteenth birthday. His name was

Warren, but he went by Puffer. (It's a long story, and disappointingly innocent.) It happened in the foyer of my parents' house, and just when things were getting good, I accidentally bit him. I would have to wait another year, until I was twenty, to have my second kiss, with a graduate student I met in college. I was so grateful and relieved that as a thank-you gift, I gave him my virginity as well—not on a silver platter, but close: on a twin bed in student housing, with the regrettable film *Niagara, Niagara* in the VCR.

Over the eight years between that harrowing night and my wedding day, I had my heart broken by Guillaume; spent one night engaged in heavy petting rituals with a future rabbi; spent three years of my early twenties with Lucas, the guy I took to the museum concert when we were kids; dated a blond Minnesotan named Karma and a well-read arborist with a dog called Index; and, finally, blessedly, met my husband. Given that I didn't have a lot of time to work with, and that I spent several years of it in monogamous situations, I think I did pretty well. I hit all the high points.

Plus, I learned some important lessons. I learned that some things, like whether or not a man makes the bed, aren't that important. I learned that men who like to dance are, in general, more fun than their non-dancing counterparts. I learned that kissing a man while leaning against a warm dishwasher is a lovely, *lovely* experience. (Go ahead! Try it! I'll wait.) I also learned—although I suppose I could have told you this years ago, even before my first date—that hell hath no fury like a woman starved.

When I was in college, I worked for two summers, as I've mentioned before, at a grocery store in northern California. My job consisted of standing behind the case of prepared salads and spooning things into to-go containers, making sandwiches, and serving rotisserie chickens from the hot case. We had several regular dinner customers, mainly single men who would come in each night for roasted chicken and grilled vegetables. I developed a friendly banter with a few—as is wont to happen when it is your job to ask people if they would prefer a breast or a thigh—and one evening, while I scooped his brown rice, one of them invited me to dinner. He seemed relatively harmless: soft-spoken, smiley, a New Age music producer in his mid-thirties with dirty blond hair and a cabin-cum-tree house on the side of nearby Mount Tamalpais. I accepted.

He invited me up to his house, where he would make dinner. It was a beautiful space, a loft of sorts with lots of bare wood and big windows, a Japanese tatami table surrounded by cushions at one end and a sprawling leather sofa and fireplace at the other. He put Van Morrison's *Astral Weeks* on the stereo—a dreamy, magical album, by the way, if you aren't familiar with it—and ushered me into the kitchen. Then he announced proudly that he'd gone to the farmers' market that morning and had come home with seven kinds of sprouts.

"Isn't that awesome?" he said. *"Seven!"*

I stared in silence as he retrieved seven small plastic bags from the refrigerator drawer. What is a person supposed to say to that? SEVEN kinds of *sprouts*. I like alfalfa sprouts, sort of, on a sandwich with provolone, tomato, and avocado. I did not, however, and still do not, have any interest in widening my sprout experience—and certainly not seven-fold. Plus, I was *hungry*. There had to be more to dinner. There had to. I smiled and leaned against the counter.

He pulled a plate down from the cabinet, set it on the countertop, and, with a delicate pinch, lifted a tuft of sprouts from one of the bags. He deposited it in the center of the plate. Then he repeated the motion with the other six bags, lifting and—slowly, gently, with enormous care—placing small mounds of sprouts around the rim of the plate. They looked like loosely formed gaseous planets in some sort of sprout galaxy, orbiting a larger sprout sun in the center. He then cut three cherry tomatoes in half and strewed them around the plate. Then he reached into the cabinet and retrieved a bottle of olive oil and another of balsamic vinegar, sprinkled them over the salad, if you can call it that, and, with a triumphant smile, handed the plate to me. I stood quietly, smiling numbly, while he assembled his own plate: much less carefully this time, just sprouts tossed haphazardly here and there. I'd had the deluxe treatment. He hadn't even saved himself a tomato. He grabbed two sets of chopsticks from a jar by the sink, nodded toward the tatami table, and dinner was served.

We were in California, so I guess I should have known what I was in for. I tried to be grateful. I knew he only wanted to impress. And he was so sweet! How can you fault anyone who takes that much care with your dinner, and who plays "The Way Young Lovers Do" on the stereo? Really, you can't.

You also, however, can't disguise the sound of an angry stomach when it growls under a tatami table. Not even the Chinese stringed instrument he kept in the corner, the one he played for me after dinner, could muffle its roar. I didn't want to seem ungrateful, but I had to go. I thanked him profusely and drove home, where I made a peanut butter sandwich and ate it at the kitchen counter, vowing silently that in my home, salad would never be a swear word.

The recipe that follows, a hearty jumble of toasted, garlic-rubbed bread, arugula, and ripe cherries, sauced with good doses of olive oil and sweet balsamic, is anything but. It's a mealtime salad, a spot-on lunch or light dinner, especially if you add goat cheese. It's handsome, delicious, and a little messy, like most good things in this life.

BREAD SALAD WITH CHERRIES, ARUGULA, AND GOAT CHEESE

*T*his isn't so much a recipe as a formula. It's the kind of thing you bang together on a summer day when you happen to have some ripe cherries and a hunk of chewy, day-old artisan bread. It's so simple that you don't really need precise quantities, although I will give you some to start with. From there, just taste and tweak to your own palate.

6 ounces rustic white bread, preferably day-old

Olive oil

½ pound cherries, preferably Bing, halved and pitted

⅛ teaspoon pressed or crushed garlic

Balsamic vinegar

Salt

Arugula

Fresh goat cheese, such as Laura Chenel, coarsely crumbled

Black pepper

Preheat the oven to 400°F.

Using a sharp knife, trim the crust from the bread, and discard the crust. Tear the bread into rough bite-sized pieces. You should have about 4 loosely packed cups' worth. Dump the bread out onto a rimmed baking sheet, and drizzle it with olive oil. Toss to coat. Don't worry if the pieces aren't evenly oiled; that's okay. Bake until crispy and golden in spots, shaking the pan once, 8 to 10 minutes.

Meanwhile, put about one-third of the cherries in a small bowl, and crush them lightly with a fork, so that they release their juices. You don't want to mash them completely; just smash them a bit.

When the bread is nicely toasted, turn it out into a large bowl. While it is still hot, add the garlic, and toss well. Set aside to cool for a minute or two. Then add the cherries, both the smashed ones and the not-smashed ones, and toss. Add 2 teaspoons balsamic vinegar and toss again. Add 1 tablespoon olive oil and a pinch or two of salt and toss again. Taste, and adjust the vinegar, oil, and salt as needed: if you taste the bread and the cherries separately, they each should taste good alone. When you're satisfied with the flavor, add about 2 handfuls of arugula and toss one last time. Finish with a generous amount of crumbled goat cheese and a few grinds of the pepper mill, and serve.

Yield: 4 first-course servings or a light meal for 2

HEAVEN

Once upon a time, not so long ago (though it feels like centuries), I lived alone in a studio apartment in Paris. It had a front door that closed only when slammed, a tiny terrace guarded by a ceramic gnome, and an almost-kitchen in an alcove in the hallway, with a two-burner electric stove, a pint-sized refrigerator, and a microwave that I could reach only when I stood on tiptoe. It was humble, but it was sweet. Moreover, it was *in France*. It could have been a shoebox and still, I would have been charmed. It was a petite (*Parisienne*-size, you could say) piece of paradise. I was twenty-two, fresh out of college, and it was my first apartment.

I had come to the end of my senior year of college with absolutely no idea what to do next. I'd majored in human biology, but I didn't want to be a doctor. I did, however, have a French minor, and that at least was something. Given the circumstances, France seemed as good an idea as any. In retrospect, I'm sure my unresolved heartache over Guillaume had something to do with it, but I tried not to think about it. I just wanted to be in Paris again. One afternoon, a girl in my French literature class told me about a program offered by the French Ministry of Education, a program through which native English speakers were sometimes hired to teach in French public schools. I applied, and a few weeks later I was assigned a post as a part-time English conversation teacher at a high school in the suburbs west of Paris. I searched around, found a furnished apartment available for monthly rentals, and that fall, I went.

It was heaven. After four years on plastic-covered university-issued twin-sized mattresses, I took to sleeping squarely in the middle of my Parisian double bed, sprawled out like a snow angel. I recorded an outgoing message on my answering machine in both English and French, finding surprising pleasure in saying my name in both languages. Because my kitchen was so small, I used the top of my dresser as a de facto countertop. I had no table to speak of, but the foot of my bed made a decent stand-in. I gave over one entire shelf of my refrigerator to cheese, each wrapped in wax paper and ripe with promise, and I was so greedy about them that I took to licking my knife to get every last nub and smear. I decided that French television, being in a foreign language and all, was instructive, so I watched as much as I could. Did you know that the French have a game show in which purple animated bloblike creatures dance around on stage with the host? And that he calls them his *"pots,"* which is French for "pals," and talks to them as though they were real? It's true. It airs every day at lunchtime, and it was my greatest weakness. On weeknights, I ate dinner with Patrick Poivre d'Arvor, also known as PPDA, the handsome anchor of the 8:00 p.m. news on TF1. Sometimes on Sundays, I dined with his weekend counterpart Claire Chazal, a distinguished blond anchor with whom he once allegedly had an affair. (And a son! The French are so good at scandal.) I had all this, right there in my little apartment. I had to break myself in half to shave my legs in the pocket-sized shower stall, but otherwise, that place was paradise.

I learned so much that year, and I don't only mean that a dinner knife, no matter how dull, can cut your tongue. I learned that I love to cook for one. I know not everyone feels this way, but here's how I see it: it's my chance, my inviolable opportunity, to eat whatever I want to. It is one of the few moments when I can be perfectly selfish without feeling guilty. No one is going to tell me that blanched green beans, three slices of fresh mozzarella doused in olive oil, and two pieces of chocolate cake are not an acceptable dinner. (They are, I promise.) What's more, if I want to, I can just sit and stare out the window. Just *tra la la*, stare out the window. I don't have to say a word. I can sink into my seat, slow down, and zone out. Or, if zoning out is not what I need, I can choose instead to focus, really *focus*, for a while. I can pay attention to only my plate. Even now that I am married, I still feel this way sometimes. Maybe it's the only child in me, but to really feel like myself, and to keep from killing anyone, I need an evening alone at the table every now and then. Food is, of course, a social thing, one of the most positive, primal ways of spending time with people, but eating alone is also an affirmation. It's a way of enjoying me.

Cooking for one could feel fruitless sometimes—it's a lot of effort for little applause—but I tried not to let that stop me. It helps that I like leftovers. I'm happy to eat the same thing, day in and day out, for a whole week. No matter how big the batch, nothing goes to waste with me around. This is a trait that would have served me well during the Great Depression, though it also comes in handy nowadays, too, especially at the end of the month, right before rent is due, during the Great Depression of my wallet. I will eat the same soup for days. Ditto for braises and stews. Some of my finest solo meals have been the simplest ones, like ratatouille, the Provençal stew of eggplant, zucchini, peppers, tomatoes, onion, garlic, and herbs. When you're living in a glorified shoebox, it's very handy to have a one-pot meal in your back pocket, and ratatouille was mine.

My studio in Paris was situated in the eleventh arrondissement, not too far from a market street called rue Oberkampf, a name that, when spoken aloud, makes you sound like you've got an endearingly fat lip. Gently curving up an ever-so-slight slope, it is lined with all sorts of shops and stands: a cheese shop here, a cheese shop there, a wine shop, a *boulangerie*, a *pâtisserie*, a butcher with a rotisserie full of chickens. But my favorite shop on Oberkampf was a greengrocer on a corner, under a myrtle green awning. Behind boxes of wares stood the shopkeeper, a man in something akin to a doctor's coat, meting out the pick of the day. He was chatty but serious, almost professorial, and liked to make small talk about carrots and politics. On my first visit, he gave me half an apricot, plump and rosy around the shoulders, to eat while I shopped. I wound up buying a dozen of them and, over the months that followed, came back for tomatoes, lettuce, cauliflower, and soft green pears. One day in mid-October, he had an especially nice display of eggplant. I bought two fat, shiny ones and, my thoughts running ahead to ratatouille, a couple of zucchini and a red pepper. Then I went home and, in my largest pot, on one of my two burners, made dinner.

Though it may sound funny to say so as a girl from the smack-dab center of America, I grew up eating ratatouille. My parents made it for dinner once a month or so, and then we'd eat the leftovers for lunches or snacks. Some nights, if they were out and I was home alone, I'd eat it over boiled Yukon gold potatoes crushed with the back of a fork. That might be how I came to like eating alone. It's hard not to when you're eating like that.

My parents had very different methods for making ratatouille. My mother's was pretty standard—a jumble of vegetables together in a pot, with olive oil for moistening—but my father, true to form, mixed things up a little. Before he put the cubed vegetables in the pot, he'd dump them into a paper grocery bag, add a couple spoonfuls of flour, fold over the top, and shake the whole thing like some sort of awkward, vegetal maraca. I guess the flour was supposed to thicken the soupier parts, but it didn't do much besides make a mess on the countertop. My mother and I used to tell him how silly it was. It didn't occur to me until now, but it must have been hard for him sometimes, being the odd man out. He and I were close, but my mother and I were even closer. Between the two of us—opinionated, critical, so similar—it must have been hard to get a word in edgewise. We had a tendency to team up to nag him about his round, low-hanging belly or his ice cream consumption, or to razz him about his ratatouille. Although in truth, it really was good.

My method for ratatouille, though, is different from either of my parents'. I like to cook the vegetables separately at first, so that each is perfectly cooked on its own, and then combine them at the end. Recently I've started taking the added but easy step of roasting the eggplant in the oven rather than cooking it on the stovetop, where it sometimes winds up spongy and weird. In the oven, it gets wonderfully silky and tender. I think it's my best version yet. When I'm home alone, it's often the only thing I want to make. I tuck a napkin onto my lap and sit down by the window, and when it's all gone, I lick my knife until it sparkles, because there's no one there to catch me.

ROASTED EGGPLANT RATATOUILLE

R atatouille is a good accompaniment for any kind of meat, but I like to serve it on its own, as a light meal, with a poached or fried egg on top. Be sure to have some crusty bread on hand for sopping up the slurry at the bottom of the bowl.

1 pound eggplant, sliced crosswise into 1-inch-thick rounds
Olive oil
1 pound zucchini, trimmed, halved lengthwise, and sliced into ½-inch-thick half-moons
1 medium yellow onion, thinly sliced
1 large red bell pepper, cored, seeded, and chopped

4 large cloves garlic, thinly sliced
5 Roma tomatoes, seeded and chopped
¾ teaspoon salt
3 sprigs fresh thyme
1 bay leaf
¼ cup finely chopped fresh basil

Position a rack in the middle of the oven, and preheat the oven to 400°F.

Arrange the eggplant rounds in a single layer on a rimmed baking sheet. Pour 2 tablespoons olive oil in a small bowl, and brush onto the eggplant. Flip the slices and brush the second sides as well, taking care that each has a thin coating of oil. Bake for 30 minutes, flipping the slices halfway through, until soft and lightly browned on each side. Remove from the oven and cool. Cut into rough 1-inch pieces. Set aside. (You can do this a day or two ahead, refrigerating the eggplant until you're ready to use it. It'll make the final dish a little quicker to prepare.)

Warm 2 tablespoons olive oil over medium-high heat in a Dutch oven or large, deep skillet. Add the zucchini and cook, stirring occasionally, until golden and just tender, 10 to 12 minutes. Remove it from the pan, taking care to leave behind any excess oil, and set it aside.

If there is no oil left in the pan, add about 1 tablespoon; if there is still some remaining, proceed to the next step. Reduce the heat to medium, and add the onion and cook, stirring occasionally, until slightly softened, 4 to 5 minutes. Add the bell pepper and garlic and cook, stirring occasionally, until just tender but not browned, about 6 minutes. Add the tomatoes, salt, thyme, and bay leaf and stir to combine. Reduce the heat to low, cover, and cook for 5 minutes. Add the eggplant and zucchini, stir to incorporate, and cook until everything is very tender, 15 to 20 minutes more. Taste, and adjust the seasonings as necessary. Discard the bay leaf, and stir in the basil.

Serve hot, warm, or at room temperature, with additional salt for sprinkling.

NOTE: Ratatouille is even better on the second day or the third. If you can, plan to make it ahead of time, so that the flavors have time to meld and ripen.

Yield: 4 servings

9:00 A.M. SUNDAY

I'd been in Seattle for only 48 hours when I met Rebecca. I was sore from driving for three days to get there from Oklahoma, and I found her name in the phone book when I went looking for a place to take a Pilates class. She owned a studio in the basement of a neighborhood center a couple of blocks from my apartment. It was decorated in a style perhaps best described as "bordello chic"—zebra stripe fabric, red paint, black fringe—and I knew we would be friends when I saw the magnet on her filing cabinet. It was a drawing of a stern-looking man in chef's whites, saying, "I know exactly what to do with fat-free food. I throw it away."

I'd come back from Paris to go to graduate school at the University of Washington, and I needed a job. Rebecca seemed to know a lot of people, so I asked if she had any leads, and she hired me on the spot. She gave me a pink feathered pen and the title "Queen of Customer Service," and with them, I ruled over the front desk. I even had my own business card, emblazoned with my name and royal handle. It wasn't easy—to know Rebecca is to love her, and to fear her a little—but for two years, I typed, filed, ran errands, and managed the studio's schedule book. Even when I left to take a position at a local publishing house, where I worked until I felt brave enough to try to write for a living, I still got to keep my title. And I was right about our friendship: it remains intact, and it has perks that no job can provide.

One Saturday night a few years ago, Rebecca invited me to her favorite restaurant for a meal of three bottles of wine, chicken liver pâté, and breaded, deep-fried, soft-boiled eggs. Somewhere in the middle of all that, she invited me to a breakfast of Dutch babies with her gay husband, Jimmy. I'd heard about Jimmy's prowess in the kitchen—namely his chocolate cheesecakes, his shortbread waffles, and his "Pink Cookies," a rich shortbread spread thickly with rosy, cherry-scented frosting—and I knew better than to refuse. Also, I am a lightweight and, when tipsy, will agree to anything remotely edible. Who could refuse a Dutch baby pancake, hot and puffy from the skillet, on a Sunday morning? Not me.

I arrived at Jimmy's apartment at 9:00 a.m. to find a table set for two and a bacon-scented haze hanging over the stove. Jimmy stood by in a starched, white apron, spatula in hand. Rebecca sat at the table with wet hair and her usual morning iced tea, obligatory straw in place.

"I have five thousand straws," she told me proudly. "All red!"

Rebecca and Jimmy have known each other since the late 1970s, when they lived in the same building in St. Petersburg, Florida. As Rebecca tells it, she knew she had to meet Jimmy when she noticed his apartment window displays from the parking lot. Sometimes they mimicked department store windows, with mannequin parts carefully arranged. Other times they were a little more understated: a Perrier beach towel hung from the ceiling and lit from beneath, sort of art gallery-meets-Saint Tropez. Their first meeting was auspicious, a long story whose details I have worked hard to forget, but whose ending involves Rebecca in a hallway without pants. For many years, Jimmy, Rebecca, and Rebecca's straight husband, John, all lived in the same building in Seattle—Jimmy on the second floor and Rebecca and John on the ninth—and even now that they live in different parts of town, they still spend the bulk of their free time together. Jimmy is the baker, John is the cook, and Rebecca is the force of nature.

"Moll, you need two husbands," Rebecca announced, stirring a snowdrift of sugar into her iced tea. "You can't expect one person to be everything for you. You need at least two. *At least.*" I nodded. She had a point. I have thought about it many times since, and I don't know that I entirely agree—so far, one husband is almost more than enough for me—but she did have a very good point. But that morning, the scent of melted butter was rising from the stove, and talk of husbands, singular or plural, had nothing on it.

Atop the stove sat two small cast-iron skillets, each containing a shimmering pool of warm butter. Using a pastry brush, Jimmy coaxed it up the sides of the skillets. Then, working quickly, he poured a thin batter—not unlike that of a regular pancake, but with more eggs and less flour—into the hot fat. He slid the skillets into the oven, shut the door with a casual backhand, and the batter slowly began to rise, like a soufflé possessed, from the foamy pool of butter. The method for making a Dutch baby, I thought, is only marginally less awe inspiring than the method for making a human one.

While the pancakes baked, Jimmy struggled unsuccessfully to keep Rebecca out of the bacon, and I busied myself with copying down the recipe on a scrap of paper by the phone. Halfway down the page, I made a startling discovery. Jimmy had accidentally *doubled* the quantity of butter called for. It was a very fitting accident, given his penchant for boosting the fat in everything: recipes, thighs, you name it. But it meant that Rebecca and I—Jimmy apparently can't bear to eat before 11:00 a.m.—would be eating *half a stick of butter each.*

In such situations, however, I find it best to skip lightly over the details. When Jimmy pulled the Dutch babies from the oven, they were tinged with gold and gorgeously rumpled, like omelets with bed hair. Rebecca and I had no trouble putting away an entire baby each. Doused with lemon juice and dusted with powdered sugar, they were miraculously light, their eggy richness countered smartly by the citrus. I scooped up every last clump of lemon-soaked sugar and scraped my plate until it shined. Rebecca downed hers in record time and then returned to the bacon.

"One thing at a time, for maximum enjoyment!" she said cheerily. She always has the best advice.

DUTCH BABY PANCAKES WITH LEMON AND SUGAR

t his recipe is based on the one Jimmy uses, only with a more moderate amount of butter. He likes to make his in two 6-inch cast-iron skillets, but I make mine in a single, deep 8-inch skillet. (A 9- or 10-inch would also work.) If you don't have a cast-iron skillet of the appropriate size, you can also use a metal or Pyrex cake pan or a pie plate.

FOR THE PANCAKES
2 tablespoons (1 ounce) unsalted
  butter
4 large eggs
½ cup unbleached all-purpose flour

½ cup half-and-half
¼ teaspoon salt

FOR THE TOPPING
Freshly squeezed lemon juice
Powdered sugar, sifted

Preheat the oven to 425°F.

Put the butter in an 8-inch cast-iron skillet and place over low heat. Alternatively, put the butter in a similarly sized cake pan or pie plate, and place it in the preheated oven for a few minutes. As the butter melts, use a pastry brush to coax it up the sides of the skillet.

Meanwhile, in a blender, mix together the eggs, flour, half-and-half, and salt until well blended.

Pour the egg mixture into the warmed skillet. Slide into the oven, and bake for 18 to 25 minutes. The mixture will rise and puff around the edges, like a bowl-shaped soufflé. The Dutch baby is ready when the center looks set and the edges are nicely risen and golden brown.

Remove from the oven. Drizzle—or splash, really; abundance is good here—with lemon juice and sprinkle generously with powdered sugar. Serve immediately.

Yield: 2 servings

*J*immy makes these cookies for Rebecca on Valentine's Day. She occasionally saves one for me, and though I am usually a chocolate chip kind of person, I have fallen hard for the pink cookie. It's rich and sweet and excessive in every way. The cookie itself is crisp and crumbly like a proper shortbread, but the frosting is pure Americana: soft and smooth, tangy with cream cheese, and scented very, very, *very* lightly with cherry—just enough, as Jimmy says, "to make it taste pink."

A note about the frosting: don't be alarmed by the amount this recipe makes. You will want it all, or most of it, at least. These cookies are meant to be frosted very generously. Without a nice, thick layer, they aren't nearly as good.

FOR THE COOKIES

3 sticks (12 ounces) unsalted butter,
at room temperature
1 cup powdered sugar, sifted
3 cups all-purpose flour
½ teaspoon salt
1 teaspoon vanilla extract

FOR THE FROSTING

8 ounces cream cheese, at room
temperature
6 tablespoons (3 ounces) unsalted
butter, at room temperature
3 cups powdered sugar, sifted
1¼ teaspoons kirsch, or more to taste,
or a capful of cherry extract
Red food coloring

To make the cookies, combine the butter and powdered sugar in the bowl of a stand mixer fitted with the paddle attachment, and beat, first on low speed, and then slowly increasing to medium, until light and fluffy.

In a medium bowl, combine the flour and salt, and whisk well. With the mixer on low, add the flour mixture to the butter mixture, beating until the flour is just absorbed. Add the vanilla and beat well to incorporate. Lay a sheet of plastic wrap on a large, clean surface, and turn the dough out onto it. Gather the dough into a ball, press it into a thick disk, and wrap it well. Refrigerate for 1 hour.

Preheat the oven to 325°F. Line 2 baking sheets with parchment paper or silicone liners.

On a clean, floured surface, roll the dough out to a thickness of ⅜ inch. (If you don't have a lot of room, cut the disk of dough down the middle, and work with only one half at a time, leaving the second one in the refrigerator until ready for use.) Using a cookie cutter, cut the dough into whatever shapes you would like. I use a 2½-inch round cutter, which, once the cookies have puffed slightly during baking, yields a 2¾- to 3-inch cookie. Jimmy uses a much bigger cutter, often in the shape of a heart.

Place the cookies on the prepared baking sheets, spacing them 1½ inches apart. Bake them one sheet at a time, keeping the second sheet in the refrigerator until the first one is done, for 16 to 20 minutes, or until the cookies are pale golden at the edge. Do not allow them to brown. Transfer the pan to a wire rack, and cool the cookies completely on the pan.

To make the frosting, combine the cream cheese and butter in the bowl of a stand mixer fitted with the paddle attachment and beat on medium speed until smooth. Add the powdered sugar and beat on low speed to fully incorporate, then raise the speed to medium or medium-high and beat until there are no lumps, scraping down the sides of the bowl with a rubber spatula as needed. Add the kirsch and a couple of drops of red food coloring and beat well. The frosting should be a pretty shade of pale pink. Taste, and if you want more cherry flavor, beat in a bit more kirsch. Generously spread onto the fully cooled cookies.

Stored in an airtight container, pink cookies will keep in the refrigerator for up to 3 days—and they're delicious cold—or you can freeze them indefinitely.

Yield: 20 to 24 (3-inch) cookies

ITALIAN GROTTO EGGS

My father had a bad back. He'd had trouble for as long as I could remember, ever since a cross-country skiing accident when I was a baby. He'd been skiing with me on his back in a frame pack, and he'd lost his balance. To keep from falling backward and crushing me, he sat down instead. After that, his back would go out sometimes, every now and then, and for a day or two he would stand crooked, his spine listing to one side. But he was a doctor, and he kept a tackle box full of pills in his bathroom drawer. He took them when he needed them. We all did. We didn't think much of it.

One night—I think it was the fifteenth of September, the day after my twenty-fourth birthday—he was in Toronto for a family bat mitzvah, and he stumbled on the stairs to his cousin's house. He'd been having back pain for a while, but he hadn't told anyone. He was never the type to talk about those sorts of things. But now the pain was so bad that he thought he might have broken something. I had moved to Seattle only a week earlier, and he and my mother called one night to tell me. It might be a broken vertebra, he said, or maybe a spinal infection. Instead, a couple of days later, a bone scan showed that it was cancer. It had started in one of his kidneys but had been growing for a while, creeping into the bones of his spine. He was a radiation oncologist, so he knew what it meant.

"What a kick in the ass," he said.

My mother told me the plan. He would have his kidney removed, and then he would be at home for a while, recovering, before the chemotherapy began. My brother David would fly in to keep him company while my mother went to work. I imagined the two of them tottering around the house, my father in a flannel nightshirt and David in a T-shirt and sweats. They would watch TV in the den, and at night, David would help him up the stairs.

But the surgery came and went, and he didn't go home. He didn't leave the hospital for five and a half weeks, and when he did, it was on a stretcher. When they opened him up to pull out his kidney, it was the size of a jumbo Kleenex box, the deep, rectangular kind they keep in hospital waiting rooms and therapists' offices. The cancer had spread to the bones of his pelvis, and to his skull, and to the skinny bone that runs along the shin. There were spots on his liver, and in his lungs.

My mother tried to be calm, counseling me to stay in Seattle. But in mid-October, I flew home for a weekend, and four days after, she called, asking me to come back.

———

For a long time, all I could think about was the duffel bag.

When my father checked into the hospital, he took a brown leather duffel bag with him. It was stained the color of melted milk chocolate, a shiny brown that bordered on red. Inside, he had packed everything that he thought he might want: a book of crossword puzzles, a bottle of cologne, his blue cotton bathrobe with the big white polka dots. He was wearing a white dress shirt and a pair of wool pants that he held under his belly with a brown leather belt. When he exchanged his clothes for a hospital gown, he folded them and put them into the bag to wait for the trip back home.

But after the surgery, he never walked, or wore those clothes, again. Bone cancer, his doctor told me, is one of the most painful kinds. It would require patches, pills, and eventually an epidural port, a coiled wire that slipped eerily into a hole in his back. Then there were the bones themselves, which were slowly ceding ground to the soft tissue of the cancer. About a month after his diagnosis, a CAT scan showed his pelvis almost completely blacked out by tumors. I remember standing by the sink in his hospital room with my mother and the doctor, looking at the scan against a fluorescent light. It was as though a storm cloud had floated across the film and settled under my father's ribs. I gasped when I saw it. My mother covered my mouth, so Burg wouldn't hear.

He couldn't stand because of the pain, but if he had, his bones would have crumbled under the weight. I didn't even know that bones could do that. I was terrified of what it might look like. But he didn't try to stand. He just lay there in the bed, propped at varying degrees of supine. Sometimes he slept, and sometimes he cried. Sometimes he just stared at us. He must have been trying to understand how we got there, to that room at the end of the oncology hall, where we read old issues of *People* to pass the time and warmed soup from the neighbors in a microwave at the nurse's station. The duffel bag sat where he had left it, on the window ledge next to the bed.

Sometimes I would open it up and look inside, overwhelmed by the rush of odors, his smell. He had expected to get up and walk the hospital halls in that robe, and to go home in the clothes he had arrived in. When he left home, he thought he was coming back. When he got out of bed that morning, when he stood in the bathroom, when he combed his hair in the mirror and stooped gingerly to pack his bag, he thought he would be back. He didn't know that he would never see the second floor of his house again, or, for that matter, anything more than a single room downstairs, the room in which we would install his hospital bed, a humidifier, and, for sixteen hours a day, a nurse.

When no one was around to hear me, I would say it aloud to myself. *He thought he was coming home.* This could have been a trip, a vacation, Paris, anywhere. The bathrobe he packed was the one he wore to make stewed prunes and, in the mornings, mugs of cappuccino for himself and my mother. I would hear him go down the creaky stairs, and then the sound of his feet on the wood floor. He would clear his throat, snort a little, and sit down with the newspaper, his knees poking through the folds of the robe. It smelled like him: a low, musky odor, masculine and pungent. When he packed that duffel bag, he didn't know that he would never wear the robe again. He didn't know that he would never put on his cologne. He didn't know that he would never do another crossword puzzle over Saturday lunch and wash it down with a beer in his favorite glass, the one with the grapevines in relief around the side. He didn't know.

For the last four weeks that he was alive, my father lay in a rented hospital bed in a room next to the kitchen. There isn't much a person wants to eat when he is hooked up to an IV drip, or when his legs feel as though they are on fire. The painkillers were strong enough to make him hallucinate—he once went on a duck hunt in his bed, pointing an imaginary gun at the fireplace and shouting *pow! pow!*—but they could barely keep up with the pain. Still, I got out of bed every morning to make his breakfast. There were plenty of people around to do it—my mother, my half-siblings, aunts and uncles, even the nurses—but I wanted to. Some mornings he took a bowl of oatmeal with half-and-half, or Cream of Wheat with fat lumps of butter. But most days, it was eggs. I would scoop the food into his mouth in quiet disbelief, watching his belly, the target of so much nagging, slowly melt away. Sometimes I would think about the last time I hugged him, standing in the driveway in early September, when I left for Seattle, and the way his gut, so distended, had pressed familiarly against mine. I didn't know then that there was a tumor behind it.

One day, he told me about the grotto. I'd come to bring his breakfast, some scrambled eggs with goat cheese and a slice of buttered toast. When he saw me in the doorway, he sighed and pointed dazedly, with one hand, toward the couch.

"Isn't it *beautiful?*" he breathed. We were sitting next to a grotto, he explained, gazing dreamily at the armchair, his voice an excited whisper. "Look at that water. It's so *blue!*"

Eyeing the plate in my hands, he asked if the picnic was ready. I nodded. Between bites, he murmured dazedly. We were in Italy, he said, and we were sitting on a blanket, and the grass around us was green and cool.

"When we finish eating, let's go for a swim in the water," he said.

I looked down to scoop up the last bite of egg. When I looked up again, he was quiet, staring at his thumbs. I slipped the fork between his lips. As quickly as it had started, it was over. He had left the grotto and come back to bed. He looked away.

I didn't say anything. I didn't want to ruin it. I wiped his mouth, and then I carried the empty plate into the kitchen. But a few days later, when I asked what he wanted for lunch, he looked at me squarely.

"Italian grotto eggs," he said. Just like that.

Maybe he knew he'd dreamed it, and he wanted me to know. Or maybe he believed that we'd really been to Italy, eating eggs and swimming. Maybe it didn't matter. Somehow his mind was working to bridge the gap between the hospital bed and a hazy, faraway place. It was a grotto in Italy, a sea cave to swim in, somewhere far from that bed in Oklahoma. I guess it was his way of escaping the body that had carried him for seventy-three years and dropped him without warning.

It could have frightened me to see him like that. Sometimes, it did. His body was giving way, literal bone by bone, and so was his mind. But I was grateful for whatever relief he found, and when I wasn't afraid, I just wanted to help him find it.

1 tablespoon (½ ounce) unsalted
   butter
5 large eggs
¼ teaspoon salt

1 tablespoon heavy cream
3 tablespoons fresh goat cheese, such
   as Laura Chenel, coarsely
   crumbled
Freshly ground black pepper, for
   serving

Melt the butter in a medium nonstick skillet over medium-high heat.

Crack the eggs into a small bowl and beat them lightly with a fork. Add the salt and cream and beat to blend.

When the pan is hot, pour in the eggs and swirl to coat. Reduce the heat to low, and using a heatproof rubber spatula, stir the eggs gently, scraping the spatula along the bottom of the skillet, until they are loosely set in large, pillowy curds. They should be slightly runnier than you want them. Remove the pan from the heat and scatter the goat cheese over the eggs. Give them one more gentle stir to melt and distribute the cheese.

Serve immediately, with additional salt and black pepper to taste and, if you like, slices of buttered toast.

Yield: 2 servings

THE MOTTLING

When someone in the neighborhood is dying, no one really knows what to do. The very brave come by to sit and visit. Others, more tentative, keep their sympathies to the phone. When my father was dying, we had a little of both. We had friends who came by and friends who called. But mainly, we had friends who cooked.

If there was anything good about that time, anything to be missed after the fact, it was the constant influx of soups, stews, roasts, cookies, and pies. I never knew how many friends my parents had until the food started arriving. The neighbors walked over with a tureen of beef stew. A bag of sugar cookies showed up, propped against the side door. A friend arrived with a car full of aluminum pans and cake boxes, enough to line the entire kitchen counter. I've never seen so much food outside of a college dining hall.

Everyone who cooked or baked for us hoped, I know, that my father would eat some, too. Sometimes he did. But mainly he ate eggs and hot cereal and cans of Ensure. (Not that he *ate* the cans, but if you've seen how thick and opaque Ensure is, you'll understand why I put it under the "eating" category, rather than the "drinking" one.) The vanilla flavor was his favorite. It smelled like a mixture of milk and chalk dust. It smelled wet and musty and oddly sweet, like nursing homes and old people, and after he would drink it, his breath would smell sweet, too. My mother told me once that he'd said to her, without the slightest wink of sarcasm, that vanilla-flavored Ensure tasted like crème brûlée. He *loved* crème brûlée. We used to joke about it. We'd retell the story to one another, laughing, saying, "Shit, if that tastes like crème brûlée, he must *really* be sick." Then, for a minute, we could forget that he was.

People took such good care of us. I can hardly tell you. It was almost comical, like something out of a sitcom or *Steel Magnolias*. There were loaves of bread and cold cuts and cheese, potato soup, and pork tenderloins. Linda Paschal brought her banana bread and her holiday sweet rolls. Barbara Fretwell brought a dried fruit pie. John Hughey, a family friend whose homemade bisteeya, chocolate bread pudding, and penchant for deep frying have made him a small-scale legend, brought over handmade tamales. Pam and David Fleischaker, old friends, brought two pies: first a fruit one and then a rum cream, topped with pistachios and bits of shaved chocolate. We ate it all.

When Thanksgiving rolled around, things quieted down for a few days. We were on our own, just me, Mom, and Burg. My brother David called from Washington, D.C., and had a local restaurant deliver our holiday dinner: half a roasted turkey, a pan of green beans almondine, mashed yams, stuffing, and pecan pie. I don't know what we would have eaten otherwise. Mom and I stood at the counter, surveying it all, peeking under the lids of the aluminum to-go containers and inhaling the familiar smells that rose on the steam.

I remember thinking that Burg wouldn't make it through the weekend. He had stopped eating. He was fading. I don't know how else to say it. You get a sense for these things. I remember talking on the phone, telling someone that he was dying. I must have had the conversation while standing in the pantry closet, because when I think of it now, I picture a row of jam jars and single-serving cans of pineapple juice. The pantry was where I went for privacy. The door had a latch on the inside, so I could safely close myself in when I needed to talk without anyone hearing me. Saying it aloud—*I don't think he's going to make it*—was almost a relief. It had been barely two months since his diagnosis, but we were exhausted. I wanted something to change: the hum from the motor on his hospital bed, the nurses that came and went, the sweet smell on his breath, something.

Early one morning, I woke to the sound of him shouting. He was babbling the way babies do, but at the top of his lungs, hooting and twittering and carrying on. It was a Friday morning, the sixth of December. Everybody else was asleep: my brothers in my bedroom, my sister in the guest room, my mom and my aunt Tina together in my parents' bed. I was sleeping on the floor in the hallway, on the foam egg-crate mattress that had lined his stretcher on the ride home from the hospital, with our dog and a couple of blankets. My stretch of the hallway was squarely above the den, where my father was, and with my head just a pillow's width from the floor, I could hear almost everything in the room below, like listening through a wall with a paper cup pressed to my ear.

Laura, the night nurse, was with him, and by the faint daylight that came through the curtains, I guessed she was probably giving him a sponge bath, her last duty before handing him over to LuDean, the day nurse. But this kind of noise was odd. His voice was almost singsong, but with an edge of panic, as though he were reciting a nursery rhyme in another language while drunk.

I tossed back the blanket and went to the stairs. When I got to the doorway into the den, I saw that Laura was just finishing his bath, straightening the fitted sheet that lay between him and the mattress. She had propped him on his side, facing the doorway. He didn't seem to be in pain, but his eyes were closed and he was agitated, jerking his head as though trying to shake off a fly, or like a Stevie Wonder video on fast-forward.

I knelt down in front of his face and stroked his beard. It was coarse and thick, a silvery gray.

"Shhh," I heard myself say, "It's okay. *It's okay.*"

It must have been as much for me as it was for him. I tilted my head to the side to match the angle of his, but he didn't seem to see me. His eyes were squeezed to narrow slits. I stroked his beard, willing his eyes to land on me. Years later, I would have a dream about this. I would be stroking a horse's cheek, but as I stared at it, the horse would morph into my father. I would wake up sobbing.

"You're calling him back, hon," Laura said. "Don't call him back. He's got the mottling, see?"

She pulled back the blankets that covered his legs. His skin was splotched with patches of reddish purple, like the strawberry birthmark I once saw on the neck of a girl in grade school, only bigger and darker, more angry looking. His knees were knobby and enormous, all shades of pink, purple, and bone white.

I had heard about the mottling. The hospice worker had brought us a little leaflet that mentioned it, a leaflet with the sort of no-nonsense title that, I imagine, is suppose to calm or soothe you in the moments before doom, like *What Happens When We Die*. The mottling is a sign that comes before death, as the circulation starts its slow grind to a halt. LuDean had told me about it, too, one afternoon a week or two earlier, when she'd seen a spot on his ankle.

"He'll get all mottled," she'd said. "That's how you know he's dying."

I know it's awful to say it, but I was so relieved that morning, when I saw the splotches. I didn't want to stop him. I was terrified of stopping him. I pulled my hand away from his face. I stood up, ran my fingers down his forearm to smooth the hair, and stepped back. Then I left the room, and I don't remember what I did.

That night, I heard Laura at the foot of the stairs. She was calling for my mother.

"Toni," she said softly, "He's going." We heard it, each of us in our beds, all the way down the hall, the way a jolt of electricity zips along a wire.

He was lying on his back, his eyes fixed on the ceiling and his mouth open, gasping. It was a strange sound, his breathing: involuntary, mechanical, ugly. I've since heard people call it "fish-out-of-water breathing," the way the lungs pull air, almost against their will, into the body. It's a rattletrap sound, a hiccup almost, a frog's ribbit, hard and curt.

We circled his bed. I stood next to Tina, I think. My mother stood next to his head, on the right. We stood there for I don't know how long, maybe half an hour, while he gasped like that. Then his breathing began to slow. At some point, my mother pressed her fingers against his neck, feeling for a pulse. And then he went silent. I don't really remember a last breath, although I don't know how anyone does. You never know which one will be the last. He just went, just like that, silent, and then my mother said, *he's gone.*

My father died at 2:35 a.m. on Saturday, December 7, 2002, at home, with his children and his wife and his sister-in-law and a night nurse named Laura, with his bed propped against a floor-to-ceiling shelf filled with books on art and history and majolica, the ceramic pottery he collected. He died a few feet from the fireplace he used to sit beside, doing the *New York Times* crossword puzzle.

He died the way I guess anyone would want to go: gently in the end, and fast. But sometimes I can't believe what he had to go through to get there, or that he became what he became: a body in a bed, immobilized, melting away. No one sits around and guesses how their parents will die. I certainly didn't. I didn't know that my father would lie down in a hospital bed and never walk again, or that he would stare at me the way he did one day, his blue eyes swimmy and knowing. But he got there. He got through it. And he got out.

I won't tell you that it was hard. You already know that. I was so numb sometimes that my hands stopped working, just locked themselves into funny, pinched fists. But then there was the gratitude, a sort of low-grade, queasy gratitude, that he was free.

Sometime around 3:30 that morning, my parents' friends Dick and Annie came over. We all sat in the den, around the hospital bed, Annie on Dick's lap, telling stories. I sat on a chair next to the bed with the dog on my lap. She tentatively toed the blankets. She'd wanted to climb onto the bed for weeks, but we hadn't let her. Even the slightest movement had made him wince. But now I let her jump. She circled between his knees and fell asleep.

I was hungry, so I went to the kitchen and poured myself a bowl of cereal.

"I don't know how you can possibly eat right now," someone said.

I don't know what I answered. I even don't know *if* I answered. I just ate. I don't think Burg would have minded. He would have taken a bite himself, if he could.

DRIED FRUIT PIE
Adapted from Barbara Fretwell

"*d*ried fruit pie" doesn't quite have the same ring as "peach pie," or "apple pie," but please trust me. This is delicious. It's surprisingly rich, plump with sticky fruit and nuts, all wrapped up neatly in a butter crust. Barbara tells me that she first made it for my parents one Thanksgiving at Lake Texoma, back when the Fretwells had a lake house there, decades ago. My father, she says, loved it.

FOR THE CRUST
½ cup ice water, plus more as needed
1½ teaspoons apple cider vinegar
3 cups unbleached all-purpose flour
2 tablespoons sugar
1½ teaspoons salt
*2¼ sticks (9 ounces) cold unsalted
 butter, cut into cubes*

FOR THE FILLING
*2 cups pitted prunes, coarsely
 chopped*

*2 cups dried apricots, coarsely
 chopped*
1 cup golden raisins
½ cup dried apples, coarsely chopped
¾ cup sugar
*1 stick (4 ounces) unsalted butter,
 melted*
½ cup walnuts, chopped
1 large egg

TO SERVE
Lightly sweetened whipped cream

TO PREPARE THE CRUST

In a small bowl or measuring cup, combine ½ cup ice water and the cider vinegar.

In the bowl of a food processor, combine the flour, sugar, and salt. Pulse to blend. Add the butter and pulse until the mixture resembles a coarse meal; there should be no pieces of butter bigger than a large pea. With the motor running, slowly add the water-vinegar mixture, processing just until moist clumps form. If you pick up a handful of the dough and squeeze it in your fist, it should hold together. If the dough seems a bit dry, add more ice water by the teaspoon, pulsing to incorporate. I often find that 2 additional teaspoons is perfect.

Turn the dough out onto a wooden board or clean countertop, and gather it, massaging and pressing, until it just holds together. Shape it into a ball, cut it in half, and press each half into a disk about 1½ inches thick. If the disks crack a bit at the edges, don't worry; just pinch the cracks together as well as you can. Wrap each disk in plastic wrap, and then press them a bit more, massaging away any cracks around the edges, allowing the constraint of the plastic wrap to help you form a smooth circle. Refrigerate for at least 2 hours. (Dough can be kept in the refrigerator for up to 4 days or sealed in a heavy-duty plastic bag and frozen for up to 1 month. Thaw it in the refrigerator overnight before using.) Before rolling it out, allow the dough to soften slightly at room temperature.

TO PREPARE THE FILLING

Combine the dried fruits in a large saucepan, and add cold water to cover. Bring to a boil over medium-high heat, then simmer for 10 minutes, stirring occasionally. Drain the fruit well in a colander. Return it to the saucepan, and add the sugar and melted butter. Stir well. Set aside to cool, stirring occasionally.

TO FINISH

Set a rack in the lower third of the oven, and preheat the oven to 425°F.

Roll 1 disk of dough into a circle wide enough to fit a 9- or 9½-inch pie plate with a bit of overhang. Transfer gently into the pie plate, pressing it smooth along the bottom and up the sides. If there is a lot of overhang, use scissors or a small, sharp knife to trim it so that it drapes only ¼ to ½ inch beyond the rim of the pie plate. Roll out the second disk of dough into a circle of the same size.

Stir the chopped walnuts into the cooled filling. (It's okay if it's still slightly warm, but it shouldn't be hot.) Scrape the filling into the prepared pie plate, distributing it evenly. Place the second circle of dough atop the filled pie, and fold and pinch the edges over the bottom crust to seal completely and form a high fluted rim. In a small bowl, beat the egg well with a fork. Brush it lightly over the top and rim of the pie. (You won't use all of the egg—just a little.)

Bake the pie for 30 minutes at 425°F. Then reduce the temperature to 375°F and continue to bake until the top is a deep shade of gold, about 10 minutes. If you're using a clear Pyrex pie plate, lift the pie and look underneath to check the color of the bottom and sides: you want them to be golden, too. If the pie seems to be browning too quickly, tent it with aluminum foil.

Transfer to a wire rack to cool completely. Serve at room temperature, with lightly sweetened whipped cream.

NOTE: Barbara tells me that she has occasionally thrown in a handful of dried cranberries as well, in addition to the dried fruits listed here. If you have some lying around, you might consider that.

Yield: 8 to 12 servings

RUM CREAM PIE WITH GRAHAM CRACKER CRUST
Adapted from David and Pam Fleischaker

*Y*ou can use a store-bought graham cracker crust, but the flavor of a homemade one is much better.

FOR THE CRUST

9 graham crackers, broken coarsely
  into pieces
2 tablespoons granulated sugar
5 tablespoons (2½ ounces) unsalted
  butter, melted and kept warm

FOR THE FILLING

¼ cup cold water
1¼ teaspoons (about half of a ¼-ounce
  packet) unflavored gelatin
1 cup heavy cream
3 large egg yolks
½ cup granulated sugar
2 tablespoons rum, preferably dark
Bittersweet chocolate, shaved or
  finely chopped
Pistachios, finely chopped

Preheat the oven to 325°F.

To make the crust, process the graham crackers in a food processor until they are very fine, about 30 seconds. Add the sugar and pulse to combine. With the processor running, add the melted butter in a thin stream. Process until the mixture looks like wet sand. Scrape it into a 9- or 9½-inch pie plate and press it along the bottom and up the sides, forming an even crust. (It can be tricky to make the sides smooth and square off the top edge, but here's a method that helps: rest your thumb along the lip of the pie plate to form a ledge, and then use a small ramekin to press the crumb mixture up the side, pinching it at the top between your thumb and the ramekin.) Bake the crust until it is fragrant and just beginning to brown, 15 minutes. Transfer to a wire rack and cool completely before filling.

To make the filling, pour the cold water into a small, microwavable bowl. Sprinkle the gelatin over the water. Set aside to soften for a few minutes; it will get thick and spongy. Meanwhile, pour the cream into the bowl of a stand mixer fitted with the whisk attachment (or any large bowl, if you plan to use electric beaters), and set aside. In a separate medium bowl, whisk the egg yolks until they lighten to pale yellow. Add the sugar and whisk well; it will be thick. Microwave the gelatin on high power for about 20 seconds, until liquefied, then pour it gradually into the egg mixture, whisking briskly. Working quickly, whip the cream to soft peaks. (It's important not to dally here, or else the gelatin will start to set, and you don't want that yet.) Gently stir the whipped cream into the egg mixture, taking care to blend them thoroughly. Add the rum, stirring gently to incorporate. Chill the filling until it starts to set: it's ready when it holds a delicate mound when nudged with a spoon.

Scrape the filling into the prepared crust. Chill until firm, 4 to 6 hours. Just before serving, sprinkle the top of the pie with a light dusting of chocolate and pistachios.

Yield: 8 servings

WHATEVER YOU LOVE, YOU ARE

My ex-boyfriend Lucas liked a band called Dirty Three. I was always fond of that name, especially for a kind of melancholic, unshaven trio, which is what they are, but they had an album title that was even better. It was called *Whatever You Love, You Are*. Isn't that perfect? That album title is probably a good part of why we got together—he told me about it on our first date—but I figure it's as valid a reason as any. I mean, think about it: whatever you love, you are. I want to believe in that.

I think about it a lot when I remember those weeks after my father died. More than anyone else I know, he was what he loved. He went after his life with both hands. He swallowed it in gulps, right up to the second they took the plate away. He never apologized, not even when I wanted him to—not for being stubborn, not for the silent treatment, not for leaving us behind. He did what he did, and he was what he was. For his memorial service, he wanted an Episcopal priest, a Catholic priest, and a rabbi. It was so weird and perfect. It wasn't so much that he really believed in any religion, I don't think, but more because he loved little bits of all of them. He *was* a little bit of all of them.

I wish you could have seen that service. We held it at All Souls Episcopal Church in Oklahoma City, and more than five hundred people came. They filled the place like football fans at a bowl game.

They filled the pews from front to back, and then they stood along the walls and in the foyer. My family processed down the aisle, twenty-seven of us in all. I wore my favorite pair of fishnet stockings. My mother wore four-inch heels. We did the best we could. It was a cold, sunny day, very clear, and afterward, when the church bells rang as we filed out the doors, the air almost shook with the sound.

The service was led by an Episcopal bishop named Shannon Mallory, a family friend who my father had, in those last weeks, named his "holy man." That he even had a holy man is hilarious—a contradiction in terms, really, since I never once saw him go to church or synagogue, and he didn't even believe in global warming, much less Jesus Christ. But Shannon was a former patient, one of the ones my father cured, and over the years, a friendship had grown between the two of them. They'd even traveled to Israel and Jordan together once, when Shannon led a tour. When Burg was sick, Shannon came by every few days, and the two of them would tell dirty jokes while Shannon drank Scotch. At the end of each visit, he would ask my father if he wanted to pray. I'd never seen my father pray before. But he would close his eyes, and then Shannon would lean over the bed, whispering softly, one hand on the crown of my father's head, their noses nearly touching.

I've been to memorial services where no one seemed to want to talk about the person who'd died, where he or she was sort of abstracted, reduced to general descriptors like "caring," or "kind," or "beloved." I wanted to talk about him. I wanted us all to talk about him. I wanted to remember how he laughed, half-gasp and half-gag; how he loved raspberries and osso buco; how he liked to read Gary Larson cartoons and had infinite patience for *A Prairie Home Companion*. I wanted to have him there with us, just for a few minutes.

So Shannon wore his robes and stood at the pulpit, talking and telling stories in his familiar, gentle voice. My siblings and I each stood up and spoke. Shannon's backup singers, as I privately thought of the priest and the rabbi, were okay, too; just right, really. The priest, like Shannon, was a former patient, but he and my father didn't know each other all that well. It was a little strange to have him there, but even that strangeness seemed fitting. Everything that had happened that fall was strange. The rabbi, for his part, didn't know my father from Adam. He even mispronounced his name during the service, referring to him as "Maurice" instead of "Morris." But that was okay, too. My father hadn't been much of a Jew for the past fifty years, so it was only appropriate that the rabbi fudge his name.

For my part, I chose a poem called "Yes, But" by James Wright, an American poet who died in 1980 after a short but intense battle with cancer, like Burg. The year before his death, Wright spent nine months traveling in Europe with his wife, waking up early to write poems. I think Burg would have liked to do that, too, if he'd had more time. He'd have eaten his weight in croissants. He would have also liked the fact that Wright's poem allowed me to say "making love" in a church in Bible-belted Oklahoma. I can almost hear him laughing now.

When I went back to Seattle, I enrolled in a grieving group at one of the local hospitals. It met every other Saturday from ten to noon. I was the youngest person in the group by a good twenty years, and I cried the hardest by far. I had the Kleenex box on lockdown.

The whole time is a blur, to be honest. The only part I remember is the baking. Those Saturday mornings, I would get up early and bake. First it was brownies, and then some kind of cookie. I remember buying strawberries, too, and making tiny fluted tartlets, vanilla bean pastry cream spooned into shells and topped with wedges of strawberry. I even made soup once, a pot of Italian vegetable soup with white beans, and forced my fellow group members to sip it from Dixie cups at ten o'clock in the morning. Someone should have had *me* on lockdown. When I called my mother to tell her, she laughed so hard that she actually hooted like an owl. My eyes were swollen from crying all the time, but I was the Official Grieving Group Food Pusher. I am *so* my father's daughter. Whatever you love, oh yes, you are.

*W*hen my father was sick, Ed Fretwell, Barbara's husband, brought us a pot of this soup. It was full of Swiss chard and carrots and plump beans, hearty and reassuring, one of the best soups I'd ever had. When the first batch was gone, we called to ask for more, and Ed delivered it the next day. He and Barbara had first tasted it, he told me, on a trip to Italy in the late 1990s, when it was served to them at a winery as a light lunch. They were so smitten that they asked for the recipe. It is best described as an Italian vegetable soup, but I call it Ed Fretwell Soup. Ed died a couple of years ago, and it feels good to remember him this way.

For the white beans, I highly recommend Rancho Gordo (www.ranchogordo.com), a California company specializing in heirloom bean varieties. I know it seems fussy to order beans by mail, but it's worth it. Their marrow beans (nothing to do with bone marrow; don't worry) are especially wonderful in this soup.

And a word about broth: I find that most commercial vegetable broths have a strange, too-strong flavor. So far, there is only one that I like: the "No-Chicken Broth" made by Imagine. But whatever you choose, be sure to taste it before you use it. If you don't like the flavor, make your own, or use water.

Last, note that this recipe makes a *lot* of soup. If you don't have a large soup pot—say, 8 quarts or even 12 quarts—I suggest halving the recipe.

1 pound dried white beans, such as
    cannellini or marrow beans
2 large cloves garlic, peeled and
    smashed under the side of a knife
3 fresh sage leaves
Water
4 tablespoons olive oil
2 medium yellow onions, finely
    chopped
4 stalks celery, finely chopped
8 medium carrots, sliced into thin
    rounds
2 medium zucchini, trimmed, halved
    lengthwise, and sliced into ¼-inch-
    thick half-moons

4 cups vegetable or chicken broth
¾ pound Swiss chard (about 1 small
    bunch), stalks discarded and leaves
    coarsely chopped
¾ pound green cabbage (about ½ of
    a medium head), trimmed and
    coarsely chopped
One 28-ounce can whole peeled
    tomatoes, drained and chopped
1 tablespoon salt
Best-quality olive oil, for serving
Finely grated Parmigiano-Reggiano,
    for serving (optional)

Put the beans in a medium bowl, and cover them with cool water by at least 1 inch. Set aside at room temperature, uncovered, for 6 hours or overnight.

Drain the beans, and put them in a Dutch oven or other (approximately 5-quart) pot. Add the garlic, sage leaves, and 10 cups cold water. The beans should be covered with water by at least 1 inch. Place the pot over high heat, and bring it to a boil. Boil for 5 minutes, then reduce to a simmer and cook, uncovered, stirring occasionally, for about 1 hour. Skim away any brownish foam that rises to the surface.

While the beans cook, start the rest of the soup. In a large (8-quart or more) soup pot, warm the olive oil over medium heat. Add the onions, celery, and carrots and cook, stirring frequently, for 10 to 15 minutes. Add the zucchini and broth, increase the heat to medium-high, and bring to a simmer. Then add the Swiss chard, cabbage, and tomatoes, cover the pot, and simmer gently, adjusting the heat as necessary, for 1 hour. At first, it will seem as though there is far too little liquid for all the vegetables in the pot, but don't worry: the vegetables will give off a good amount of water as they cook, and it'll even out in the end.

After 1 hour, add the cooked beans and their cooking water, discarding the sage leaves. Add the salt and stir well. Simmer for another 30 minutes to 1 hour, stirring frequently, until the beans and vegetables are very tender and the broth has taken on a creamy pale orange hue. Taste, and add salt as needed.

Serve with a hearty glug of good olive oil over the top of each bowl and a dusting of Parmigiano-Reggiano, if you like.

NOTE: Refrigerated, this soup will keep for up to a week, and it gets better with each passing day. It also freezes nicely.

Yield: 10 to 12 servings

SUMMER OF CHANGE

I remember saying to people, during that year that I lived alone in Paris, that the city felt like my second home. It was a plain enough thing to say, but in retrospect, it seems odd that I should have said it, since I hardly even know where my first home is. I guess it's Oklahoma, technically, but that never seemed quite right. My parents were from the East Coast, and they never really thought of themselves as Oklahomans, so I didn't either. I was raised to know that I would leave, and that, in fact, I was *supposed* to. It never occurred to me to stay.

I think that's why I'm such a sucker for the Bruce Springsteen album *Born to Run*. Swap out Springsteen's motorcycle and the backstreets of mid-seventies New Jersey for an airplane and mid-nineties Oklahoma, and you've got me. Mine is not quite so sexy a story—no chrome wheels or wind in my hair—but you get the idea. Six days after my nineteenth birthday, I was gone. I spent the next four years in college in California, with a stint in Paris in the middle. Then, when college was through, there was Paris again. I'm still not sure where home is. It might be Seattle, though I can't be certain. My second home, though, is always the same. Paris.

There's been so much said and written about Paris that it's daunting to hazard a statement of my own. That city just has something. I can't think of any other place so idealized, so longed for, so sighed over. My Paris isn't always such a sweet one, with kisses à la Doisneau on every street corner, but I like it better that way. It's the place where I've been loneliest, and where I've been happiest. Sometimes I've been both at the same time. It's where my father introduced me to croissants and *pain au chocolat.* It's where I met my first love, and where, six weeks later, when he stopped calling, I sat on a bench at the Champ de Mars and filled an entire Kleenex mini-pack with my snot and tears. It's a place where even crying feels romantic somehow, where heartbreak makes you feel like a part of history. It's who and where, for a long time, I wanted to be.

Whenever I don't know what to do, Paris is where I've gone. I guess it shouldn't have surprised me to find myself there in the summer of 2004. When my father died, everyone told me the same thing: *Don't make any big decisions for the first year and a half. Don't change anything. Just get through it.* Not knowing what else to do, I obeyed. I went back to Seattle. I went back to school. But every time I thought about the years that lay ahead, the dissertation and the defense, my eyes glazed over. I was on track to be a cultural anthropologist, but I hardly knew what for. I didn't want to teach. I wasn't even sure I was interested in anthropology. What I was really interested in, it turned out, was France. So a year and a half after Burg died, I went to Paris.

I had gone to graduate school to study power relations and the body, the way that medicine and other social institutions act on our bodies to mold them into docile "subjects." Just writing that, just now, I almost nodded off. That's how excited I am, and was, about what I was doing. I'd started down that path because of a philosopher named Michel Foucault, a Frenchman with some very dark, intriguing, and, some might say, sexy ideas about the way societies function. He also happened to have a seemingly bottomless supply of black turtlenecks and a penchant for social deviance. He was fascinating, an object of study in himself. The salient part, though, is that he was French. I think that's why I followed him down the path in the first place. I planned a dissertation in which I would apply his theories to a study of national health insurance in—you guessed it—France. My three years in graduate school, I now know, amounted to one big excuse to go back to Paris.

So I saved my money, and in the summer of 2004, I went for five weeks. I was ostensibly there to do pilot research, preliminary studies for my dissertation. I would write my master's thesis upon my return, take my general exams, and then, assuming all went well, return to France for more extensive research. These five weeks were to be the foundation for all of it. The timing was perfect: the National Assembly, France's equivalent to our Congress, was in debate over the social security system, one part of which is national health insurance. The first morning I was there, one of the experts I wanted to meet was on television, even, talking about the very issues I wanted to understand. I couldn't have planned it better if I'd tried.

That first week, I worked so hard. I read the papers, collected posters and signs, and conducted interviews. I'd rented the same tiny studio that I lived in two years earlier, and my landlord, who lived next door, was an especially good interview subject. He worked for the government. It was like taking candy from a baby. My research was all but doing itself. It was easy. It was perfect. I was bored stiff.

To reward myself for such diligent work, I'd spend afternoons visiting chocolate shops or taking long walks through the city, stopping at *boulangeries* here and there to sample the wares. I wrote long e-mails home, detailing my lunches, snacks, and dinners. I sat on a bench in the Luxembourg Gardens and read cookbooks until dark. By the second week of the trip, I knew I was doomed. I'd stopped buying the newspaper. My research notes were crowded with addresses for pastry shops and kitchen supply stores. I wasn't even pretending anymore. I was quitting graduate school.

Paris has a way of getting your priorities straight. For a place that clings vehemently to its history, it certainly helped speed mine along.

My friend Elizabeth likes to call it my "Summer of Change." That sounds a little like the title of a Judy Blume novel, a coming-of-age story with budding breasts and first crushes, but it fits. Liz lived down the hall from me during our freshman year of college. In the summer of 2004, she and our friend Doron, who studied with me in Paris during our junior year, happened to be in Paris at the same time that I was. She was there to go to design school, and he was doing an internship at a law firm, and they were sharing a sixth-floor walk-up on rue des Rosiers. For those who like falafel, you'll recognize the address. Their apartment was only three doors down from the famous L'As du Fallafel, purveyor of some of the finest fried chickpea balls this side of Israel. Even if all you knew was that, you could guess what kind of summer it was.

The first night I was in town, they invited me to dinner. Liz served salmon with caramelized onions and baby potatoes tossed in butter with fresh herbs. We drank until one in the morning. It was only a matter of time before I was baking lemon cakes in their oven and drinking gin and tonics with Liz in the late afternoon while we waited for Doron to get home from work. At night we would sometimes get together for roasted chicken from the butcher shop on rue Oberkampf or a puréed soup with bread and cheese. Liz was having a torrid love affair with the food mill.

Halfway between our apartments was boulevard Richard Lenoir, where each Thursday and Sunday row upon row of covered stands would magically sprout from the pavement, blossoming into the city's largest outdoor market. From the Place de la Bastille to the Bréguet-Sabin Métro station, tables unfurled to offer crates of fruits and vegetables, some still splotched with dirt and smelling appealingly of damp soil. Other booths proffered neatly arranged bottles of olive and nut oils, display cases full of sausages and sauerkraut and pâté, straw mats covered with cheese in various stages of ooze, and troughs mounded with nuts, dried fruits, and olives. Liz and Doron had grown especially fond of one Italian vendor who sold a spectacular soppressata. It was heinously expensive—two dozen slices weighed in at 18 euros—but oh, was it ever fine. Anyway, as we discovered, the expense could be easily offset by washing it down with cheap champagne. On Bastille Day, we had an indoor picnic that went on all day. We had goose liver pâté, duck pâté with pistachios, a thick slice of Comté, an even thicker wedge of bleu d'Auvergne, baguettes, *tomates confites,* red radishes with salt, champagne, and a DVD of *Six Feet Under,* the first season. One Sunday I made ratatouille, and we ate it on a blanket in the Place des Vosges, with slices of soppressata and Comté from our favorite cheese lady and wine drunk from yogurt jars. I had never before, nor have I since, been so happy to have no idea what I was doing with my life.

My mother came to visit during my last week. One night, we dressed up and went to dinner at Le Repaire de Cartouche, one of my favorite restaurants. I had taken my father there in the spring of 2002, at the end of my time working in Paris, when he came for a visit. He was tired during that trip, and he had nerve pain in his feet, but we didn't think much of it. Of course, when he was diagnosed with cancer four months later, we put two and two together: the nerve pain had been from the tumors in his spine. But he was seventy-three that spring, and it didn't seem weird to me that, at that age, he should be tired, even though he never had been before. He loved Le Repaire de Cartouche. He ordered marinated sardines and tuna with an eggplant tapenade, and we both had rhubarb clafouti for dessert. He wrote everything down on that trip, every dish at every meal, every last detail duly noted. Now I know where I get it.

That night, after dinner, my mother and I walked to the Pont de Sully, one of the bridges that spans the Seine. The wind was blowing from behind us, and we stood quietly for a moment, looking to make sure that no one could see. Then my mother reached into her purse and pulled out a plastic freezer bag, the better part of my father's ashes. She unzipped it and held it over the ledge, and when the wind came up just right, we tipped it and let him float down into the river.

I say that Paris is the place where I've been loneliest, and also where I've been happiest. But what I mean is harder to say. The thing I call loneliness is delicate and lovely, like a blown-out eggshell. It's both empty and hopeful, broken and beautiful. Paris couldn't be anything else for me now, because it's full of my father. That night on the bridge, I could almost see him, waving over the water.

The day before I left to return to Seattle, I had lunch with my friend Chris. He's an American and a technology writer, and he moved to Paris a number of years ago with his wife Martine, a Pilates instructor and fellow writer. I met them when I was working in Paris and went looking for a place to take Pilates mat classes. (I don't really meet *everyone* through Pilates; it just seems that way.) They're about the most gorgeous couple you can imagine, lean and beautiful and *très Parisien* in all the right ways, in spite of their American accents. That late-summer day, Chris and I met for a send-off coffee at a café in the Marais. We sat on the terrace with our tiny cups, and I told him that I was going to leave graduate school.

I wanted to do something with food, I said. That was what I kept coming back to, after everything else. At the end of the day, when I was exhausted and fed up and unsure of everything, food was a certainty. It was what I thought about, what I cared about, what I wrote about, what got me out of bed in the morning. (I mean that. I get up for the sole purpose of eating breakfast. I don't know why else you would.) It was so obvious, and so utterly terrifying. In my wildest dreams, the ones also populated by lions and masked men chasing me with live chainsaws, I thought I might want to write for a food magazine. But I had no idea what to do.

"Why don't you start a blog?" he suggested. "It'll give you something to be accountable to, so you can't give up right away. And it'll be a kind of portfolio. You can show it to editors someday."

I had no real idea what a blog was. Maybe a clue, but only the foggiest. Chris told me how to set it up and assured me that it would be easy.

So I flew home. The next day, I started a blog. I'd sneaked a sachet of my favorite chocolate-dipped orange peels from Paris in my suitcase, and it was sitting on my desk that day. Not having much else in the way of title ideas, I named my blog "Orangette," after the French name for those orange peels. It was a pretty name, I thought, and since my hair color is a vague shade of orange, sort of auburn-meets-red-meets-brown, it seemed fitting. "Tomme de Savoie" was the only other contender. It's the name of one of my favorite cheeses. I worried, though, that no one would be able to pronounce it, and I wasn't terribly keen on being known as "Tom de Savings," or "Tummy D. Savoy." Who knows, maybe I missed the boat on that one. But I don't think so.

DORON'S MEATBALLS WITH PINE NUTS,
CILANTRO, AND GOLDEN RAISINS

*t*his recipe was, relatively speaking, one of the first I wrote about on my blog. A few months after our summer in Paris, Doron e-mailed to tell me about a dinner he'd made, a meal of Mediterranean-style meatballs with a lemon-and-garlic yogurt sauce.

"It was one of my finer moments," he wrote. Then he described the recipe.

Doron makes these versatile meatballs with ground turkey, but I've tried them with chicken, too, and they're especially good with lamb. It's hard to go wrong. One pointer, though: if you go with turkey or chicken, use a mixture of breast and thigh meats. Many butchers offer both, and the extra fat in the thigh helps to keep the meatballs moist. I usually use about half breast meat and half thigh.

Also, about bread crumbs: they're easy to buy, but they're just as easy to make. When you have a day-old baguette or other plain bread lying around, trim off and discard the crusts, cut the soft center into coarse cubes, and spin them in a food processor until you have fine crumbs. (Only process a couple of handfuls at a time, though, or the machine tends to overheat.) Stored in the freezer, they will keep for a couple of months.

FOR THE YOGURT SAUCE
1 cup plain yogurt (not low fat or nonfat)
3 tablespoons lemon juice
1 medium clove garlic, minced
¼ teaspoon ground cumin
¼ teaspoon salt

FOR THE MEATBALLS
½ cup minced yellow onion
¼ cup chopped fresh cilantro leaves
½ cup chopped pine nuts

½ cup golden raisins, halved or coarsely chopped if large
½ cup fine bread crumbs
1 large egg, lightly beaten
½ teaspoon salt
⅛ teaspoon ground cumin
⅛ teaspoon freshly ground black pepper
1 pound ground turkey, chicken, or lamb (see headnote)
About 4 tablespoons olive oil

First, make the yogurt sauce. In a small bowl, combine the yogurt, lemon juice, garlic, cumin, and salt and whisk to combine. Set aside at room temperature to let the flavors develop while you make the meatballs.

To make the meatballs, combine onion through black pepper in a large bowl. Add the ground meat and, using your hands, break it up into small chunks. Then massage and gently knead the meat to incorporate the ingredients. Mix until combined, but do not overmix: meat gets tough easily. With damp hands, gently pinch off hunks of the mixture and roll into 1½-inch balls. Set aside on a large plate. (Raw meatballs can be covered and refrigerated for up to 1 day. Or place them, not touching, on a rimmed baking sheet and freeze until hard, then transfer them to a heavy-duty plastic bag and freeze for up to 2 weeks.)

Warm 2 tablespoons of the oil in a heavy large skillet over medium heat. Add about half of the meatballs, taking care not to crowd them. As they begin to color, turn them gently with tongs and lightly shake the pan to roll them around, so they get some color on every side. Don't worry if a few of the pine nuts fall out into the pan; that happens. The meatballs are ready when they're evenly browned and feel pleasantly firm, but not rock-hard. You can also cut one or two of them in half, if you like, to make sure they're cooked through.

Transfer the finished meatballs to a plate lined with a paper towel. If the skillet looks dry, add the remaining 2 tablespoons oil. Cook the remaining meatballs.

Serve hot, warm, or at room temperature, with the yogurt sauce.

NOTE: Leftover meatballs are delicious. I eat them cold, straight from the refrigerator, or warmed a touch in the microwave, with a dunk in yogurt sauce.

Yield: about 30 small meatballs, enough for 4 servings

PRETTY PERFECT

I have this funny thing about recipes. When I find one that I like, I have a hard time trying others. Take lentil soup, say. If I make a lentil soup recipe and like it, I'm apt to stick by it, for better or for worse. Sometimes, after quite a while, I will cave in and try a new one, but in most cases, I would be just as happy to rest on my laurels and sit there, eating that same lentil soup, forever. This is not good behavior, I am told, for someone who supposedly cares about cooking. I'm supposed to be more curious, more devil-may-care, more like my father. Sometimes I am. But most of the time, I'm not. I'm loyal and sentimental and possibly even boring. When something clicks with me, I want to keep it around. That goes not only for recipes but also for facial cleansers, chocolate, and men.

But about the recipes. My sister Lisa's Scottish scones are another good example. I prefer scones over all other morning breads, and of the specimens I have sampled, hers are my very favorite. They are solid, tidy things, with a dense, tightly woven crumb that tears apart into fat, flaky layers. They bear a close resemblance to biscuits, only a little less dainty and delicate. They're the kind of thing you'd expect to eat before setting out for a rousing, ruddy-cheeked hike in the Highlands. Scones seem to run a spectrum these days, with the fluffy muffin type at one end and, at the other, the sturdy, Old World biscuitlike variety. My sister's rest delectably among the latter, which is exactly where I want them. Forever.

This can be tricky, as you might guess. I have a lot of cookbooks, and they demand my attention. You wouldn't believe how pushy they are. They lie next to my bed like fat, lazy dogs. They stretch and yawn all over my lap. Sometimes they even yap about scone recipes that aren't my sister's. And sometimes, because I am occasionally sort of curious, I listen to them. I try something new. And then I go back to those same scones.

Like Doron's meatballs, Lisa's scone recipe was one of the first I posted on Orangette. It's a classic. My sister got the recipe from a Scottish girlfriend of hers, and with it, this girlfriend offered a piece of advice that I should probably pass on to you: do not knead the dough more than twelve times. That's the magic number, she said; any more, and the scones will be tough. I tend to lose count and therefore cannot confirm the truth of this, but Lisa swears by it, and she would want me to tell you. She's a wonderful cook and baker, so really, listen to her. She has five children and a job in a museum on Long Island, but still she manages to grow her own asparagus and rhubarb and make eggplant salad, blackberry upside-down cake, and Indian-style chicken with cumin. She was twenty-two when I was born, the first child from our father's first marriage, and though we live on opposite sides of the country and in very different circumstances, we have been trying to spend more time together in recent years. I grew up an only child, but I like being able to say that I have a sister now. I have a little fantasy that one day we will meet for a weekend in New York, just the two of us, and we will eat pastries and go to museums, and she can tell me everything she knows, which is a lot more than I know, about art history. But that would take quite a bit of orchestration, so instead we write letters and talk on the phone about recipes, which is a close second.

In our family, Lisa's scones have come to be a Christmas tradition, unspoken but sacred. Each December, she takes the basic formula and spins it into a half-dozen multihued varieties, from dried apricot to cinnamon, blackberry, raspberry, currant, and dried cranberry. Then she tucks them carefully into plastic bags and freezes them until Christmas Eve. If she is traveling for the holidays, they come with her, naturally, in a cooler in the trunk. Come Christmas morning, when the coffee machine sputters to life, we spread the bags on the countertop and circle them like vultures, ready to claim our share. Warmed briefly in a low oven, they're perfect for eating with one hand while tearing at wrapping paper with the other. For me, actually, they're pretty perfect in general, which is why I have such a hell of a time getting excited about another recipe.

That said, if you like a scone that bursts with butter—a scone-cum-muffin, I would say—these may not be for you. They will happily accept a pat of butter, but they don't foist it upon you. I think of them as the ideal blank slate, because you can flavor them with almost anything. Maybe that's why I never get tired of them. One of my favorite versions includes bits of sweet-hot crystallized ginger and the merest slip of lemon, wintry and warming. If you're the sentimental type, like some of us, there's no need, ever, to do them another way.

*F*eel free to play with the flavorings in this recipe. In lieu of the lemon and ginger, you could try orange zest and currants, or Meyer lemon zest, or diced dried apricots, or dried cranberries or cherries, or pistachios, walnuts, or almonds. I also love this recipe with a couple of handfuls of whole, frozen berries, even though they make the dough a mess to work with. Don't thaw them first: the colder, the better. The dough will be wet and sticky, and you won't be able to knead it much, but the finished product, filled with jammy pockets of soft fruit, is worth the trouble.

2 cups unbleached all-purpose flour	*2 teaspoons grated lemon zest*
2 teaspoons baking powder	*¼ cup finely chopped crystallized*
½ teaspoon salt	*ginger*
4 tablespoons (2 ounces) cold unsalted	*½ cup half-and-half, plus more for*
butter, cut into ½-inch cubes	*glazing*
3 tablespoons sugar	*1 large egg*

Preheat the oven to 425°F.

In a large bowl, whisk together the flour, baking powder, and salt. Using your hands, rub the butter into the flour mixture, squeezing and pinching with your fingertips until the mixture resembles a coarse meal and there are no butter lumps bigger than a pea. Add the sugar, lemon zest, and crystallized ginger and whisk to incorporate.

Pour ½ cup half-and-half into a small bowl or measuring cup and add the egg. Beat with a fork to mix well. Pour the wet ingredients into the flour mixture, and stir gently to just combine. The dough will look dry and shaggy, and there may be some unincorporated flour at the bottom of the bowl. Don't worry about that. Using your hands, squeeze and press the dough into a rough mass. Turn the dough, and any excess flour, out onto a board or countertop, and press and gather and knead it until it *just* comes together. You don't want to overwork the dough; ideally, do not knead more than 12 times. There may be some excess flour that is not absorbed, but it doesn't matter. As soon as the dough holds together, pat it into a rough circle about 1 inch thick. Cut the circle into 8 wedges.

Place the wedges on a baking sheet lined with parchment paper or a silicone baking mat. Pour a splash of half-and-half into a small bowl. Using a pastry brush, gently brush the tops of the scones with a thin coat to glaze. Bake for 10 to 14 minutes, or until pale golden. Transfer them to a wire rack to cool slightly, and serve warm, with butter, if you like.

NOTE: If you plan to eat them within a day or two, store the scones in an airtight container at room temperature. For longer storage, seal them in a heavy plastic bag or container, and freeze them. Before serving, bring them to room temperature. Either way, reheat them briefly in a 300°F oven. They're best served warm.

Yield: 8 medium scones

PROMISE TO SHARE

Idon't know of any more appropriate way of saying this, so I'm just going to do it: I hate, *hate*, the notion of a secret recipe. I don't usually throw the h-word around like that, but this is one instance where I've got to put my foot down. I do not like secret recipes.

The whole idea is sort of ridiculous. Recipes are by nature derivative: rare is the recipe that springs, fully formed, from thin air, without the influence, wisdom, or inspiration of other prior dishes. Recipes were made to be shared. That's how they improve, how they change, how new ideas are formed and older ones made ripe. The way I see it, sharing a recipe is how you pay back fate—in the karmic sense, if you believe in such things—for bringing you something so tasty in the first place. To stop a recipe in its tracks, to label it secret, just seems mean. And isn't cooking about making people, on some level or another, feel good? It seems to me, then, that it only makes sense to give people the means to continue feeling good. By which I mean the recipe.

Anyway, one person can only cook for so many people, but by giving away a recipe, you can become, as word of the recipe spreads far and wide, the Amazing Cook Who Had That Amazing Recipe. Just imagine it. It's our best shot at fame. What on earth did you think I was giving you all these recipes for?

Sharing is nice. Take it from me. I learned the hard way, because for the early part of my life, I was really, really bad at it. I can think of several instances in which a grade-school classmate, having forgotten his or her pencils at home, tried to borrow one from me. I'd shake my head and refuse, reminding my poor, innocent classmate that we were supposed to come to class *prepared*. By some miraculous stroke of luck, I was not maimed and killed by my peers, à la *Lord of the Flies*, and I lived to tell this story today. But I won't tempt fate again. I've become a pretty good sharer. In fact, I actually like sharing. I've made such strides that sometimes I even show up for meetings unprepared, sans pen or pencil, which makes me feel liberated and wild, like wearing racy lingerie under my clothes.

But what I really wanted to tell you about, or rather *who*, is my father's younger brother, my uncle Arnold. He's a very good recipe sharer.

Arnold, who I call Arnie, is an excellent home cook. He lived in New York until several years ago, when he retired and moved to Maine, to a little house that he and his wife Reva call "The Bear Cottage." The two of them are terrific to eat with, mainly because they *ooh* generously and pause in mid-sentence to moan appreciatively over things. They love to cook and they love to eat, and luckily, they also love to share.

At least once or twice a month, Arnie sends me a new recipe to try. I can't begin to keep up with him, but it's always a treat to get his letters, with recipes for things like cioppino, or beef-and-bean chili with bittersweet chocolate, or Indonesian spiced chicken. Arnie is also full of smart kitchen tips, which he regularly throws in. Take note, for example:

> *The next time you make a fruit crisp, if you're tired of cutting/ rubbing the butter into the dry ingredients for the topping, try the Maine Weisenberg Method. Freeze the stick(s) of butter. Combine all the dry ingredients in a work bowl. Lay a grater across the bowl. (If you use a box grater, chill that in the freezer, too.) Coarsely grate the frozen butter from the small end of the stick, so that the shreds are only an inch or so long. Every ¼ or ½ stick,*

stir the butter shreds under the dry mixture until you're done.
Dump it onto your prepared fruit and bake.

Unc Arn

I haven't tried his method yet, but Arnie usually knows his stuff, so I'll bet it works like a charm. And in case you're wondering why his last name is spelled differently from mine, the answer is that my father's last name was misspelled on his birth certificate. He didn't know that, however, until he was in his twenties and in the process of finishing medical school and, according to my mother, he didn't have the money or the desire to go to the trouble of changing it. So he was a Wizenberg in a family of Weisenbergs. I've always liked that.

Arnie also has quite a way with fish. Some time ago, he gave my parents a recipe he'd dreamed up for fillets of salmon poached in apple cider and then sauced in a cider-cream reduction. I'm not much of a sauce person, so it sounded a little fussy to me, but the idea stuck there, in one of the dusty back corners of my mind, and not too long ago, I decided to give it a try.

My mother calls this recipe "Salmon with Apple Glaze," but Arnie calls it "Saumon Gelée à la Louis XIV," a completely fanciful title that, as it turns out, actually kind of suits the dish. It's very elegant and impressive, and were a hungry king to stop by to water his horses, it would not be a bad thing to make him for supper. It starts with a few fillets of the best salmon you can find—I like king or sockeye and always buy wild when I can—and a jug of fresh cider. You don't want the kind with spices added, nor do you want regular apple juice, the kind babies drink from bottles. This is the perfect occasion to buy some real unpasteurized cider, if you can get your hands on it. Here in Seattle, I make do with a local unfiltered brand in the refrigerated section at the grocery store.

The rest is very straightforward. You poach the fish in the cider, remove it from the pan, and then reduce the cider to a pretty syrup. To that, you add a good glug of cream, and then you let it simmer a little while longer. What you wind up with is a moist, perfectly tender piece of fish, coddled gently in a warm cider bath and then wrapped in a silky caramel-colored sauce that's both sweet and savory and entirely sigh inducing. In fact, I should warn you in advance that the sauce is quite beguiling. You will be tempted to get greedy with it (maybe even hide in the pantry with the skillet and a spoon), but please, save some for your fellow diners. As long as you promise to share, I will, with no further ado, give you the recipe.

CIDER-GLAZED SALMON,
OR SAUMON GELÉE À LA LOUIS XIV
Adapted from Arnold Weisenberg

*f*or this recipe you'll need a large (12-inch) skillet with a lid. The pan should be large enough to hold the salmon without crowding and to provide plenty of surface area for boiling down and thickening the sauce.

*1 tablespoon (½ ounce) unsalted
  butter*
*1 medium shallot, peeled and halved
  lengthwise*

2 cups fresh unfiltered apple cider
4 (6-ounce) salmon fillets
Salt
½ cup heavy cream

In a large, heavy skillet, combine the butter, shallot, and cider. Place over medium-high heat, and bring to a simmer. Simmer for 5 minutes, then remove and discard the shallot.

Place the fillets gently in the pan. Spoon a bit of the liquid over them, so that their tops begin to cook. Cover and simmer very gently. The fillets will cook for 8 to 10 minutes per inch of thickness. To test for doneness, make a small slit with a paring knife in the thickest part of the fillet: all but the very center of each piece should be opaque. (It will keep cooking after you pull it from the heat.) Transfer the cooked salmon to a platter, and cover loosely with aluminum foil to keep warm.

To prepare the glaze, raise the heat under the pan to medium-high, add a pinch of salt, and simmer, stirring frequently, until the liquid is reduced by about two-thirds. It should be slightly thickened and should just cover the bottom of the pan. Reduce the heat to medium, and add the cream. Stir well to combine. Boil, stirring frequently, for a few minutes, until the mixture darkens to a pale golden caramel—like those

Brach's Milk Maid caramel candies, if that helps—and is reduced by one-third to one-half.

Place the salmon fillets on 4 plates and top each with a spoonful of sauce. It should coat them like a thin, loose glaze. Serve immediately.

NOTE: If you'd like to make this for only 2 people, halve the amount of salmon, but not the sauce quantities.

Yield: 4 servings

WITH CREAM ON TOP

Sometimes I worry that with all I've written about my father, you might get the wrong impression. He was a real character, a very kind person, and even sort of a sap, but he could also be very difficult. He was not some mythic figure sent from on high. He and my mother almost separated when I was ten. The night before I left for college, when I was overwhelmed and scared and wanted his sympathy, he told me coldly, "You'd better get used to it, because this is the way life is." I hated him for saying that, though I don't think he really believed it. No one who lived as large, or ate as many croissants, as he did could possibly believe that life is cruel. But he could be gruff and hard all the same.

The thing is, now that he's gone, I don't really remember the bad things. When someone dies, we tend to tell the same stories over and over: the happy ones, or the funny ones, or, at the very least, the poignant ones. We turn those stories this way and that, studying them like diamonds or ancient scrolls, taking note of every detail. We don't tell the sad stories, or the ugly, warted ones. After a while, they fade like old newsprint, and we start to forget.

Part of what I love about writing is that it helps me to remember things. A computer or a scrap of paper is about eight million times more reliable than my brain. But sometimes, when I sit down to write, the stories are already half-gone. This happens especially often with the ugly ones, the ones I hid away behind something prettier or more important. When I go to look for them, they aren't there anymore. So it's hard for me to show you exactly who my father was, because I don't know anymore. And, to be perfectly honest, I don't want to. I'm not interested in wrapping him up in a box with a tidy bow. He would hate that.

One of the details I remember about my father is that he loved cream. In retrospect, it's kind of an endearing quality, I think, and very illustrative of his priorities, but at the time, it was an ongoing source of tension. He always had that big gut, that sagging shelf above his skinny birdlike legs, and he didn't seem the least bit interested in doing anything about it. It looked precarious, like a glass of water balanced atop a teetering stack of papers, and given his substantial back problems, it was. It's not uncommon, I understand, for doctors to be bad at taking care of themselves, and my father certainly was. Both he and that gut of his were maddeningly stubborn. My mother and I used to struggle to hold our tongues when he took a third scoop of ice cream or, late at night, sneaked into the kitchen to eat a bowl of cereal doused in heavy cream.

Of course, none of that, not his belly or any amount of cream, is what killed him. The cancer had its own plans, and it didn't need any help. And in light of that, I'm actually sort of glad he didn't listen to us.

Until a couple of years ago, I used to be a little scared of cream. It was probably a reaction, now that I think about it, to my father's decadent tastes, although at the time, I thought I was just being sensible. Once, at a bistro in Paris, I ordered a *velouté de potimarron,* a velvety pumpkin soup, and when it arrived at the table, my stomach did a flip-flop. It coated the spoon like crème anglaise, and its color tended more toward white than any shade of winter squash I'd ever seen. I only took three bites, though I had to admit, it was delicious. Of the remainder of the evening, the only thing I remember is the man sitting next to me, who leaned into my ear and breathed lustily, *"Ma cherie, tonight you are Cleopatra.* " I was going through a smoky eye makeup phase.

But if ever there were a reason to change my tune, creamwise, it's winter. The cold months make us all feel a little hungrier, I find, and a little more generous with ourselves and our measuring cups. A couple of winters ago, I discovered that I like to be especially generous with cabbage. I like to give it the better part of a cup of cream.

I first tried braising vegetables in cream because of food writer Molly Stevens, who wrote an entire book about braising. She has a recipe for cream-braised Brussels sprouts, which is insanely good, but I think green cabbage is even better. Cabbages may be homely, hard-headed things, but with a little braising, they're bewitching. Cut into wedges and cooked slowly in a Jacuzzi bath of cream, they wind up completely relaxed, their bitter pungency washed away and replaced with a rich, nutty sweetness. My stomach coos like a baby at the thought of it.

My father would have loved cream-braised cabbage. I'll bet he would have served it with one of his roasted chickens and some boiled, buttered potatoes. Just thinking about it makes me want to go fix myself a bowl of cereal with cream on top. I just might.

CREAM-BRAISED GREEN CABBAGE

t his recipe calls for a fairly small cabbage. I like to use small ones because they're often sweeter and more tender than their big-headed siblings. If, however, you can only find a larger cabbage, you can certainly use it. Just be sure to use only as many wedges as fit in a single layer in the pan, and take care that each wedge is no thicker than 2 inches at its outer edge. Otherwise, the cabbage won't cook properly.

You can also try this method on halved or quartered Brussels sprouts.

1 small green cabbage (about 1½ pounds)	*¼ teaspoon salt, plus more to taste*
3 tablespoons (1½ ounces) unsalted butter	*⅔ cup heavy cream*
	1 tablespoon fresh lemon juice

First, prepare the cabbage. Pull away any bruised leaves, and trim its root end to remove any dirt. Cut the cabbage into quarters, and then cut each quarter in half lengthwise, taking care to keep a little bit of the core in each wedge. (The core will help to hold the wedge intact, so that it doesn't fall apart in the pan.) You should wind up with 8 wedges of equal size.

In a large (12-inch) skillet, melt the butter over medium-high heat. Add the cabbage wedges, arranging them in a single crowded layer with one of the cut sides down. Allow them to cook, undisturbed, until the downward facing side is nicely browned, 5 to 8 minutes. I like mine to get some good color here, so that they have a sweetly caramelized flavor. Then, using a pair of tongs, gently turn the wedges onto their other cut side. When the second side has browned, sprinkle the salt over the wedges, and add the cream. Cover the pan with a tight-fitting lid, and reduce the heat so that the liquid stays at a slow, gentle simmer. Cook for 20 minutes, then remove the lid and gently, using tongs, flip the wedges. Cook for another 20 minutes, or until the cabbage is very tender and yields easily when pierced with a thin, sharp knife. Add the lemon juice, and shake the pan to distribute it evenly.

Simmer, uncovered, for a few minutes more to thicken the cream to a glaze that loosely coats the cabbage. Serve immediately, with additional salt at the table.

Yield: 4 to 6 servings

HAPPINESS

The word *happiness* has many definitions. For some, it involves cotton candy and peonies and babies that coo. For others, it involves ice cream, reruns of *Law & Order: Criminal Intent,* and warm sun on your face in early March. I'm quite certain, though, that if you looked it up in one of those visual dictionaries, what you'd see is a pan of slow-roasted tomatoes.

I first tasted slow-roasted tomatoes one hot summer several years ago, the summer after I returned from working in Paris and before I moved to Seattle. I was in Oklahoma, staying with my parents for a few months, and one day, a glut of tomatoes from the garden sent us running for the cookbook shelf. Each spring, my father used to start tomato plants in tiny pots in the laundry room, and by mid-July, they were so big, so top-heavy, that they would droop over the driveway until he tied them to the fence. That summer was an especially good one. The fruits were sweet and fat, coming ripe by the dozen. We needed to get rid of a bunch of them all at once, so we set out for ideas. We'd scoured two shelves of cookbooks when we stumbled upon a technique called slow roasting. It called for the tomatoes to be halved lengthwise and put into a low oven for several hours, so that their juices went thick and syrupy and their flavor climbed to a fevered pitch.

Following the loose guidelines, we sent two pans of tomatoes into the oven, and six hours later, we opened the door to find them entirely transformed. They were fleshy and deep red, with edges that crinkled like smocking on a child's dress. When we bit into them, they shot rich, vermilion juice across the table. We were sold.

Over the course of those few months, we must have roasted a half-dozen sheet pans' worth. We ate them plain, straight from the pan, or with mozzarella and basil. We put them into sandwiches. We used them to sauce fresh pasta that my father had flattened with a rolling pin and cut into small, rustic rags. It was a very good summer. Which is a good thing, as it turns out, because it was his last.

One day that fall, when he was lying in the hospital bed in the den, he had a dream about the tomatoes.

"There were so many," he told me sleepily, staring out the window. "We must have grown ten *thousand*."

I followed his eyes to the spindly patch outside. One could do much worse, I decided, than to go out that way, on a swan song of ten thousand tomatoes.

I think of Burg now every time I see a flush of those red fruits. In honor of that summer, I try to slow-roast them whenever I can.

I make mine the same way that we did back then, but in recent years, I have begun to add a few pinches of ground coriander. It's an idea I borrowed from a sandwich shop in Paris called Cosí, where one of the offerings is *tomates confites à la coriandre*. I used to ask for them fanned atop a smear of fresh ricotta or goat cheese, and the bright fragrance of the coriander always seemed to give the tomatoes a subtle boost.

Slow-roasting tomatoes may take time and planning, but straight from the oven, it's instant gratification. It's almost impossible to keep stray fingers out of them. They're like rubies in fruit form. And though they're delicious plain, their sweet acidity also plays remarkably well with other flavors, especially those dishes at the rich, robust end of the spectrum. I've served them alongside cheese soufflés and plates of pasta with pesto. When teamed up with fresh goat cheese, basil, and arugula, they make for a delicious, if drippy, sandwich, and laid over the top of a burger, they're like ketchup for adults. You can whirl them in the food processor with some basil and Parmesan and turn them into a pesto of sorts. You can even make them into a pasta sauce. Just slice a handful into a bowl with some capers, slivered basil, and sea salt, and add splashes of balsamic and olive oil. It's the sauce we ate all those summers ago atop Burg's fresh pasta, and it works on pretty much any noodle that happens to land in the pot. And on nights when the stove is too much to consider, few things make for a happier picnic than a hunk of crusty bread, a wedge of blue cheese, and some slow-roasted tomatoes. You don't even need a patch of grass. I can tell you from experience that the living room floor works fine.

With a little foresight, you can have them always in the refrigerator, ready and waiting. I've never been one to believe, anyway, that happiness can't be planned. I think my father would agree.

t his formula is loose enough that it can hardly be called a recipe. I've tried it in many permutations, and with good results every time. Sometimes I've roasted the tomatoes for 6 hours; other times, I've roasted them for 4. (You could even try 8 or 10 hours, if you want. What's the worst that could happen?) Sometimes I've set the oven to 200°F; other times I've set it to 250°F. I've roasted 10 tomatoes one day and 28 the next. I've even carried my experimentation into winter, when the tomatoes are far from ideal, and have come away with summery results.

The quantities listed here are intended to be a starting point. I like to use Roma tomatoes, but you could use almost any. Romas have very little juice and dense, meaty flesh, meaning that they roast very nicely. And unlike their more delicate, juicy cousins, decent Romas can be found almost year-round. That's good to remember, should you find yourself with a midwinter tomato craving.

3½ pounds ripe Roma tomatoes   *Salt*
   (about 20 tomatoes)   *Ground coriander*
1 tablespoon olive oil

Preheat the oven to 200°F.

Wash and dry the tomatoes, trim away the stem end, and halve them lengthwise. Place them in a large bowl, and, using your hands, toss them gently with the oil. Arrange them cut side up on a large baking sheet. Sprinkle with salt and ground coriander, about a pinch of each for every 4 to 6 tomato halves.

Bake until the tomatoes crinkle at the edges and shrink to about half of their original size, 4 to 6 hours. They should still be juicy in their centers. Remove from the oven, and set aside to cool to room temperature.

Put them in an airtight container, and store them in the refrigerator for up to a week.

Yield: about 40 tomato halves

SLOW-ROASTED TOMATO PESTO

a plain slow-roasted tomato is hard to beat, but should you want to take yours a step further, try this riff on pesto. It makes a great spread for a sandwich, especially when there is goat cheese or fresh mozzarella involved. It's also good as a condiment for pan-fried polenta. And like the slow-roasted tomatoes themselves, you can use it as a sauce for pasta. Just thin it with a splash of olive oil and some water from the pasta pot, and it's ready.

½ cup olive oil

1 teaspoon lemon juice

¼ teaspoon salt

2 medium cloves garlic, peeled and
   trimmed

2 cups packed basil leaves

3 cups slow-roasted tomatoes (about
   36 halves; see preceding recipe)

½ cup tightly packed finely grated
   Parmigiano-Reggiano

In the bowl of a food processor, combine the olive oil, lemon juice, salt, and garlic. Pulse until the garlic is finely chopped. Add the basil leaves and process until smooth, scraping down the sides of the bowl with a rubber spatula as needed. Add the tomatoes and process well. Add the Parmigiano-Reggiano and pulse to combine. Taste, and adjust the seasoning as necessary.

Stored in an airtight container in the refrigerator, this pesto will keep for up to a week.

Yield: about 2½ cups

BABY STEPS

I've never liked the word *blog*. It's kind of weird and lumpy. When you say it, it tumbles out of your mouth with an unbecoming thud. Plus, the whole concept is a little weird: a Web site where a person can write about whatever they want to, inviting comments and feedback from the whole world. At their best, blogs are smart, funny, and informative. At their worst, they're blush-worthy rants written at 2:00 a.m. after a bad breakup.

I tried to steer mine somewhere in between. I write about food and cooking, and in that sense, I aim to be informative, but I write about my life some, too, since it intersects with food roughly three times a day. I don't think many of us are terribly interested in recipes that have no stories or real-life context. For me, the two are inseparable. One is pale and boring without the other.

But still, having a blog is strange. I never know whether to be proud (*I'm young and hip! I'm with it! I have a blog!*) or sheepish (*So, uh, yeah, I have, uh, a blog? I take pictures of my dinner. But enough about me! Let's talk about you.*). It's a classic love-hate relationship. And like the human-to-human kind, the human-to-blog kind is oddly addictive. It's hard to beat the rush that comes when you press "Publish," sending your words out into the ether, or the satisfaction that stems from someone leaving a comment on your site. There's always a twinge of fear—

Will anyone read this? Will I alienate all my friends?—but so long as it's only a twinge, it's tolerable. Delicious, even.

I guess you could say that having a blog is a little like the windows of a house I used to live in during my sophomore year of college. I loved opening them wide during the day, so that the smell of the eucalyptus trees outside could drift in and sweep out the rooms. But occasionally I would come home and find a squirrel on my desk. A live squirrel. He would have climbed up the tree outside and jumped in through the window, and now here he was, rifling with his tiny, scratchy claws through whatever he found, tearing up every paper and scrap. Blogging is a little like that. It's an incredible pleasure to open the window, to put yourself out in the world that way. It's even better than the scent of eucalyptus. But occasionally you come home and find a squirrel on the desk, so to speak: a nasty comment, maybe, or even worse, something you wrote yourself, probably late at night, when you should have been sleeping, something that makes your cheeks hot.

I didn't know what to expect when I started Orangette. But I certainly didn't expect the e-mail that flew in through the window on April 3, 2005.

> *Hello,*
>
> *I'm sure you get this all the time, but your site is wonderful. My friend Meredith (who's a poet/writer and a damn good pastry chef) found it while searching for a French lemon yogurt cake recipe for a dinner party we're having. She texted me right away to tell me that I had to look at it. We relate to you because your writing is exactly how we feel and talk about food and life. And it seems that we've all spent time in France. I was in Paris for a semester last year; she was in Aix-en-Provence. I forget where you said you were. My name is Brandon, by the way (if you didn't infer that from the e-mail address), and I'm a musician (composer) getting my master's part-time in NYC, while being a full-time food snob. Anyway . . .*
>
> *The main problem is that you live in the wrong city. Spring's*

starting to show its beautiful face here in "The world's second home." (It's our new slogan—apparently "The Big Apple" was outdated.) Also, if you were in NYC, I would like nothing more than to take you out to Balthazar for some French martinis and a Balthazar Salad. Hope you're enjoying the day as much as you can, with the clouds and all.

~b

Well. This was certainly something new. I wasn't sure how to feel. He could be anyone. For all I knew, he could be twenty-two and an underwear model, or he could be eighty-two, with sweaters that smell like mothballs. Even worse, he could be some sort of Internet serial killer, stalking his prey among the food blogosphere, following the scent of banana bread and Ed Fretwell soup.

But I was strangely intrigued.

He's a musician, I thought. I like music!

He's a composer. He must be smart!

He mentioned Balthazar. How bad could he be? I'd had a terrific meal there once, cold seafood and a beet salad, on a trip to visit my sister. It was big and bustling, French to the core, all polished wood and tile and café tables.

I had no idea who this person was, and the mention of this Meredith girl made me suspicious—was she his girlfriend, or what?—but still, I was intrigued. I decided to write back. I'd write a little low-key letter, just to say thank you, and maybe ask about his music. That's all.

Hi Brandon—

Thanks for your e-mail, and no, I don't get that sort of thing all the time! It's always so nice to know that people are reading and enjoying my site. Thank you for letting me know.

And please thank your friend Meredith on my behalf for sending you over. It's good to meet fellow food-loving Francophiles! I see that you were in Paris for a while. Where in the city were you? I was there for two quarters as an undergrad, living in the 15th with a host family, and then I lived and worked there for almost a year after graduation, from late 2001 to mid-2002. I rented a little studio in the 11th. I miss it terribly, but Seattle grows on me all the time. If I'm going to be in the States, this isn't a bad place to be. I've toyed with the idea of New York, but I'm a West Coast girl at heart. I do love Balthazar, though, and I'd take you up on your offer in a heartbeat, were I in the area . . .

Speaking of which, where are you doing your master's? And what type of pieces are you composing? I'm not well versed in the world of classical music, but I have a weakness for nights at the symphony. Is that the sort of stuff you're working on?

Have a great week,
Molly

See that bit about the symphony? Total lie. I don't know what got into me. I didn't know whether to pat myself on the back—*go get 'em, girl!*—or to punch myself in the eye. In the end, I did neither. I sat by the computer all day, waiting for his name to appear in my inbox. And that night, it did.

Hello Molly,
Thank you for writing back so quickly. It was so much fun to call Meredith and tell her that our good friend Molly e-mailed me. She had no idea that I wrote to you!

On Paris . . . I still dream of the macaroons at Ladurée, the hot chocolate at Angelina's, the exotic creations of Pierre Hermé, the smell of flaming Calvados on crêpes at Crêperie Suzette (did you ever go there?), the falafels with salade turque in the Marais, the view from the escalators in the Centre Pompidou. I could go on forever . . .

On music . . . I'm currently studying at the City University of New York, taking classes at Brooklyn and Hunter colleges. I'm studying with an amazing woman from Cuba whom I refer to *as the Buddha, because of her never-ending knowledge of all things. I play saxophone, but as for the type of music I write, I guess it's considered classical. Or "art music." I usually write for choirs or orchestras or chamber groups, although sometimes I use electronics or make sound sculptures or installations. I guess I write pretty out-there music. But I try to keep an eye on the beauty of the outcome. For a food analogy: I won't create salads with raw chicken, lychee, pork rinds, and lemon zest with a motor oil-goat cheese-olive dressing, just because no one has done it before. I try to make "dishes" that taste like nothing else, but that also taste good. Being a composer is really no different from being a chef or a choreographer. Anyway, enough about music and too much about me.*

How are you? I hope you're having a great day.

~b

Oh my. This was very interesting. This was very good. Ladurée? Pierre Hermé? And Crêperie Suzette? That place was a ten-minute walk from my old apartment. I used to pass it almost every day. Sometimes, especially in the winter, I would stop at the to-go window for a hot crêpe smeared with apricot *confiture*. It came folded in a thin paper sleeve, and I would eat it as I walked, holding it in one hand and my soggy umbrella in the other. I had forgotten how much I loved that.

I kind of liked this guy.

So I sent another letter, and he, for his part, replied. Then there was another, and another. Soon he knew that my mother was an identical twin, that she had once owned a brown faux-fur dress and wore it to a Christmas party where she danced with the man who would become my father, and that I was conceived in Marin County, California. He knew that I used to have a T-shirt from Marin Brewing Company, a brewery near the town where my parents did the deed, that said BREWED IN MARIN across the back, and that I loved it, because I was. Soon I knew that his parents were former hippies and that he had been a vegetarian since birth; that he had been in a serious long-term relationship that had ended about a year before, in Paris; and that he was conceived in Allendale, New Jersey.

"Every time we passed a particular house, my mom would say, 'Did you know you were conceived there? Right in that little white house?' This was before I even knew what it meant to be conceived."

I really liked this guy.

One day, he happened to mention that he'd been on Friendster, the major social networking site at the time, and that, oh, what a small world, one of his friends was So-and-So, who was friends with another So-and-So, who was a friend of mine. I was never a big fan of Friendster, but I certainly did love it that day, when I logged onto my account and clicked through, friend to friend to friend, to Brandon's profile, where he'd posted two photographs of himself.

In the first, he was halfway out of the frame, smiling and seemingly laughing. He had hazel eyes and brown hair that fell in loose curls to his earlobes. There was a good-sized freckle on his left cheek, next to a dimple—he had dimples! on both sides!—and he had nice white teeth. (My mother always told me to look at the teeth.) The second shot was in black and white. He was looking squarely at the camera, mouth relaxed and lips slightly parted, and wearing what appeared to be lightly tinted, John Lennonesque glasses and that same, lovely, messy hair. I could forgive him for the glasses, I decided, because of that hair. He was adorable. He was handsome. He was hot. I wrote him another letter.

But I was starting to get nervous. I still hadn't heard his voice, and for all I knew, he could be some frisky teenager, setting up a very elaborate ruse. I really didn't think so, but still. Also, I had noticed in his Friendster profile that under "Hobbies and Interests," the first item listed was "dinner parties." I'd never heard a straight man say such a thing. I was worried. Then again, he also listed as interests "hot sauce," "beer," "bread," "bourbon," "anything with the consistency of salsa," and "thinking too much." I decided to give him my phone number.

The next night, he sent me a text message that read, simply, "Baby steps . . ." I was a goner. Using the number in my cell phone memory, I called him the next afternoon, and we talked for three and a half hours. Three days later, he called to tell me that he was coming to Seattle. He'd been out in New Jersey, he said, visiting his parents, and his father happened to mention that he was taking a business trip to Seattle in a week or so, and would Brandon like to come along? He could get a companion fare. It would be easy.

So it was that on April 25, barely three weeks after that first e-mail, I walked into the lobby of the Westin Hotel in downtown Seattle, where his father had booked a room, and met Brandon. He was about 5'10", wearing a leather jacket the color of dark chocolate and a pair of old jeans. His smile was bigger, giddier, than in the photograph, and his hair was wild and curly, just brushing his shoulders. He was still wearing those weird glasses, but *the hair*, people, *the hair*. I wore my favorite jeans and my purplish leather ankle boots with the pointed toes, the ones I call my Peter Pan Boots. We eyed each other shyly, grinning, as I walked toward him through the revolving doors. I was so nervous that I could hardly see straight. He discreetly looked me up and down (a move he still denies, though we both know he did it) and wrapped me in an enormous hug. He is a very good hugger.

Then I realized that I'd forgotten to put money in the parking meter. I told him to hold on, that I would be right back, and I ran, my boots slap-slapping the pavement, down the block to the car. It occurred to me only as I was walking back to the hotel, trying to catch my breath and checking to make sure that I hadn't sweat through my shirt, that he might think I'd fled the scene.

If he did, he didn't say a word. He was waiting, smiling, on a bench in the lobby, with a shoulder bag at his feet. We walked out onto the street, yelling over the noise of the monorail above, and I pointed us toward the new downtown library. It had opened not long before, and it was impressive, a massive, misshapen Rubik's Cube on a hill amidst the skyscrapers. Talking all the while, we absentmindedly took it in, the mezzanine with its curving red hallways, the chartreuse escalators. On the top floor, under the sloping windows, we sat in foam chairs that looked like Lego bricks and talked about hometowns and secrets. He told me that as a kid, he used to shoplift candy bars and eat them in the bathroom, because his mother wouldn't let him have them. In high school, he confessed, he sang in a rock band called "Um. . . ." I admitted that I'd been a debutante in the Oklahoma City Beaux Arts Ball. I am not really debutante material, but the chair of the selection committee that year was the mother of my senior prom date Billy, and I think she had something to do with it. My invitation was nearly revoked when I showed up for bow practice the day before with my nose pierced, but on the night of, no one said a word, and I got to come out, my arm looped over my father's, in my big white dress. My mother occasionally still runs into people who remember me as The Girl Who Got Away with a Nose Piercing at the Beaux Arts Ball. As far as secrets go, my debutante days lie at the dark end of the spectrum, but Brandon didn't flinch. We bought cups of gelato and sat on the Harbor Steps, facing the water, and talked some more. Then we went to Pike Place Market to buy ingredients for dinner.

We weren't aiming high, and I was too nervous to have much of an appetite, so we decided to make a salad. It was early spring, and ramps—those skinny wild leeks, like scallions with flat leaves—were in season. We bought a small bunch, along with some romaine and a fat avocado. Then we stopped for a round of Cowgirl Creamery's Mt. Tam cheese—made in the county where I was conceived! Oh, the coincidence—and, on the way back to the car, a baguette and beer.

I let Brandon take the lead on dinner. By this point, anyway, I could hardly look him in the eye. I knew a kiss was coming. I just didn't know when. I felt bashful, impatient, itchy with anticipation. I put my head down and tried to focus, slicing the avocado. Meanwhile, he whisked together a dressing, a slurry of lime juice, olive oil, soy sauce, and Vietnamese chile-garlic hot sauce from my refrigerator door. I warmed the baguette in the oven, put the cheese on a plate, and set the table. He went to the refrigerator to retrieve two beers. When he turned around to open them, I knew I had to do it. I asked if I could kiss him. He smiled and pulled me in, setting the beers on the counter behind me, and then he leaned down and kissed me. Then he kissed me again. We looked at each other, giggled, and leapt in the air, and then he danced me around the kitchen.

The next morning, we retrieved our dirty dinner plates from the kitchen table, wiped up the crumbs, and walked, wide-eyed and woozy, into we didn't know what.

i wrote about a version of this cake on my blog on August 1, 2004, and it's the reason Brandon's friend Meredith—and, by extension, Brandon himself—found me. I owe this cake quite a debt of gratitude. It may be simple, but to me, it borders on the magical.

This type of cake is an old-fashioned classic in France, the sort of humble treat a grandmother might make on a Sunday afternoon. Traditionally, the ingredients are measured in a yogurt jar, a small glass or ceramic cylinder that holds about 125 milliliters. But because most American yogurts don't come in such handy, multipurpose packaging, I've rewritten my own recipe to use cups.

You could certainly eat this cake plain, but I like to finish mine with two glazes: first, a lemony syrup that soaks into the still-warm cake, and second, a thin, glossy icing applied once the cake is fully cooled. Together, they're stupendously good. But if you're short on time or ingredients, you can certainly get away with only one of them.

FOR THE CAKE

1½ cups unbleached all-purpose flour
2 teaspoons baking powder
Pinch of salt
2 teaspoons grated lemon zest
½ cup well-stirred plain whole-milk
    yogurt (not low fat or nonfat)
1 cup sugar

3 large eggs
½ cup vegetable oil, such as canola

FOR THE SYRUP

¼ cup powdered sugar, sifted
¼ cup lemon juice

FOR THE ICING

1 cup powdered sugar, sifted
3 tablespoons lemon juice

Preheat the oven to 350°F. Grease a 9-inch round cake pan with butter or cooking spray. Line the bottom of the pan with a round of parchment paper, and grease it too.

In a medium bowl, whisk together the flour, baking powder, and salt. Add the lemon zest and whisk to mix thoroughly.

In a large bowl, combine the yogurt, sugar, and eggs, stirring to mix well. Add the flour mixture and stir to just combine. Add the oil and stir well. At first, it will look like a horrible, oily mess, but keep going, and it will come together into a smooth, pale yellow batter. Pour into the prepared pan.

Bake for 25 to 35 minutes, until a toothpick or cake tester inserted into the center comes out clean. Do not overbake.

Cool the cake in the pan on a wire rack for 15 minutes. Run a thin knife around the edge of the pan, and invert the cake onto a wide, flat plate or pan. Remove and discard the parchment paper. Invert the cake back onto the rack so that it sits upright, with the shinier, slightly domed side facing up. Set the rack over a rimmed baking sheet.

In a small bowl, whisk together the syrup ingredients. Spoon the syrup slowly atop the warm cake. Some of the syrup will run down the sides and onto the baking sheet; don't worry. Cool completely.

In a small bowl, combine the icing ingredients. Whisk well to dissolve the sugar completely. Spoon the icing over the cooled cake.

Serve immediately—the icing will still be soft and a bit juicy—or wait until the icing has firmed up, about 1 hour. Whichever way you like.

VARIATION: Instead of making a lemon-flavored cake, try orange or tangerine, or Meyer lemon, when in season. You can also try replacing the vegetable oil with a fruity, round-flavored olive oil; it brings a subtly richer flavor and wonderful fragrance. And for an especially delicate, sweetly fragrant cake, try replacing ½ cup flour with ½ cup very finely ground blanched almonds.

Yield: 8 servings

LIKE WILDFLOWERS

The day after Brandon and I met, I asked my friend Keaton to join us for a drink after work. I was already crazy about him, but I needed a second opinion. It's a good idea to get one when you've been diagnosed with a serious illness, and the early pangs of love are not much different.

Keaton and I became friends during our junior year in Paris, although we first met when we were freshmen. We took a political science class together, and I noticed her because one day she sat next to the guy I had a crush on. She was beautiful. Also, she had a Fugazi patch on her backpack. I had spent the better part of my teens listening to Fugazi, a band from Washington, D.C., and I knew for a fact that they didn't sell any band merchandise. The patch on her backpack had to be unauthorized, a fake. I gave the guy a polite hello and then slouched to the other side of the auditorium to quietly fume that this girl with the fake, *fake!* Fugazi patch had stolen him. What a hussy.

But two years later, we found ourselves in Paris together, and I had to admit, against my better judgment, that I liked her. I couldn't help it. I even told her, giggling, about my fury over the Fugazi patch. She confided that the guy I'd had a crush on was actually the resident assistant from her dorm, and that he was kind of strange. She was terrific. For six months, we palled around Paris, teaming up for research projects and sharing packets of Peanut M&Ms from the Métro vending machines. She was with me when I met Guillaume, and when he disappeared, and when we came back to the States, we drew together in the campus housing lottery and wound up sharing an apartment. It was in a dark, gloomy building on the edge of campus, but we did our best to make light of the brown shag carpet and the mold on the bathroom ceiling. I taught her how to sear tuna in a cast-iron skillet, how to roast Brussels sprouts and potatoes, and how to make my family's favorite cranberry chutney with crystallized ginger and dried cherries. She shared her formula for spinach salad with green apples, toasted walnuts, and blue cheese and made me giggle every night when she put in her mouth guard (she grinds her teeth when she sleeps) by saying "I love biscuits," which came out as "I love bis-CUSTH." I love that girl. Also, because no one ever gets her name right, when she introduces herself, she says, "Hi, I'm Keaton, like Buster Keaton." I just love that.

When I decided to go to graduate school, part of the reason I chose Seattle was because Keaton lives here. She's the kind of person you want to have around, especially if you might be needing advice on important matters. And especially when those matters concern your heart and a man who, only three weeks earlier, you hadn't known existed.

So, at around five in the evening on the second day of his visit, Brandon and I met Keaton at a bar called the Alibi Room, underneath Pike Place Market. When we arrived, she had already ordered a beer and made herself at home, and she jumped up, smiling, to shake Brandon's hand.

I hardly remember what happened after that, except that Brandon handily passed her inspection. It was so easy, so fun, the three of us sitting there together, as though we'd done it a million times before. And you know that expression, "to spread like wildfire?" Well, at one point during the evening, Keaton told us about some bit of news she'd heard at the office, and about how, she said, "it spread like *wildflowers*!" Then she paused and wrinkled her brow, sensing that something was amiss, and we dissolved into howls. *Spread like wildflowers.* Isn't that great? It's so much better than wildfire, and yet still fitting.

Sometimes, when I tell people about Brandon, I think of that night. I like to tell them that he spread like wildflowers through my life. Because he did. He does.

CRANBERRY CHUTNEY WITH CRYSTALLIZED
GINGER AND DRIED CHERRIES

W hen I gave Keaton the recipe for this chutney, she fell instantly in love, and so does pretty much everyone who tastes it. It was originally intended to go with Thanksgiving turkey, but it's delicious with almost anything, from biscuits to sweet potato soup. Brandon and I like it best as part of one of our favorite lunches, a thrown-together meal we call "toasts." We take whatever bread happens to be sitting on the counter, slice it and toast it, and turn it into small, open-faced sandwiches dressed with whatever cheeses or spreads can be found in the refrigerator. In the fall, this chutney is a special treat, dolloped onto toasts smeared with fresh goat cheese.

My mother doesn't remember where she first found the recipe, which is now written in her handwriting on an old slip of paper. But we've been making it for long enough, and I've tweaked it enough, that it feels like ours. The original version calls for raspberry vinegar, which Brandon tells me is *"so eighties."* If you happen to have some in your pantry, by all means, use it, but if you don't, feel free to substitute a mixture of white distilled vinegar and raspberry preserves. It works just fine.

Also, keep in mind that this chutney reaches its thick, jammy, finished consistency only as it cools, so it will still be somewhat loose when you first remove it from the heat.

24 ounces apricot preserves

¾ cup raspberry vinegar, or ¾ cup white vinegar plus 1½ teaspoons raspberry preserves

Pinch of salt

¼ teaspoon ground cloves

¼ cup Grand Marnier

2 (12-ounce) bags fresh cranberries, picked over

½ cup finely chopped crystallized ginger

1¼ cups dried tart cherries

In a large, heavy-bottomed saucepan, combine the apricot preserves, raspberry vinegar (or vinegar and raspberry preserves), salt, cloves, and Grand Marnier. Stir to mix, and place over medium-high heat. Bring the mixture to a boil, and cook for 10 to 15 minutes, or until it has thickened slightly. It will bubble aggressively, and you should stir regularly to keep it from scorching.

Reduce the heat to medium, add the cranberries, and cook until they are soft but not popped. I know that they're ready when I hear one or two of them pop; that's a good indicator that most of them must be getting pretty soft. Add the ginger and cherries, stir well, and remove from the heat.

Cool completely before serving. The chutney will thicken considerably as it cools.

NOTE: Stored in an airtight container in the refrigerator, cranberry chutney will keep for at least a week, if not indefinitely.

Yield: about 5 cups

DELICIOUS IN ITS WAY

P opular wisdom has it that long-distance relationships are a bad idea, and popular wisdom is often right. Dating over a distance is painful, expensive, and, much of the time, doomed to fail. It is a lot of things, and easy isn't one of them. But for me, it's a little more complicated. I may be the first person in history to say this, but I like long-distance relationships.

I don't, of course, say that lightly. Being separated from someone you love is nothing to sneeze at. I spent the better part of my early twenties living that way, and I was glad to see it end. At age twenty-two, a couple months out of college, I ran into Lucas, my childhood crush, and we fell in love. A month later, I left for a year of teaching in France. Then, when I went to Seattle, he got a job in Mississippi. We were like checkers on a board, jumping around and over each other, but never landing in the same spot. And in retrospect, I'm not so sure we were supposed to. When his Mississippi gig was finished, he joined me in Seattle, but we only lasted a year. Doomed was an apt descriptor.

But that didn't stop me from diving in again. When Brandon and I first met, we used to joke, wincing all the while, that we lived as far apart as we possibly could without needing a passport to visit. But we threw caution to the wind, and with it, ourselves. We took turns flying to see each other, me this month and him the next. I brought coffee beans from Seattle in my carry-on. He stuffed his suitcase with pastries from Balthazar and bottles of Brooklyn Brown Ale. We made friends with our flight attendants and credit card companies. He flew to Oklahoma for Thanksgiving with my family, and I sat with him in a noisy auditorium in northern New Jersey, watching his little sister's school play. We got used to greeting each other with bloodshot eyes and to saying good-bye in public places with fluorescent lights and PA systems. It was painful, to say the least, and certainly expensive, but in a small, secret way, I liked it.

For as nice as it is to wake up next to someone and to spoon while you fall asleep, there is something to be said, too, for being apart. For one thing, it left plenty of time for missing him, which, when done right, could be delicious in its way. Take love poems, for instance. They were made for long-distance relationships. I combed the shelves for my old favorites—Anne Sexton, Robert Hass, and "Slow Dance," by Tim Seibles, because it has that part about couscous—and I sent them to him slowly, one at a time. I bought new underwear and practiced making eyes at the mirror, like Brooke Shields in those early eighties Calvin Klein ads. I spent hours daydreaming, devising elaborate plans of seduction, each with its own soundtrack and choreography. When we were together, the days had a sense of gravity that was exquisite and awful. They were finite, and we filled them to the brim.

When we were together, we were always on vacation. (If one of you is living out of a suitcase, it's only fair for the second party to get into the spirit.) We ate accordingly. In Seattle, we splurged on dinners out, and I showed up late for work. I sat on the couch and wrote while he cooked in my kitchen, spelling out MOLLY in pizza dough on the counter. One night, we undertook a rigorous taste-test of malted milk powders, making four different chocolate milk shakes. (Carnation won, in case you wondered.) In New York, we had no schedule. He only had classes two days a week, so we had plenty of time, albeit not much money. He lived on West 123rd Street, not far from the enormous Fairway Market, and sometimes we would wake up late and walk to get a jug of orange juice, a bunch of radishes, a baguette, and some butter.

Back at home, we ate lazily at the wobbly table with the window open, the box fan blowing, and my bare feet on his lap. We'd spend the day wandering or skimming through museums (he has since told me that he once thought about proposing to me, and I'm *so* glad he didn't, under the big whale that hangs from the ceiling in the American Museum of Natural History) and then, at dusk, stop at Fairway again for the makings of dinner. It was some sort of salad, usually, something easy to eat with leftover baguette and sharp cheddar.

One such night, I climbed into his lap in the middle of dinner and told him, with a prickle of fear, that I was falling in love.

t he French have been eating radishes this way for time eternal, for breakfast or an afternoon snack, or with the evening aperitif. There's no hard-and-fast rule for how to do it. You can make a little tea sandwich of it, assembled on soft bread or baguette, or you can eat the radish whole, on its own, dragged through a dish of soft butter and dipped in salt. For breakfast, Brandon and I do something in between. We slice the radishes thinly and put them on the table with a couple of knives and the butter dish. Then we tear hunks from a baguette and top them, bite by bite, with butter and radish and salt. But on evenings when we're having friends over, we'll make things a little more refined, slicing the baguette thinly and giving it a quick toast. What follows is this last method, but you're welcome to do whatever you want.

Baguette
Radishes

Good-quality unsalted butter,
preferably cold
Fleur de sel, or another crunchy salt

Preheat the oven to 350°F.

Using a sharp serrated knife, slice the baguette into thin rounds. I usually aim to slice mine about ⅓ inch thick. Arrange the slices in a single layer on a baking sheet, and bake them until they are pale golden around the edges, just a few minutes. Watch carefully to make sure they don't burn: you want them to toast lightly, so that they crisp just a little, but you don't want to turn them completely dry and crunchy. Remove the pan from the oven, and cool to room temperature.

Meanwhile, trim the radishes and slice them thinly—as thinly as you can, like a communion wafer—into rounds.

When the baguette slices are cool, shave a slice of butter off the block—this is why it's helpful to have the butter cold, so you can peel off thin slices—and smear it onto the bread. Don't worry about really spreading it: I like the way it looks and melts on your tongue when it just sort of sits there. Arrange a few radish slices on top. Sprinkle with salt.

Repeat with the remaining baguette slices and serve.

ROUGH GOING

B randon came into my life with relatively few flaws, as these things go. His hygiene is pretty good, give or take some minor stubble. He doesn't snore, except when he has a cold. He'll even watch Pedro Almodóvar movies with me, which, for an American male, is really saying something. But he does have one major flaw. He doesn't like Bruce Springsteen. *Bruce Springsteen.* What kind of person grows up in New Jersey and comes away disliking the Boss? I can hardly listen to "Glory Days" without pumping my fist, and I'm from Oklahoma. My sister has had a crush on Springsteen for decades. She once saw him in a restaurant in New York, and even though she's not much for stalking celebrities, she couldn't resist asking for his autograph. She even touched his leather jacket. If I were her, I wouldn't have washed my hand for at least a week. Brandon just doesn't get it.

To tell you the truth, now that I think about it, there's another flaw, too, one that's almost worse. It's raw cabbage. Brandon *loves* it. I, on the other hand, do not.

Cabbage is delicious when it's braised, sautéed, steamed, or stewed, but certainly, definitely, not raw. To me, uncooked cabbage conjures up visions of sneeze guards and salad bars, where it always lurks amidst the lettuce, gnarled and dry at the edges. And once in the mouth, it's not much better. It's starchy and stiff, like a Styrofoam packing peanut that's been stepped on. When it's especially conniving, it shows up in the cheerful guise of coleslaw, hidden stealthily under a cloak of mayonnaise. I'm usually of the belief that mayonnaise can make anything better, but with cabbage, it's questionable.

You can imagine, then, the depth of my displeasure when Brandon suggested, one day not long after we started dating, that we make a salad of shredded red cabbage. I gasped.

"But with lemon juice and garlic and grated Parmesan? It's *so good*!" he chirped.

Apparently, it was a formula he came up with in college. He liked to approach the dining hall, he says, as though it were a grocery store of sorts, taking a little something here and another something there and assembling them into a meal. Such was the case with the cabbage salad. His dining hall had a salad bar stocked with particularly pert shredded cabbage, and one day he served himself a big heap. Then he reached above the sneeze guard to a basket of decorative fruits and pulled down a lemon. He used a dinner knife to saw it in half, and then he squeezed it over the cabbage. He added a drizzle of olive oil, decent shakes of salt and pepper, and, from the pizza station, a spoonful of shredded Parmesan. The resulting concoction, a sort of Italian-style slaw, became his dining hall routine. And it's been a recurring element in his repertoire ever since.

Needless to say, this was a problem, especially on top of his dissing of Springsteen. It was rough going for a while.

Then he told me the story about Clarence Clemons, the saxophonist for Springsteen's E Street Band. Once, when Brandon was sixteen and on a trip to Boca Raton to visit his grandparents, he went to a blues show and wound up chatting with the band. They mentioned that they'd left their saxophonist back in New York and asked him, just like that, if he might want to play with them the following night, when they would be the opening act for Clarence Clemons, who was touring solo at that point. Brandon said yes, and so it was that he came to open for the esteemed Mr. Clemons.

This might, I told myself, be the closest I ever get to Bruce Springsteen. I had to give Brandon and, by extension, his cabbage salad, another chance. He was worth it. Anyway, there's only so long you can stand between a man and his eating habits—and, incidentally, his ugly striped shirt with the stretched-out collar. And his old green sweater with the holes in it. And just so you know, you also cannot make a man notice when the bathtub needs to be scrubbed, or when his side of the bed has started to look like a small graveyard for books and dirty socks. For his part, Brandon would like to add that you cannot, after a certain hour, stand between a Molly and her bed. You also cannot beat her at cards without her getting grumpy, and you cannot convince her to go out for drinks after dinner, because she prefers to have them before. We teach each other all kinds of things.

Anyway, one day at the farmers' market, when I saw a basket of red cabbages, I bought one. It was an especially petite, midwinter specimen, and with the help of our sharpest knife, Brandon quickly reduced it to a pile of purply ribbons. Then he poured equal parts olive oil and lemon juice into an old jam jar, along with a dose of fiery garlic for good measure. He tossed the whole mess together with a palmful of grated Parmesan and a few turns of the pepper grinder, and we sat down to the simplest of winter dinners: a loaf of crusty bread, a plate of cheeses, and red cabbage salad.

I was amply prepared to despise it. For the sake of saving face, I almost wish I could tell you that I did. But I didn't despise it at all. In fact, I ate a second helping. The cabbage was surprisingly sweet and crisp, as it is at the peak of its season, each shred plump and dense. Flecked with shards of Parmesan and black pepper, bright with lemon and garlic, it made a lip-smacking salad, one worthy of being eaten by the scoopful.

Sometimes, when we're sparring for the last shred in the serving bowl, I don't even care about Springsteen. And that, you know, is saying a lot.

C abbage is at its sweetest during the colder months of the year, making this pretty salad a good one for winter. Be sure to choose heads of cabbage that feel firm and heavy, with smooth, tight leaves. Remember, too, that small heads often taste sweeter and milder than their larger siblings, so for this salad, they're your best bet.

You will probably have a bit of dressing left over, but it's easy to dispose of. For a quick lunch, I like to use it to dress a can of drained, rinsed chickpeas, which I then top with some shredded Parmigiano-Reggiano.

2 tablespoons olive oil

2 tablespoons fresh lemon juice

¼ teaspoon pressed garlic

⅛ teaspoon salt

1½ pounds red cabbage

¼ cup finely grated Parmigiano-

Reggiano

Freshly ground black pepper

First, make the dressing. In a small bowl, whisk together the olive oil, lemon juice, garlic, and salt. Set aside while you prepare the cabbage.

Pull away any bruised leaves from the outside of the cabbage, and trim its root end to remove any dirt. Cut the cabbage into quarters. Working with one quarter at a time and using a large, sharp knife (my mother, who also loves this salad, swears by a serrated bread knife), slice the cabbage as thinly as you possibly can, as though for coleslaw. Slicing it very thinly is crucial; if you slice it too coarsely, it won't absorb the dressing as well. Ideally, no sliver should be thicker than ¼ inch. Discard the white cores.

In a large serving bowl, toss the cabbage with a large spoonful or two of the dressing. Add the Parmigiano-Reggiano and toss to distribute evenly. Taste, and add dressing as needed. Season generously with pepper, and serve.

Yield: 4 servings, as a first course or side dish

BONUS POINTS

Experimentation is not my strong suit. This means, on the one hand, that I'm every D.A.R.E. parent's dream child. I have only been drunk once, and it was at a dinner party with my mother, which hardly counts, and though I did try smoking pot one time, it was from a cheerful yellow and white pipe named Colonel Mustard, which definitely doesn't count. But when it comes to the kitchen, my difficulty with experimentation tends to get me into trouble. It means that I am, in most cases, not so daring.

In my defense, I come by it naturally. Like my mother before me, I'm a baker by nature: precise, obedient, and fiercely devoted to my digital scale. My mother taught me early on that a recipe should always be followed strictly the first time through, with no tweaking or second guessing. You give it an honest try, see how it goes, and then you can tinker to your heart's content. If, of course, you're into that. I've been known to throw an extra handful of chocolate chips into my banana bread, but in general, I find a deep, abiding satisfaction in following instructions.

This concept is a source of perpetual amusement for Brandon, who might have never, had I not come along, carried out a recipe as written. While I hunch over a cookbook, hanging on every word, he's at the stove with his fingers in the pot. If I'm reaching for a calculator, he's sniffing the spice jars. I can make a proper soufflé, but he can turn tamarind, roasted garlic, and Parmesan cheese into a sauce that'll make you shed a tear. If I get a gold star for reading comprehension, he gets detention, and then a MacArthur "Genius" Grant.

It's okay, I guess. We're a perfect pair and opposites attract and so on and so forth. But deep down, no one likes a teacher's pet, including the pet herself. And slavishly following instructions is only sexy if you're cooking in your underwear.

So I've been working on it. I've been working on experimentation. I see it as an investment not only in our relationship but also in my cooking skills. It hasn't always been easy, but I'm getting there.

One day early on, I called Brandon in New York to report that I'd tried a new cookie recipe, and that I'd tweaked it on the very first go.

"Really?" he asked incredulously. "What did you do?"

"Well, the recipe called for 2 cups of rolled oats, but I used 1½ cups rolled oats and ½ cup quick-cook!" I announced triumphantly. "*And*— get this—I used dark brown sugar instead of light brown."

He still chuckles about that.

But it wasn't long before I gave the genius a reason to be jealous. I made a soup flavored with vanilla bean. It doesn't sound that daring to me now, which I will take as a sign of my progress, but back then, it was big. Especially because I was sick at the time with mononucleosis that *he* gave me, I should note, after he got it from his friend Gratia, whose flute he'd been playing (isn't that slang for something?), who got it from her German boyfriend Winfried. It was a special international strain, extra nasty, so I get bonus points.

It was November of the first year we were dating, and I was in the mood for soup. That I was in the mood for anything is pretty impressive, I think, since I was so sick and exhausted that, most days, I came home from work, sat on the couch, and cried. I contemplated walking down the street to a café for some lentil soup or split pea, but there was a butternut squash on the counter, and squash soup sounded good. My mother has long made a wonderful version with apples and onions and curry, and just thinking about it made me feel better. So I shuffled into the kitchen and took stock of the pantry, where I found that I had only pears, not apples, and that my curry supply seemed to have been depleted on Brandon's last visit.

Then I remembered a soup I'd eaten in a restaurant a few weeks earlier, before all the night sweats and crying on the couch. It was a butternut soup with pear and vanilla bean, pale gold and frothy with cream. It was utterly galvanizing. I could do it. Yes I could.

So, using my mother's recipe as a guide, I got to work. I substituted pears for the apples, skipped the curry, and instead, I slit open a vanilla bean. Then I put it into a pot with some half-and-half, warmed it on the stove, and let it steep until it smelled like an old-fashioned candy store. When I stirred it all together, the soup and the steeped half-and-half, a ghost of steam rose from the pan, lifting with it the loveliest scent. It was earthy but delicate, sweet but savory, astoundingly appealing. I felt as though I'd just discovered a new constellation, or a sack of gold coins in my bedroom closet. It was momentous.

I'm not sure what I did next, but I'm pretty sure I went back to the couch with a mug and spoon and sat there for a long time. I may have also fallen asleep. But then I called Brandon to gloat.

"Hot *damn,* " he said. I wasn't sure whether he was referring to the soup or the cook, but I took it as a solid endorsement.

ℐ hortly after I first made this soup, Brandon called to report that he'd gone to the Union Square Greenmarket, and that he'd bought fifteen pounds of squash, which he was now in the process of lugging back to his apartment, 109 blocks north.

"Will fifteen pounds be enough," he asked, panting, "for that butternut soup with vanilla bean?" I *howled*. As it turns out, there is something to be said for paying attention to ingredient lists and recipe instructions. Victory is mine.

If you don't like the idea of seeing vanilla seeds in your soup, feel free to strain the infused half-and-half through a fine sieve or cheesecloth before adding it to the soup. Also, keep in mind that this soup is even better on the second or third day.

3 tablespoons olive oil
One 2 pound butternut squash, peeled, seeded, and cut into 1-inch cubes (about 4 generous cups)
2 firm-ripe pears, peeled, cored, and cut into 1-inch cubes (about 2 cups)
1 medium yellow onion, peeled and coarsely chopped

1 cup apple cider or unfiltered apple juice
4 cups vegetable or chicken broth
½ teaspoon salt
½ cup half-and-half or cream
1 vanilla bean
Finely chopped fresh chives, for garnish

Heat the oil in a Dutch oven or small stockpot over medium-low heat. Add the squash, pears, and onion and stir to coat with oil. Cook for 10 to 15 minutes, stirring occasionally, until the onion is soft and transparent and the pears are starting to fall apart.

Add the cider and bring the mixture to a boil over medium-high heat. Add the broth, reduce the heat to medium-low, and simmer the mixture, partially covered, for about 30 minutes, until the squash is tender.

Using a blender or food processor and working in small batches—don't fill your blender jar more than one-third full; hot liquids expand—purée until very smooth. Return the soup to the stockpot and add the salt. Continue to cook, uncovered, over medium-low heat, until the soup has reduced to about one-half to one-third of its original volume. Stir occasionally. The final consistency is up to you; when it reaches a thickness that seems right—not too thin, not too thick—it's ready.

While the soup is reducing, put the half-and-half in a small saucepan. Using a sharp knife, split the vanilla bean in half from tip to tip. Using the back of your knife, scrape the tiny black seeds out of the pod. Scoop the seeds and the pod into the saucepan with the half-and-half, and warm it over low heat, swirling occasionally, until it steams. Do not allow it to boil. Pull it from the heat, remove and discard the pod, and whisk to break up any clumps of seeds. Set aside.

When the soup has reduced to your desired thickness, stir in the infused half-and-half. Taste, and adjust the seasoning as necessary.

Serve, garnished with a sprinkling of fresh chives.

Yield: 4 to 5 servings

HERBIVORES ONLY

I guess it's a product of our time, or a generational thing. Or maybe it's just a matter of pheromones. Whatever the reason, I keep falling in love with vegetarians. Lucas was one, and a vegan, even. He had the bumper stickers to show for it. We used to share pints of soy ice cream on his corduroy couch, and for his birthday I baked him an entirely dairy- and egg-free chocolate cake. And before he came along, I had a wicked crush on a vegetarian rock star, which isn't quite love, but it still counts. And once, in college, I asked out an outspoken vegetarian in one of my classes. He was very handsome, with chiseled cheekbones and wavy auburn hair. I told him about a bar I knew and asked if he wanted to have a beer. He was too busy, he replied, but could I remind him in a couple of weeks? Remind him. Can you imagine? I *really* needed a beer after that, and a lobotomy. So that counts, too.

I spent nine years in the vegetarian camp, from age sixteen to shortly before my twenty-fifth birthday, so I guess I'm predisposed. I have dated a couple of meat-and-potatoes types, just to see what it was like, but fate has it that my love is meant for herbivores only. One could argue that my sample size is too small for statistical significance, but now that I've met Brandon, I don't intend to make it any bigger. It's significant enough for me. In the nearly three decades since his birth, Brandon has not once eaten meat, but his palate has ventured further than that of many omnivores, mine included. If push came to shove, I'd take Brandon over a plate of sausage any day, and I love sausage more than almost anything.

Maybe it's a result of my own years as a vegetarian, but when we eat together, I don't feel as though anything is missing. We eat a lot of eggs, and interesting cheeses, and those tiny French lentils, the green ones that are good with vinaigrette. I do occasionally wish there were another meat-eater around when I make a roasted chicken, but it's a relatively minor problem, as these things go.

Plus, Brandon once showed up at my door with a quarter pound of a very rare type of cured pork, and nothing makes a girl feel googly-eyed like getting pork from a vegetarian. Especially if he's just visiting, only for ten days, so the gesture is especially poignant. And even more if, over the span of those ten days, he makes her a batch of pita, a vat of hot sauce, ten *canelés,* two lunches of Thai green papaya salad, rocky road candy with homemade marshmallows, a quart of milk chocolate ice cream with cocoa nibs, cilantro chutney, sticky tamarind sauce, and the finest chana masala ever to flirt with her lips. There's no reason to ever look elsewhere. Or to leave the house again, except for groceries. It would be a shame to squander precious time on things like seeing friends, eating in restaurants, and fresh air. Brandon is all a person ever needs. That, and his chana masala.

Brandon is certainly not the first person to make chana masala, and he doesn't have any particular pedigree, ethnic or otherwise, to lend him an air of authority in Indian cookery. But he does have a very precise palate, and that carries him a long way. I may be the more orderly of our couple, but next to his palate, mine is a proverbial bull in a china shop, rubbing clumsily against a rabble of spices. I chew and swallow, but he *concentrates,* teasing apart layers of flavor. He claims it has to do with his training in music: that learning to listen closely for notes, to parse a piece of music, gave him a fine-tuned ear that, apparently, had a trickle-down effect on his tongue. I don't know. I just know that when he starts surveying the spice rack, I set the table, sit down, and watch.

What happens is a kind of dance, I guess you could say. He hops around, cabinet to stove to cutting board to cabinet, tasting and tweaking and tasting again. It's all very cute, as long as you don't interfere. In the case of the chana masala, the dance begins with a pot of onions, cooked until they teeter on the edge of burnt. I've heard that my father's mother, when describing how to make one of her recipes, would always start by saying, "First, you brown an onion," and if that's true, she and Brandon would have been fast friends. After the onion comes a small but spirited parade of spices, a tin of tomatoes, and some cilantro, cayenne, and chickpeas. Then things simmer for a little while, during which time you can safely enter the kitchen to do some dishes or kiss the cook, which will cause him to wrinkle his brow and mumble about cumin. It's a show worth paying admission for.

Very often, I find, restaurant renditions of chana masala are evidence of alchemy gone astray. They pound your tongue with a ton of tomato or smother your taste buds under a slick of oil. Brandon's does neither of these things, and I don't say that only because he bribes me with milk chocolate ice cream or because, in moments of weakness, I like to watch him sleep. His chana masala is a beautiful thing. It's worth keeping around, as is the man who made it.

$\mathcal{W}$ hen I'm not hovering next to him with a pen and paper, Brandon makes his chana masala entirely by feel and taste. The recipe that follows is our joint effort to make it reproducible for those who, like me, love a reliable recipe. You should feel free, however, to tweak as you see fit. It's The Brandon Way.

This chana masala can be served in two different styles: with some whole milk yogurt to smooth and soften the flavors, or *sans* yogurt, served with a squeeze of lemon. I prefer the former, but Brandon leans toward the latter. Either way, this dish is better the second day, or even the third.

¼ cup olive oil

1 medium onion, coarsely chopped

2 medium cloves garlic, minced

1 teaspoon cumin seeds

½ teaspoon ground coriander

¼ teaspoon ground ginger

1 teaspoon garam masala, plus more
   for serving

3 green cardamom pods, lightly
   crushed under the side of a knife

1 teaspoon salt, or to taste

Water

One 28-ounce can whole peeled
   tomatoes

1 tablespoon coarsely chopped cilantro
   leaves, plus more for serving

Pinch of cayenne or red pepper
   flakes, or more to taste

Two 15-ounce cans chickpeas,
   drained and rinsed

⅓ to ½ cup plain yogurt (not low fat
   or nonfat; optional)

A few lemon wedges (optional), for
   serving

Pour the olive oil into a Dutch oven and warm it over medium heat. Add the onion, and cook, stirring occasionally, until it is deeply caramelized. It's okay if it's even charred in spots. Be patient. The more color, the more full-flavored the final dish will be.

Reduce the heat to low. Add the garlic, cumin seeds, coriander, ginger, garam masala, cardamom pods, and salt and cook, stirring constantly, until fragrant and toasty, about 30 seconds. Add ¼ cup water and stir to scrape up any brown bits from the bottom of the pan. Cook until the water has evaporated completely. Pour in the juice from the can of tomatoes, followed by the tomatoes themselves, using your hands to break them apart as you add them. (Alternatively, add them whole and crush them in the pot with a potato masher.)

Raise the heat to medium, and bring the pot to a gentle boil. Adjust the heat to maintain a simmer, add the cilantro and cayenne, and continue to cook gently, stirring occasionally, until the mixture reduces a bit and begins to thicken, about 5 minutes. Add the chickpeas, stirring well, and cook over low heat for 5 minutes. Add 2 tablespoons water and cook for another 5 minutes. Add another 2 tablespoons water and cook until it is absorbed, a few minutes more. This process of adding and cooking off water helps to concentrate the sauce's flavor and makes the chickpeas more tender and toothsome. Taste, and adjust the seasoning as necessary.

Stir in the yogurt, if you like. Or leave it out, and serve instead with a lemon wedge on the side. Either way, sprinkle it with a pinch or two of garam masala and some chopped cilantro.

Yield: 4 servings

SPECIAL GAME

E very now and then, Brandon and I like to play a special game. It
has no real name, but if I were to give it one, it might be called
the "Your Partner Has No Past" game. It goes something like this:
whenever one of us mentions a previous boyfriend or girlfriend, the
other feigns complete incomprehension. For example:

> MOLLY: Oooh! I love this song! Turn it up! [*Ex-boyfriend*] put it on
> a mix tape for me when we first met.

> BRANDON: What? Who did? You mean I did? I did, right?

It's not so much that we dislike knowing about each other's previous
significant others. In fact, I take a real interest in the topic. Who doesn't
want to know all her predecessors' faults and shortcomings, or the story
of the foolish English girl who broke his heart at age sixteen? (Hannah
Baldry was her name, although you have to pronounce it "Hannah
Bowwwldry," with a British accent.) It's just that it's fun to pretend that
your partner sprang from the ether, pure and wise and perfectly formed,
the way Athena emerged from Zeus's head. Pretending that we have no
past makes us look very talented and precocious, like minor geniuses in
the romance department. To wit:

MOLLY (*breathily*): You're such a good kisser. It's really amazing, since I was your first kiss.

BRANDON: Isn't it? And *you*, I have to say, are so good at spooning. It's kind of crazy how good you are, especially when you've never done this before.

Quite fun, as you can see. You should really try it, so long as both players are in on the plan. Otherwise, it could get messy.

But all that said, I have to admit that I am actually quite grateful for Brandon's ex-girlfriends, and one of them in particular. Her name is Gillian. Without her wise tutelage, he tells me, he would be "a terrible hippie," whatever that means. He would never have done any homework or made it through college, and he would douse all edibles with inedible amounts of vinegar. I owe her a lot. But more than anything else, I owe her, or, technically, her parents, for teaching Brandon about shaved fennel salads.

Back when Brandon and Gillian were together, her parents owned—and perhaps they still own—a CD-ROM of Julia Child's series *Cooking with Master Chefs*. In one of the episodes, Alice Waters teaches Julia how to make a salad of shaved fennel, mushroom, and Parmesan. Gillian's parents were quite taken with the idea, and it quickly became a regular in their repertoire. They once served it to Brandon, and today, one breakup and several years later, it is a regular in our repertoire, too.

After summer's lettuces are gone and before winter's red cabbage arrives, fennel is our early fall standby. It's crisp and fragrant and cheering for the jaw. Shaved into slivers and layered on a platter, drizzled with olive oil and lemon and scattered with curls of Parmesan, it's what salad looks like when it wears white after Labor Day.

We often serve it with slivered mushrooms, à la Alice, but as we discovered on a whim one October afternoon, we like it even better with Asian pears. We stumbled upon the idea when we happened to finish off a Sunday lunch of fennel salad with some slices of an Asian pear. Much to our surprise, the juicy, perfumed crunch of the pear was delicious with the clean, aniselike flavor of the fennel, and a new salad was born. It makes a handsome lunch for two, along with a baguette, a pat of butter, and some chocolate for dessert.

If you're anything like us, it might even inspire a special game, something involving forks, stealth, and the last bite of salad.

*a*s you may have noticed, Brandon and I eat a lot of salad. Between the two of us, we could keep a small farm in business. Much of the time, in fact, we don't so much cook as *assemble*. It's sometimes a little disconcerting, given that we supposedly like to cook, but it's nice to eat simply. A good salad is nothing to scoff at.

As salads go, this one is especially elegant, with its layered presentation. But if you're short on time, you can certainly toss it. As for variations, you might try substituting aged Gouda for the Parmesan, or replacing the Asian pear with thin shavings of cremini mushroom.

1 medium fennel bulb, about 10 ounces	*Crunchy salt, such as Maldon or fleur de sel*
1 small Asian pear	*Wedge of Parmigiano-Reggiano cheese*
Olive oil	
Lemon	*Freshly ground black pepper*

First, prepare the fennel. If it still has long stalks and fronds, cut them off and discard them. (Or use them for something else, like a homemade stock.) Using a vegetable peeler or small knife, trim away any bruises or brown spots on the bulb's outermost layer of "skin." Cut it in half from root to stalk, and trim the root end. Using a sharp knife or a mandoline and working with one-half of the bulb at a time, slice the fennel very thinly, ⅛ to ¼ inch thick. You're not going for *quite* paper-thin—that's almost too fine and will tend to make the fennel watery—but you want it to be close. Set aside.

Next, prepare the Asian pear. Using an apple corer, remove and discard the core. Then cut the pear in half from top to bottom. Using a sharp knife or a mandoline, slice it very thinly, just like the fennel. Set aside.

Assemble the salad in layers on a large platter. First, make a wide layer of fennel slices. Drizzle lightly with olive oil. Then place a layer of Asian pear on top of the fennel. Drizzle lightly with lemon juice, and season with salt. Using a vegetable peeler, shave thin ribbons of cheese on top of the pear. Add another layer of fennel, followed by a light drizzle of oil, and then another layer of pear, lemon juice, salt, and cheese. Repeat until you run out of ingredients. You might have two layers, or you might have many more; it doesn't matter. Finish the salad with a good drizzle of lemon juice and a hearty splash of oil, and garnish with a few shavings of cheese.

Serve immediately, with salt and pepper to taste.

Yield: 4 first-course servings or a light meal for 2

THE DIAMONDS

My father was not known for having a particularly impressive memory. If you had something important to tell him, there was no need to hurry, because at least eight times out of ten, he wouldn't remember it anyway. In most cases he promptly forgot, or else he buried it beneath another wisp of information, never to be seen again. Someone might have called with exciting family news, but my mother and I would never hear it. Burg was a dead end. My uncle Arnie took to facetiously calling him "Radio Free Wizenberg," because he was anything but. He would have made a terrific career criminal, the kind who conveniently forgets which bank he robbed and who his accomplice was. He not only failed to remember his children's birth dates, but he also occasionally referred to my brother David as "Midnight," the name of the family dog, circa 1965.

So it didn't surprise me that he forgot about the diamonds. Sometime during college, I think it was, he had called to tell me about them. He'd just come from an estate sale where he'd found a pair of small diamond studs that were relatively cheap, as these things go. He knew I didn't have my ears pierced, but he bought them anyway, figuring that I might want to use the stones for something else. He would give them to me, he said, the next time I was home.

But then, of course, he forgot. And lo and behold, I, being his daughter, forgot, too. (With that kind of genetic stock, I didn't stand a chance.) Years went by, and those diamonds might as well have never been.

We could have been a terrific slapstick duo, the two of us. I can see it now, the first episode of our show. We're walking down the street, both in oversized pants and suspenders, when we stumble upon a suitcase with a label on the side that says CONTENTS: GOLD. We leap on it, slapping our thighs and cheering, and set to work jiggling the latch. But after a few minutes, when it still hasn't budged, boredom starts to set in. We lose interest. We forget why we were there. We stand up, shake out our coats, and while the audience squeals in disbelief, shouting for us to turn around, we set out cheerily in search of some doughnuts.

The year after Burg died, my mother, my brothers, my sister, and I met in Oklahoma to go through his belongings, his clothes and shoes. Mom found the diamond earrings in his bathroom drawer. He'd put them in his cufflinks box, apparently, a clear plastic case with small compartments built for fishing flies, now filled with knickknacks and lapel pins. They were hidden in a silk bag, but she recognized them. She gave them to me, gently prodding my memory, and I brought them home to Seattle. I put them in a drawer under my bathroom sink. I didn't know what to do with them, but I liked having them there. They felt like a secret that only my father and I would know.

I told Brandon about the earrings earlier than I meant to, maybe two months after we met. It just slipped out. He was in town to visit and, while walking around the neighborhood one afternoon, had found six vintage champagne glasses, the wide, shallow kind with a hollow stem, for fifty cents each. They were glamorous and pretty, the sort of thing a flapper would hold in one gloved hand. They reminded me, I told him, of something my father would have brought home. They reminded me of the costume jewelry he bought for my mother, and of the diamond studs in my bathroom.

Several months later, in January, Brandon was in Seattle again. When I got home from work, it was already dark outside, and he was in the kitchen, working on dinner. While we waited for the timer to ring, we sat down on the couch. My hands were cold, and he rubbed them for me. In the little apartment I lived in then, my desk was directly across from the couch. On top of the desk I kept a row of photographs. The largest, taller than all the rest, was a 5 × 7-inch black-and-white shot of my dad in his doctor's coat in one of those wobbly plastic frames. This is probably way too precious to admit, but I always felt like he was watching me from up there, looking down over the living room with its hopeless, stained carpet, making sure everything was safe.

"I had a talk with your dad today," Brandon announced, nodding toward the desk.

I guess it would be smart, or maybe just minimally sane, to say that I was surprised. Or that it was creepy to have my boyfriend tell me that he'd been chatting with my dead father. But I wasn't surprised. I was charmed. Brandon had always asked questions here and there, wanting to know more about Burg. It didn't surprise me that he might sit down at my desk one day while I was at work and study the face in the photograph. I wanted him to.

"What did you two talk about?" I asked nonchalantly, smiling a conspirator's grin.

"Oh, nothing," he said shyly. Then he stood up and pulled me into the kitchen.

I don't like mysteries very much, not outside of movies or books, but I decided to let it be. In fact, after a day or two, I'd completely forgotten about the entire conversation. Brandon is lucky I didn't start calling him "Midnight."

It seems a little strange to tell the story this way now, when, as I was living it, it didn't feel so neat and chronological at all. Even though I had wanted for months to marry Brandon—and had been, in small, subconscious ways, waiting for him to hurry up and ask me— still, it caught me by surprise. I didn't put it all together until well afterward. When Brandon walked me across the Brooklyn Bridge that afternoon in March, almost a year after we met, and steered me up the hill to Brooklyn Heights, to a bench on the promenade, I had no idea. When he knelt in front of me and put his head in my lap, I had not the foggiest. I was thoroughly absorbed, in fact, in staring at a fleck of dandruff tangled in one of his curls. When he pulled out the blue leather box with a ring inside, a dainty, antique ring with two triangular sapphires and a small diamond in the middle, I still didn't understand. Even when he said, "It's one of your father's diamonds," I didn't put it together. I didn't understand that, that day when he had talked to my father, he had been asking if he could marry me.

What I did instead was yell, "Are you *crazy?*" Then I looked at him, and then behind him, at the water, and up and down and all around, and giggling, out of breath, said yes.

When I tell people the story of our engagement, that Brandon took the diamonds from my bathroom that January and carried them around New York City for two months, looking for an antique setting that would fit them—or one of them, at least—because he knew that was what my father would have wanted, they never know what to say. Sometimes they swoon. Sometimes they sigh. But sometimes they look at me hard. Wasn't I upset, they ask, that

Brandon took them without telling me, that he *stole* those diamonds from me?

I never know what to say to that. It didn't even cross my mind. They were never mine, I say. I was just their caretaker. They were meant for him all along.

*A*fter Brandon and I got engaged, we went to his apartment and opened a bottle of champagne, and then we took the subway to Avenue J for pizza at DiFara. On the ride home, we shared a couple of chocolate truffles and leaned sleepily into each other over the hard plastic seats. It was strange and surreal, and just right.

When I went back to Seattle a few days later, I ate this salad for two weeks straight. My binge of sorts had nothing to do with wanting to fit into a wedding dress (we weren't getting married for almost a year and a half, anyway) or with any nervous lack of appetite. I was just overwhelmed. I couldn't do anything else. So I made salad, and then I made more salad. I ate it straight from the serving bowl while sitting on the floor, my back against the couch, watching *Jeopardy!* and shouting answers at the screen.

The components of this salad are not the most obvious partners, but don't let that dissuade you. Tossed together in a classic vinaigrette, they meld almost seamlessly: crunchy with creamy, bitter with mellow. Anytime I serve it to someone, they ask for the recipe.

You can eat this salad as a starter or side dish, but I like it best as a light meal, with a hunk of crusty bread or a few roasted potatoes on the side.

Note that there will be more vinaigrette than you need for one salad. Extra vinaigrette can be stored in the refrigerator indefinitely and used on almost any salad.

FOR THE VINAIGRETTE
1 tablespoon Dijon mustard
3 tablespoons red wine vinegar
½ teaspoon salt
5 tablespoons olive oil, plus more to taste

FOR THE SALAD
8 red radishes

1 medium radicchio (about 10 ounces)
4 Belgian endive (about 1 pound)
A good handful of cilantro leaves, from about 20 sprigs
1 medium avocado
½ cup crumbled French feta, or more to taste

First, make the vinaigrette. In a small bowl, combine the mustard, vinegar, and salt. Whisk to blend well. Add the olive oil and whisk vigorously to emulsify. Taste, and adjust as needed. Depending on your vinegar, you may need more oil. I often add 2 additional teaspoons, but it varies. This is a more acidic dressing than some, but it shouldn't hit you over the head with vinegar.

Keeping your serving bowl close at hand, prepare the vegetables. Once sliced, some of them will brown more quickly than others, so I work in a certain order. First, trim the radishes and slice them very thinly into translucent wafers. Toss them into the bowl. Next, quarter the radicchio from stem end to tip, and peel away any raggedy outer leaves. Working with one quarter at a time, slice it crosswise into ribbons roughly ¼ inch thick. Toss the radicchio into the bowl. Next, slice the endive crosswise into ¼-inch-thick strips, discarding the root end. Add it to the bowl. Add the cilantro leaves and toss with vinaigrette to taste.

Quarter the avocado from stem to base and discard the pit. Cut each quarter crosswise into ¼-inch-thick strips. Distribute them evenly over the salad, and top with the feta.

Serve immediately.

NOTE: This salad takes very well to substitutions and additions. If you can't find French feta, which is creamier and less salty than the Greek kind, try some crumbled fresh goat cheese instead. If you have a fennel bulb, cut it into slivers and toss it into the bowl. Leftover roasted chicken, torn into bite-sized pieces, is delicious here, too, as is smoked trout.

Yield: 4 good-sized servings

SUGARHOUSE

You know the old saying. "Women marry their fathers," it goes, with a cheery undertone of doom, the idea being that women choose men who are, in certain ways, subtle or not so much, like the men who raised them. I always thought I was different. I thought I was original. I chose a composer, a vegetarian with long hair. My father was a doctor and a lifetime meat-eater. I doubt he ever, not even accidentally, let his hairline consort with his shirt collar. But then there was the issue of the maple syrup. When I agreed to marry Brandon, I had no idea about that.

I don't know how I could have missed it, but I did: the way he poured it onto his plate, in puddles big enough to drown in, like India during monsoon season. Or the way he inspected the label so carefully, and the liquid inside, as though it might contain impurities or an impostor. Or the fact that he brought his own maple syrup when he moved from New York, a little metal can with a sticky screw-top lid and a horse and buggy on the side. The syrup had been made, he told me proudly one morning, by a friend of his grandfather's who owns a "sugarhouse," as they're called, in Putney, Vermont.

My god, I thought, *I'm marrying a maple syrup snob.*

And then, a few seconds later, *OH SHIT. I'm doing it. I'm marrying my father.*

Don't even get me started on the way he ties his shoelaces (in bunny ears, just like Burg), or the way he laughs at his own jokes (with an approval-seeking ear-to-ear grin, just like Burg), or the way he revels in other people's junk, thrift shops and antique shops and estate sales. Really, don't ask. I don't know.

But you should see him with his maple syrup. He's kind of adorable. I'm allowed to say that, right? Apparently, he made maple syrup as a project in elementary school, and if that's not adorable, I don't know what is. (They also made butter and bread.) In high school, his favorite after-school snack was a toasted sesame bagel dipped in a bowl of maple syrup. And his favorite dessert was a plain sliced banana, abundantly sauced with it.

"We kept multiple grades in the house at all times," he told me dreamily one night, just before drifting off to sleep. "Grade A Light Amber, Grade A Medium Amber, Grade A Dark Amber, Grade B . . ." It was like he was counting sheep. I do love this man.

His mother's signature dessert is a whole wheat angel food cake sweetened with maple syrup instead of sugar, and frosted with maple whipped cream. It's been the family birthday cake for years. It even won a prize at a bake sale once. I've got my work cut out for me.

But Brandon's very favorite vehicle for maple syrup is almost no work at all. It's a tender, open-crumbed corn bread with a ribbon of cream through its center, and it's a cinch to make. It begins with a fairly basic cornmeal batter, but it gets turned upside down, literally, by the addition of a cup of cream just before it goes into the oven. The thick liquid seeps down into the batter, forming a layer of smooth, milky custard sandwiched by corn bread. It's magic. And it soaks up syrup better than any pancake, bagel, or banana.

Served warm on a Sunday morning, or reheated, even, on Monday, it's the sort of breakfast that good marriages are built on, I hope.

CUSTARD-FILLED CORN BREAD

*t*his corn bread, inspired by a recipe from Marion Cunningham's classic *The Breakfast Book,* is also sometimes called Spider Cake. I've seen many formulas for it, but this one is my favorite. We like it for breakfast, of course, but it might also be nice with a bowl of soup. Just be sure, whatever you do, to have some maple syrup on hand.

Also, don't be worried by how runny this batter is. That's just how it is.

---

3 tablespoons (1½ ounces) unsalted
   butter
1 cup unbleached all-purpose flour
¾ cup yellow cornmeal, preferably
   medium ground
1 teaspoon baking powder
½ teaspoon baking soda
2 large eggs

3 tablespoons sugar
½ teaspoon salt
2 cups whole milk (not low fat or
   nonfat)
1½ tablespoons distilled vinegar
1 cup heavy cream
Pure maple syrup, for serving

Preheat the oven to 350°F. Butter an 8-inch square or 9-inch round pan. Put the buttered dish in the oven to warm while you make the batter.

In a large microwavable bowl, melt the butter in the microwave. Take care to do this on medium power and in short bursts; if the heat is too high, butter will sometimes splatter or explode. Or, alternatively, put the butter in a heatproof bowl and melt it in the preheated oven. Cool slightly.

Meanwhile, in a small bowl, whisk together the flour, cornmeal, baking powder, and baking soda.

When the butter has cooled a bit, add the eggs and whisk to blend well. Then add the sugar, salt, milk, and vinegar and whisk well again. Whisking constantly, add the flour mixture. Mix until the batter is smooth and no lumps are visible.

Remove the heated pan from the oven, and pour in the batter. Then pour the cream into the center of the batter. Do not stir. Carefully slide the pan back into the oven, taking care not to knock it, and bake until golden brown on top, 50 minutes to 1 hour. Serve warm, with maple syrup.

NOTE: Covered with plastic wrap, this corn bread will keep at room temperature for 1 day. Covered and refrigerated, it will keep for up to 3 days. Leftovers are delicious both at room temperature or warmed in a low oven. Brandon likes to put a slice into the toaster oven and let it get a little crispy on the edges.

Yield: 6 to 8 servings

THE CHANGE THING

I love the concept of routines. For some people, like skydivers and storm chasers, it may sound like torture, but to me, it's reassuring. I love having a routine, even if it's just the order in which I wash my face and brush my teeth at night. It makes me feel human. It's a reminder that I am still alive and still me, because depending on the day, it can be hard to keep track. Anyway, there are enough things to think about in this world. The beauty of having routines and habits lies in letting my hands and feet think for me, and in giving my brain a break. My predilection for routine may make me a little boring, but it does keep my teeth nice and clean.

I've never been very good at change. Just ask my mother. During college, I called her at the beginning of every quarter, crying, whimpering incoherently about my new schedule, my new classes, and the end of life as I knew it. Each time, she'd remind me, with the sort of patience that only saints and mothers have, that this happened last quarter, and the quarter before it, and that it was just "the change thing, Moll. You'll find a *new* routine." I'd nod and blow my nose and feel much better for approximately three months, until the next quarter came around.

I'm also the girl who took the same lunch to school every single day for the first fourteen years of her life. Every *single* day. The contents of the brown bag were as follows: carrot sticks, two cookies, and Peter Pan creamy peanut butter on whole wheat bread. There was no jam, no jelly, no crunchy peanut butter, no natural peanut butter, no white bread, no seeded bread, and *no* change. Sometimes I think my taste buds may be the eighth wonder of the world. How they survived such monotony is one of the great mysteries of our time. Someday, after I'm gone, people will gather to study my tongue. They'll peer hopefully into my mouth, the way I look under the bed when I've lost something, and they'll cluck approvingly, noting that my teeth were indeed very clean.

I am happy to report, though, that in recent years, I've been working on getting friendlier with change, and with its cousin, flexibility. Growing up has helped a lot. Plus, all that crying got kind of exhausting. It's a lot more fun this way. No one ever got laid because they wrote it into their day planner.

Which, I guess, brings me to a larger, more serious point: that it's hard to love someone, I've found, when you're preoccupied with holding your entire world firmly in place. Loving someone requires a certain amount of malleability, a willingness to be pulled along, at least occasionally, by another person's will. When Lucas and I lived together, I was so uptight that when I came home from grocery shopping, I would sit down with the calculator and make an itemized list of what he owed me, every last cent. It seemed very important at the time, although I have since thought about sending him a thank-you note for not killing me.

When I met Brandon, I didn't want to be that person anymore. I didn't want to mistake accounting for intimacy. I wanted things to be easier. Which meant, I knew, that *I* had to be easier—about everything. It has taken some practice, admittedly, but I am making progress. Just the other day, for example, I didn't even flinch when he used the last of my peanut butter for one of his soba noodle salads. That's how I know we're going to be all right. Because being the person I want to be feels easier when he is around.

But I do still love my routines. I'm not an entirely new person. And I'm not ashamed to admit that I often put my taste buds to the test of boredom. I can't help it. When I like something, I want to eat it all the time. Nearly every morning, I sit down to the same breakfast—some whole grain cereal, a few spoonfuls of granola, and either plain yogurt or milk—in the same red glass bowl, and nearly every morning, it makes me irrationally happy. That carries me through to lunch, when I sit down, usually, to a bowl of soup, a hunk of bread, and a few slices of cheese. The formula changes with the seasons, but as a general principle, it holds true for most weekdays, if not the occasional Saturday, too. Sometimes Brandon even joins me.

Soup is a perfect lunch food. It's filling, but unlike a salami sandwich with provolone and sautéed peppers (which would be my second choice), it never makes you want to unbutton your pants or sleep for the rest of the day. My favorite take on the theme is a tomato soup with slices of sweet fennel, fennel seeds, and a few sprigs from our thyme plant on the side stoop. When I was fifteen, I wrote a poem about wanting to immerse myself in a vat of marshmallow fluff, but today I'd much rather take a warm soak in gently simmering tomato soup, preferably with an eye pillow. I'd be happy, in fact, to do it every day. I doubt it would ever get old.

TOMATO SOUP WITH TWO FENNELS

t his rustic, chunky soup is quick to make, and a single batch yields a good amount, so you'll have lunch to last all week. And, like most soups, it only gets better with time, as the flavors meld.

When it comes to serving it, you have a number of options. You can serve it plain. You can drizzle it with olive oil. You can crumble a little fresh goat cheese into the bowl, or you can top it with some grated Parmesan. Or, for an adult version of old grilled cheese-and-tomato soup combination, try smearing a piece of toasted baguette with goat cheese, and dunk it in the bowl as you go.

3 tablespoons olive oil	1 teaspoon chopped fresh thyme
1 large yellow onion, quartered and	leaves
thinly sliced	2 teaspoons fennel seeds
2 medium fennel bulbs (about 1¼	Two 28-ounce cans whole peeled tomatoes
pounds), trimmed, quartered from	Water
root to stalk, and thinly sliced	¾ teaspoon salt, or to taste
4 medium cloves garlic, finely	Sugar, to taste
chopped	Red wine vinegar, to taste

In a large (5-quart) pot or Dutch oven, warm the oil over medium heat. Add the onion and fennel, and cook, stirring occasionally, until the onion just starts to soften, about 5 minutes. Add the garlic and cook, stirring frequently—garlic has a tendency to burn—until the onion is translucent and very soft, 5 to 8 minutes more. Add the thyme and fennel seeds and cook until fragrant, about 2 minutes.

Using your hand to hold back the tomatoes, pour the liquid from the tomato cans into the pot. Stir well. Crush the tomatoes in their cans, using your hands or a potato masher to tear and mash them into small chunks. Add the tomatoes to the pot. Then fill 1 empty tomato can with cold water and pour it in, too. Bring to a boil. Then adjust the heat to maintain a gentle simmer, and cook, uncovered, for about 45 minutes.

The soup is ready when the fennel is very tender and a spoonful of the tomatoey broth tastes like a good, full-bodied soup. (If it hasn't cooked long enough, it will taste watery and raw, like tomatoes straight from the can.) Add the salt. Taste and adjust as needed. If the tomatoes need a little sweetness, add a pinch or two of sugar. If the soup tastes a little bland, add a small splash of vinegar. I often add a bit of both.

Serve hot.

Yield: 6 to 8 servings

BONNE FEMME

I love traveling with my mother. I don't mean any offense to Brandon, of course. It's just that my mother and I have had decades to sync up our priorities. They are as follows: eat, walk, eat, walk, window shop, window shop, and then walk to dinner. As you might guess, we do especially well in France.

My mother speaks barely a word of French, but she laces up one of her tiny, adorable pairs of Pumas and hits the streets with the air of someone who *knows*. She is not afraid. She can tackle the Parisian Métro. She can decipher the majority of a restaurant menu. She can go into Monoprix with a grocery list and come out at least somewhat victorious. She plays the part so well that Parisians have even been known to stop her on the street for directions. That's got to be satisfying, although I wouldn't know, because they never stop me. They always think I'm English or Irish, because of my red hair.

My mother believes that language barriers were made for overcoming. She has a good grasp on the essentials, like the requisite *"Bonjour, Madame"* when entering a store and *"Merci, au revoir"* upon leaving. If need be, she'll even mime. For a while, she was determined to learn how to order her own coffee in a café, which is tricky, since what she wants is not a simple *café*, but a double espresso with a pitcher of warm milk on the side. Nevertheless, she really tried. She braved my drills with only a minimal amount of giggling. But when push came to shove, she could never remember which word came first. She may be a go-getter, but *"un double café avec un petit pot de lait chaud"* was a bit much to ask. So I order for both of us, and that's okay. Once the coffee is se-curely in her hands, she sits on a café terrace like a true, seasoned *Parisi-enne*.

You can imagine, then, how quickly I said yes when she offered, as a pre-wedding gift, to take me to France for ten days. It seemed intui-tive to go back to the country that had, so many times, been my incuba-tor and my catalyst. Every girl needs a little incubating from time to time, especially when she's about to become someone's wife. She needs ten days with her mother, a solid supply of baguette sandwiches, some well-aged cheese, a lot of chocolate, and some old-fashioned, fat-rippled, devil-may-care eating, which, for future reference, is im-mensely fortifying.

Not long ago, I exchanged letters with a friend who was preparing for his first visit to Paris. Without intending to, he said something that sums up pretty much everything I could possibly want to tell you about my own travels, and especially that trip with my mother.

"The only reason I travel," he wrote, "is for an excuse to eat more than usual."

I love that. I mean, it's not like I *need* an excuse, but France is cer-tainly a convincing one. It's basically a cheese cellar the size of Texas. That's a part of why I love it so much. I couldn't tell you what the inside of Notre Dame looks like, but I do know how to get from the greengrocer on rue Oberkampf, the one with the green awning, to that terrific *fromagerie* way down in the 7th, near Le Bon Marché. I also know a word that you might want to remember, if your priorities are anything like mine. The word is *bouchon*.

When my mother and I first started planning our trip, Paris wasn't even in the picture. To tell you the truth, it was sort of an afterthought. My first priority was Lyon. I'm not sure how I got this particular bee in my bonnet (and it's shocking, really, given my feelings for Paris), but somewhere, sometime, someone told me that the best food in France could be found in Lyon, churned out of kitchens that haven't changed for decades and served up by sturdy proprietresses who shuffle around in their slippers. Someone told me about *bouchons*.

The *bouchon*, simply put, is a Lyonnais twist on the classic French bistro. It's similar, but louder, more communal, and with ruddier cheeks. I've read a few different explanations of the *bouchon*'s origins and history, but most agree that the concept is a very old one, dating from the seventeenth and eighteenth centuries, when silk workers passing through town would be fed and watered in rustic local inns. The term derives from the word *bousche*, an old-fashioned name for a bundle of straw, which would be hung outside an inn to indicate that food and wine were served inside. By extension, the establishments themselves came to be called *bouchons*. The word *bouchon* also means "cork," as in the thing you yank from a bottle of wine, but apparently that comes from a different linguistic root.

Tucked away in the narrow streets of Lyon, an ancient city split by two rivers, modern-day *bouchons* still dish out the same sort of humble food that was served centuries ago. They're famous for a type of cooking called *cuisine de bonne femme*, a particularly generous and hearty style that operates by the motto, "Waste not, want not." They serve lots of pork, lots of offal, and lots of wine, all on red-checked tablecloths with lace curtains in the windows, wooden chairs and wobbly tables, and worn, dented flatware. They're the kind of place where you make friends with the table next to yours, where you eavesdrop to hear what's been ordered and trade oohs and ahhs as dishes are delivered. They're my kind of place.

If you've read this far, you know that I prefer home cooking over restaurant fare almost any day. But *bouchons*, bless them, are the best of both. They serve the kind of rustic, heartening food that I dream of making, and I don't even have to lift a finger.

Just imagine this: you and your dining companion (your mother, let's say) sit down at a checker-top table and order a carafe of (cheap!) Côtes du Rhône. With it comes complimentary pork cracklings, enough to fill a basket as big as a newborn baby. This alone is worth the train ticket from Paris. Did I mention, too, that they are crisp and prettily browned, the color and shape of walnuts, and that on your tongue, they melt dead away? You will have to warn your mother, twice, not to spoil her dinner.

Next comes the first course, served family style to every table, whether you ask for it or not. The waitress comes by with four dishes, which she sets down with a businesslike clunk. One might be a platter of local salami and cornichons, another a white ramekin packed with housemade boar terrine. You might also get a bowl of lentils with shallots and vinaigrette, or a frisée salad that the two of you will talk about for days, spotted with bits of salty ham and hard-boiled egg and sauced with a mustard dressing. There's no fussy presentation to besmirch with your fork, nor is there any gnashing of teeth over what to order. You eat what you're given. The well-starched businessmen across the room toast and loosen their ties, and the middle-aged Frenchwoman next to you pulls her knees up to sit cross-legged in her chair.

Next might come *oeufs en meurette*, eggs poached in red wine and served in a beefy, brothy sauce spiked with *lardons*. Your mother will scold you for scraping the bowl too loudly, but ten seconds later, she'll do the same. You can swat her hand if you want to.

When it comes time to order the main course, the waitress will recite the options at tableside and wait patiently while you translate for your mother, who only understood about half of her spiel, which, come to think of it, is actually a lot. You hem and haw. You could have the chicken liver, or *tablier de sapeur*, a local specialty of breaded, fried tripe. Or there's a rich, inky stew of pork cheeks, or maybe *tête de veau*, bits of meat from a calf's head that—just warning you—sometimes jiggle like Jell-O on the plate. You will be tempted by the chicken liver, and your mother will consider the breaded tripe, but you both settle on *quenelles de brochet*, pike dumplings served in *sauce Nantua*, a creamy slurry infused with crayfish. When you love crayfish sauce, you make sacrifices.

Then comes the cheese. Every table gets their own platter, which is roughly the size of a dinner plate. If you're in the first seating of the night, the plate will be pristine: six or seven creamy rounds, blocks, or pyramids, utterly perfect and untouched, all for your pleasure. It's good to be prepared for this, or else you might squeal with glee when the waitress sets it down. If you're in a later seating, the platter might be slightly picked over, but it's still beautiful in its way, like a well-worn shoe.

And then, just when you think it can't get any better, it's time to place your dessert order. I highly recommend a wedge of lemon tart or, even better, the chocolate mousse, which comes messily crammed into a small cup with a spoon stuck bolt upright in its center. But watch for your mother's wandering hand. She's out of control when there's chocolate around.

The whole thing will top out somewhere around twenty-five euros per person, which will make your heart pound with gratitude. Just make sure you have a place nearby to sleep it off, because that's going to be important. In a pinch, try one of those cheap hotels by the train station. That's what we did. It took every ounce of fortitude I had (which, by this point, after so much hearty eating, was really quite a bit) to board the train back to Paris the next day. The *bouchon* changed everything.

Suddenly all I want in life is a checkered tablecloth and a pair of fuzzy slippers, and a *bouchon* to shuffle around in. Sometimes I lie awake at night, wondering how Seattle might take to *la cuisine de bonne femme*, and how communal cheese platters and a hostess in house shoes might sit with the health department. I am still trying to come up with a proper way to thank my mother, although I have a hunch that a recipe for that frisée salad might be a good way to start. That, and a big bowl of chocolate mousse.

Y ou can get a great mustard vinaigrette in almost any kitchen in France, but making one in the States is a little trickier. Different brands of Dijon mustard taste remarkably dissimilar, which is a real problem when you're trying to replicate a specific, and specifically French, flavor. I have tried many different brands, and my favorite is called Roland Extra Strong Dijon Mustard. It has a wonderful flavor, strong and insistent, but without too much acidity or bitterness. It can be a little tricky to find, but it's worth the trouble. If your local store doesn't carry it, ask if it will. Or ask for a slightly more common brand, Beaufor, which is very similar. In a pinch, I also like Maille brand, which is even easier to find. I do not, however, recommend Grey Poupon for this vinaigrette recipe. It tends to have a harsh, bitter flavor.

For a vegetarian version of this salad, substitute shavings of Parmigiano-Reggiano for the ham.

2 large eggs
1 medium head frisée (4 to 6 ounces)
⅔ cup cubed cooked ham

2 tablespoons Dijon mustard (see headnote)
1 tablespoon plus 2 teaspoons red wine vinegar
3 tablespoons olive oil

First, cook the eggs. Put them in a small saucepan, and add cold water to cover. Put the pan over medium-high heat, and bring to a boil. When the water boils, remove the pan from the heat, cover it, and let it sit for exactly 12 minutes.

While the eggs cook, prepare the frisée. Remove any bruised leaves, and trim away and discard the stem end. Using your hands, separate the leaves. If any of them are more than about 4 inches long, tear them in half; otherwise, leave them alone. Put the frisée in the basket of a salad spinner. Place the basket inside its bowl, and fill it with cold water.

Swish the leaves around a bit, and then let soak for a minute or two. This will allow any dirt to fall to the bottom of the bowl. Pull the basket from the bowl, and shake it to remove excess water. Dump the water from the bowl, replace the basket, and spin until the leaves are dry. Turn them out into a serving bowl.

When the eggs are ready, drain off the hot water immediately, and rinse with plenty of cold water. When they are cool, crack their shells and peel them. Coarsely chop them, and add them to the frisée, along with the ham.

In a small bowl, whisk together the mustard and vinegar. Add the oil, and whisk well to emulsify. Drizzle a large spoonful or two over the frisée, and toss well. Taste, and add more dressing as needed.

NOTE: Leftover vinaigrette will keep for up to a week in the refrigerator and is also very good on Bibb lettuce, especially with toasted walnuts.

Yield: 2 large servings or 4 side-dish servings

SO MUCH BETTER

When Brandon moved to Seattle, he brought a lot of New York with him. He brought the pink checked shirt that only he can wear well, his favorite old leather jacket, and a pair of red sneakers that look like part of a Spider-Man costume. He brought a bottle of hot sauce, a dented aluminum bowl that he uses for tossing salads, and a set of fancy skillets and saucepans scrounged up at T.J. Maxx. He also brought a deep-seated need for pizza, the kind that only an East Coaster can know. A couple of months after he arrived, I came home from running errands to find him jury-rigging the oven in our new apartment. He wanted, he explained, to make it climb past its factory-set ceiling of 550°F to something closer to 800. He'd taken an old white T-shirt, wet it under the faucet, and draped it over the thermostat prong, hoping to trick the oven into preheating longer and hotter. I came home shortly after the oven hit 700 and the T-shirt started to singe, filling the kitchen with an odor not unlike burnt hair. Sometimes I do miss those long-distance days.

But it is nice to have him around. Before Brandon moved to Seattle, I liked my city quite a bit. I thought I would probably stay here for a while, although I wasn't sure. But when he joined me, I fell in love. When you want someone to like your city, you go to great lengths to show him all of its best features, which has the unintended but very

267

welcome side effect of making you feel pretty smitten with it yourself. We went to Gasworks Park and watched the seaplanes come in on Lake Union. We sneaked wine into Golden Gardens, a strip of public beach on Puget Sound, and watched the sailboats come and go. We rented a rowboat and paddled around. We walked to the farmers' market on Sunday morning and spent way too much money on wild mushrooms. We had time now for that kind of thing, for everything.

When Brandon moved to Seattle, he made more friends within the first three months than I had in four years. He spread like wildflowers, in every way. I guess I could have been jealous, but since he shares them all with me, I can't complain. We may not have any proper family particularly close by, but we have a family of friends, which I am just as happy with. Especially because they're the kind of family who will come to dinner on short notice and don't even mind that last night's dishes are still in the sink.

Take our friend Olaiya, for instance, whom Brandon met about two months after he moved here, when he was working at a local restaurant. Olaiya was hired shortly after he was. Like Brandon, she had just moved to Seattle, only instead of New York, she was coming from Brussels, where she had lived for four years. Before that, she lived on the East Coast, and before that, she grew up in Wichita, Kansas, which means that, like me, she is, or was, a girl of the Great Plains. She is also a very, very good cook. Often, on nights when none of us is quite sure what to eat for dinner, she comes over and we take turns staring at the refrigerator until something materializes. One night, to go with a dinner of burgers from the grill, she roasted some sliced cauliflower until it was caramelized and then doused it with a sort of salsa verde, a lime and olive oil dressing spiked with garlic, cilantro, and jalapeño. It was so good that we wound up scooping the last crispy bits of cauliflower from the bowl with our fingers. She is a keeper.

Then there's Sam, a New Jersey native who arrived in Seattle by way of Poland (he likes a circuitous route) around the same time that

Brandon did. They met in late August, when Brandon was cutting back his schedule at the restaurant to start school again, a PhD program at the University of Washington. Sam was hired as his replacement. On his first day of work, Brandon was in charge of training him, and they hit it off right away, swapping the kind of stories that guys from Jersey like to tell. That afternoon, when Brandon came to pick me up at work, he brought Sam. We drove him home, and Sam told me about a book he'd been reading by Verlaine, I think, or one of those other French poets I'd had to study in college, and I remember thinking, *Hmm, that's very interesting.* And also, *Hmm, that sounds like torture.* I soon learned that Sam consumes books the way most of us consume food, which, though I do prefer to eat, is a quality I much admire. He is one of the most fascinating people I have ever met. He also makes a mean bowl of tabouli and the best sweet tea this side of the Mississippi. He and Brandon invented a ritual called Roadhouse, whereby we sit on Sam's back porch, drinking tea and listening to old country and blue-grass on the turntable. Before Sam, the only country music I knew was what I had heard in Oklahoma as a kid, and I hated it, but I now have a soft spot for Merle Haggard and Gram Parsons. I think it was the sweet tea that did it.

In the months before our wedding, Sam and Brandon played tennis almost every night, trading off between the community courts in his neighborhood and ours. There has never been better comedy than the two of them on a tennis court. When they serve, the ball actually bounces once before it crosses the net, and Sam does this fun hop thing when he hits the ball. They would come home sweaty and half-starved, and we'd open a bottle of something cold and throw together dinner. Our favorite meal that summer was one of the simplest: a few zucchini sliced into long strips on a mandoline, sautéed and then tossed with hot spaghetti and pesto. We called it "zucchini noodles," for the way the long slivers of squash mimicked the shape of the spaghetti. We must have eaten it a dozen times.

There is an infinite number of reasons, I think, for loving someone. I love Brandon for lots of things, not the least of which is the fact that we found each other at all. But if I had to name just one reason, it would be this: because he made my home—my city and my little place within it—feel, for the first time, like home. It sounds sappy to say it so plainly, but I think you know what I mean. I wasn't lonely before he came along. I had no real complaints or grievances. Seattle was good to me. But with him, and everything that comes with him, it's so much better.

CARAMELIZED CAULIFLOWER WITH SALSA VERDE

I 've been roasting cauliflower for a long time, but until I met Olaiya, I'd never thought to serve it with a dressing. Needless to say, I've now changed my ways. This recipe needs no real guidelines other than this: be sure to make the salsa verde before roasting the cauliflower, so that it has time to sit. The garlic and lime need to mellow and meld, and you'll notice a marked difference in the flavor after about 30 minutes.

FOR THE SALSA VERDE
1 medium jalapeño, ribs and seeds removed, finely chopped
3 tablespoons finely chopped cilantro leaves
2 medium cloves garlic, minced with a pinch of salt
3 tablespoons fresh lime juice

4 tablespoons olive oil
Salt to taste

FOR THE CAULIFLOWER
1 medium cauliflower (2 to 2½ pounds)
2 to 3 tablespoons olive oil
Salt to taste

First, prepare the salsa verde. In a medium bowl, combine the jalapeño, cilantro, garlic, lime juice, and olive oil and whisk to combine. Add two pinches of salt, or more, to taste, and whisk well. Set aside at room temperature for at least 30 minutes and up to an hour.

Preheat the oven to 450°F.

Wash and dry the cauliflower well. Put it on a cutting board, stem side down, and slice it vertically, top down, into ¼-inch slices. You'll only get about 4 intact slices, and the rest will be a hash of cauliflower crumbs. That's okay. Put the cauliflower in a large bowl and toss with 2 tablespoons olive oil. (I find that my hands work best for this.) You want each little bit of cauliflower to get a thin coat of oil. If necessary, add 1 more tablespoon. Spread the cauliflower in a single layer on a heavy sheet pan, or if the pan seems crowded, use 2 pans. You don't want it packed too tightly, or the cauliflower will steam rather than roast. Salt it lightly.

Bake until the cauliflower is tender, golden, and even deeply browned in spots, 20 to 30 minutes, turning once with a spatula. Salt lightly again.

Serve cauliflower hot or warm, with salsa verde on the side for drizzling.

Yield: 4 side-dish servings or 2 larger servings

ZUCCHINI NOODLES WITH PESTO

I f you don't have a mandoline slicer, this recipe alone is worth the investment. We like Benriner brand, from Japan, which will only set you back about thirty-five dollars.

FOR THE PESTO

2 cups tightly packed basil leaves,
  washed and dried well
½ cup olive oil
3 tablespoons pine nuts
2 medium cloves garlic, minced
½ teaspoon salt
½ cup Parmigiano-Reggiano

FOR THE NOODLES

3 medium zucchini, trimmed (about
  1½ pounds)
3 tablespoons olive oil
¾ pound dried spaghetti or other long
  noodles
Salt
Finely grated Parmigiano-Reggiano,
  for serving

First, make the pesto. Put the basil leaves in a large heavy-duty ziplock plastic bag. Press all the air from the bag, and seal it carefully. Put the bag on the countertop or floor and, using a rolling pin, pound the bag until all the leaves are bruised. This helps to release their flavor.

Put the pounded basil, olive oil, pine nuts, garlic, and salt in the bowl of a food processor. Process to a smooth, creamy consistency, stopping once or twice to scrape down the bowl with a rubber spatula. Transfer the mixture to a medium bowl, and stir in the Parmigiano-Reggiano. Set aside.

Put a large pot of salted water over high heat.

While the water heats, prepare the zucchini. Using a mandoline slicer fitted with the julienne blade, carefully slice the zucchini into long, skinny noodles, each the width of a strand of spaghetti.

Warm the oil in a large skillet over medium heat. Add the zucchini "noodles" and cook, stirring occasionally, until tender but not mushy, 5 to 8 minutes.

When the pot of water boils, drop in the spaghetti. Cook until al dente. Using a pair of long-handled tongs—or, if you have one, a wire strainer with a long handle, also called a "spider"; that's what works best—scoop the pasta directly from the pot into the skillet of cooked zucchini. Doing it this way, rather than draining the spaghetti into a colander, means that each strand brings with it a little bit of its cooking water, which will loosen up the pesto and help it to form a nice sauce. Add ½ cup of the pesto and toss the mixture well to ensure that each noodle—zucchini and spaghetti alike—has a thin, even coat of sauce.

Serve immediately, with additional salt and lots of grated Parmigiano-Reggiano at the table.

NOTE: You will likely have some pesto left over, but in our house, that's never much trouble. Just cover its surface with a sheet of plastic wrap to prevent oxidation, and store it in the refrigerator for up to 4 days.

Yield: 4 servings

A BIG DEAL

You're ready to marry someone, I figure, if you're willing to go into debt with him. It may not be a terribly romantic way of gauging things, but it's as good as any. Buying a house or a car or a fancy television is not as quaint as falling asleep in his arms or soaking together in a bathtub filled with bubbles and rose petals, but it's a serious commitment, a way of promising to continue to love each other—at least for the term of the loan.

When Brandon and I bought a car together, we'd already been engaged for a year, but in some ways, it felt even more affirming than the white dress waiting in my closet, the wedding bands in their velvety boxes, and the invitations in the mail.

Not that it was an easy decision. Our old car, or rather, *my* old car, a used two-door that my father had bought for me when I was sixteen, had suddenly reached the point in its lifespan when its total worth was approximately that of a head of cabbage, but it required about a thousand cabbages' worth to keep it running. I didn't want to get rid of it, but we had to. So we parked it on the street out front, called the American Cancer Society, filled out the donation paperwork, and waited for the tow truck to come.

In the meantime, we contemplated just how badly we really needed a car. Maybe we could live without one. We could save money. We could be ecologically correct. We could be *progressive!* People in New York and Paris don't need cars, we told ourselves, and maybe we didn't either. The Seattle bus system is a little less efficient than the Metropolitan Transportation Authority, but we have friends without cars who make do. We thought we'd give it a try.

And to tell you the truth, in a small, dark way, I wasn't sure we were *ready* to buy a car. We'd never put our names side-by-side on any sort of legally binding document. If we were to call off the wedding, our names would still be there together, legally bound, even if we weren't. We decided we should take some time to ride the bus, just to make sure.

This, however, was late May. The flowers were in bloom, and so were the trees, but Seattle, being the Rainy City it is, wasn't quite on the bandwagon. When it comes to summer, Seattle tends to hang from the tailgate for a while, bumping along, dragging its heels, until finally— sometime around July 4, usually—it decides to climb on board. This particular May, every time we went to leave the house, it started raining. It was in this hostile climate that Brandon and I considered our newly carless situation. For the better part of two weeks, while we dutifully checked bus schedules and stood at our chosen stops, it rained. It rained almost constantly. Every time we stepped out the door, there it was. *Drip drop, drip drop.*

One Sunday afternoon in the midst of all this, Olaiya called to invite us to dinner. We had a few hours before we would need to catch the bus, and I was in the mood for baking, so I offered to bring dessert. We had a bag of pistachios sitting on the counter, and I'd been thinking of turning them into a cake. And apricots were coming into season. We had some in a bowl on the table, and they were still a little sour, but with some heat, they would sweeten up nicely. A cake, I decided, would be the perfect place for them. So while the rain beat against the window-panes, I flicked on the oven and got to work.

I whizzed some pistachios in the food processor until they turned to powder. Then I folded them into the batter, now a pale, speckled shade of green, and grated in some nutmeg for extra warmth. At this point in the season, I would take all the warmth I could get. Then I halved and pitted the apricots, nudged a blob of honey into their upturned wells, and nestled them into the batter. As the cake baked, the apricots sunk slowly, hiding themselves from view. It wasn't what I had intended—I wanted a cake with a pretty, apricot-dotted top—but it was sort of charming. Anyway, I could hardly blame them. I wanted to burrow into that warm batter, too.

I pulled the cake out of the oven exactly ten minutes before our bus was due at the nearest stop, two blocks away. Not knowing what else to do, I pulled out a paper grocery bag, pushed a folded-up newspaper all the way to the bottom to reinforce it, and gently, suited up with my oven mitt, set the cake on top of the newspaper. Then I laid a plastic grocery sack loosely across the cake to protect it from splashes, and we grabbed our umbrellas and ran.

Have you ever tried to carry a freshly baked, still-steaming cake in a paper bag under a too-small umbrella in a rainstorm? Also, have you ever sat in front of a drunk on the bus and watched him fondle your fiancé's chin-length hair? And have you ever held a still-hot cake on your lap, now without its (soaked, torn, discarded) paper bag, anticipating that at any second, you might need to leap from your seat to avoid being fondled yourself? I have. That's all I want to say about that.

We did make it to Olaiya's, I'm pleased to report, and with the cake still intact. Despite all that it had suffered, it was exactly what I hoped it would be. The apricots had stopped their descent somewhere near the equator of the cake, and when we cut in, they revealed themselves like buried treasure. We ate half of the cake that night and left the rest with Olaiya when we headed out to catch the bus. One cake-related transportation fiasco was enough, we figured. Better not to risk another.

Instead, we huddled together in a corner of the humid bus all the way home. Then we filled the bathtub and soaked until our feet were warm again. The next morning, we took the bus downtown and bought a car.

*C*efore you assemble this cake, be sure to taste one or two of the apricots. If they're on the tart side, you might consider doubling the amount of honey.

I like to serve this cake on its own, unadorned, but if you want to dress it up, you could dust it with powdered sugar. You could also serve it with a dollop of loosely whipped cream. For a fancier, more festive treatment, you could even try making it into a layer cake. Double the recipe, omitting the apricots and honey, and sandwich the layers with strawberry or raspberry jam that you've pressed through a sieve to remove the seeds. Coat the whole thing in whipped cream or any other frosting you like.

¾ cup shelled raw pistachios

1 cup unbleached all-purpose flour

2 teaspoons baking powder

¼ teaspoon freshly ground nutmeg

¼ teaspoon salt

½ cup whole milk

¼ teaspoon pure vanilla extract

1 stick (4 ounces) unsalted butter, at
   room temperature

1 cup sugar

3 large eggs

5 ripe apricots, halved and pitted

1 tablespoon honey

Set an oven rack to the middle position, and preheat the oven to 350°F. Butter a 9-inch round pan, and line the bottom with a round of parchment paper. Butter the paper; then dust the pan lightly with flour.

In the bowl of a food processor, pulse the pistachios until very finely ground. Take off the lid every now and then and rub a pinch of the ground nuts between your fingers: if they feel too coarse, keep going, but if they feel fine, like sand, they're ready. Add the flour, baking powder, nutmeg, and salt, and pulse once or twice to mix.

In a measuring cup, combine the milk and vanilla.

In a large bowl, beat the butter and sugar until pale and fluffy. Add the eggs one at a time, beating well after each addition. Add the flour mixture in three batches, alternating with the milk, mixing at low speed to just combine. Do not overmix. If any streaks of flour remain, use a rubber spatula to fold them in. Pour the batter into the cake pan, and shake the pan a bit to ensure that the batter is evenly spread.

Arrange the apricots cut side up on a cutting board or countertop. Using the tip of your finger, smear a blob of honey into the center of each, dividing it evenly among the ten halves. Gently arrange them cut side up on top of the batter.

Slide the cake into the oven, and bake until a toothpick inserted in the center comes out clean, 35 to 40 minutes. The apricots will have sunk into the batter, but don't worry: they will reveal themselves in each slice. Cool the cake in the pan on a rack for 10 minutes, then run a thin knife around its edge and release the sides of the pan. Continue to cool the cake until you are ready to serve it.

Serve warm or at room temperature.

Yield: 8 servings

FREEZE FRAME

Getting married is tricky. In case you haven't tried it yourself, let me tell you a little about it.

First, when you get engaged, a few things happen. You agree to marry someone, for starters. Also, your head sort of explodes. Third, you are handed a ticket—rather sneakily, I should note, with no warnings at all—to an amusement park ride known as *THE WEDDING*. If you were to pass it at the fair, you'd know it by the pink flashing lights and the neon sign of two doves in silhouette, kissing. It's at times mildly disorienting, and it can even tend toward terrifying, with tears, beers, pimples, and speeding tickets. But if you stay in your seat until the very end, it turns out to be pretty fun.

When Brandon and I got engaged, we didn't know any of that. We knew only that we wanted to be married in the summertime, and that we wanted our wedding to be a big party. We wanted to gather our families and friends around us somewhere special, where we could spend a weekend in celebration. We also wanted to show off a little. Contrary to what I was saying just a second ago about Seattle and its surroundings (that it rains and rains and rains), it can also be absolutely gorgeous. We wanted to gather in a place with a view, with water and mountains both, somewhere big enough to fit us all but small enough to feel cozy.

We looked here and there, searching for just the right spot, but it wasn't as easy as we had hoped. We were either stuck with a yacht club, or with a public park teeming with barbecues and Frisbees. But then, one fortuitous evening, our friends Ashley and Chris told us about their wedding, which they had held two years earlier in Bellingham, a college town on the coast about ninety miles north of Seattle. (We didn't know them then, so we weren't there.) They held the ceremony in a small, secluded park by the water, they said, and the reception was a short walk away, in the Bellingham Cruise Terminal, where ships leave for Alaska and the nearby islands. It had exposed brick walls and steel beams, a grand staircase in the center of the building, and a fifteen-foot domed window that looked out onto the piers. They'd even found a caterer there, someone who sourced almost everything from local farms, served it in hand-carved wooden bowls, and passed champagne and Rainier cherries in the park before the ceremony. That was the clincher.

Borrowing shamelessly from their blueprint, we began to put the pieces into place. We drove up to Bellingham and blocked rooms at three small hotels. We hired a photographer. I bought a dress. We asked Ashley, a graphic designer, to do our save-the-dates, invitations, and ceremony programs. If she was bothered by the fact that we were essentially stealing her entire wedding, she didn't say a thing. When I came over to proofread the programs, she even gave me strawberries and ice cream.

So in many ways, it was a piece of cake. We were planning the wedding we wanted. We had all the right people to help. We had a few arguments over frivolous things, like honeymoon destinations and the cost of flowers, but we talked our way through them, and figuring out how to do that made us feel even more sure of each other. But still, it was hard. However you look at it, an engagement is a limbo period, a space in between. For someone who has a hard time with change, it's torture. Being engaged is one big, drawn-out transition, a single change that takes months to enact. Sixteen months, in our case.

Don't get me wrong: I loved seeing that ring on my finger. I loved knowing that we were getting married. But what I didn't love was the way that being engaged held us in a sort of freeze frame and, at the same time, kept us running—breathless, driven, determined—toward one single day, the day that would take us, *ta daa!*, from this state to the next. Getting married is not for pansies. The way I see it, it's a little like Valentine's Day. If you allow it to, it can feel kind of stale and stilted, like a test to show how impossibly romantic you can be. So much rides on the wedding—on what is said, what is worn, the tiniest nuances— but in the end, it's just a single day. Granted, it's a day to celebrate your love for someone in the presence of everyone you care about, but still, it's just one day.

When people would wish us well, they would often say something like, "Oh, I just *know* your wedding day is going to be PERFECT! It's going to be BLISS! It's going to be the BEST day of your life!" Brandon and I would always giggle about that, even though the gesture was very nice. For one thing, there's the word *bliss*, which makes my toes curl. It reminds me of diamond company commercials and bath beads. But even more than that, if the best day of our lives is our wedding day, we thought, what the hell comes afterward? We would have a lot of so-so years to look forward to. We wanted to have a beautiful wedding, but it didn't need to be utter perfection. It needed to celebrate what we bring to each other in the truest way possible, and with some good food and dancing. But it didn't need to be the best day *ever*. In fact, we sincerely hoped that, in the long-term scheme of things, it wouldn't be.

Sometimes, when the planning would get the best of us, or when I would start crying about hotel rooms or table linens, Brandon would look at me and say, "This is BLISS!" and then everything would feel much better.

To tell you the truth, I don't think a wedding, no matter how nice, could have anything on any number of other, more ordinary days. Like the day after our engagement party in Oklahoma, the day that Brandon spent sitting on the floor of my mother's kitchen, wrestling contentedly with a rusty bolt in my father's old espresso machine. He spent hours sitting there, watching us come and go, rigging and wrenching and wielding a can of WD-40. When he finally pried the bolt loose, the machine shuddered to life with a squeal and a roar, a sound none of us had heard since my father died. Brandon worked the knobs with a sort of sweet, fearful reverence, and my mother fawned over her cappuccino for hours.

Or like that one Saturday in July, a couple of months after Brandon moved to Seattle and a year before our wedding. We left home in the morning and drove north to Bellingham to meet with the caterer. We had a bag of spicy peanuts in the console, and I was wearing a new pair of flats. We stopped at Goodwill near Mount Vernon and bought a yellow Pyrex dish that I love, and then we ate spaghetti with pesto at a place called D'Anna's. Our canopy bed at the Best Western was nearly four feet off the ground, and it had a set of wooden steps that leaned up against it. The next morning, when I tried to climb down, I banged my hip on the bedside table and got a bruise the size of a baseball. After I stopped whimpering, we laughed about it for a long time. Then, after breakfast, we went out for ice cream. We ordered two scoops, one of which I can't remember and the other being vanilla with black pepper, and then we sat on the curb outside, eating them from a frilly glass dish, the kind they use at old-fashioned soda fountains. I think of that day a lot.

If we could have a wedding like that, we would be all right. More than any amount of bliss, that would be us.

*I*t may sound like a strange union of flavors, but vanilla and black pepper make a stunning ice cream. When you take a bite, what you get first is the vanilla, but as you swallow, a mild wave of peppery heat washes over your tongue. After we tasted it at Mallard Ice Cream in Bellingham, we knew we had to replicate it at home. We first tried steeping whole peppercorns in the hot milk base, but the flavor was too soft and floral. Ultimately, we wound up adding the pepper at the very end, once the custard was cool, so that it retained its raw, familiar bite. It would be delicious with a rich chocolate cake or brownie, or sandwiched between two chocolate shortbread cookies.

Oh, and if you accidentally boil or curdle your custard, here is a trick I learned from pastry chef David Lebovitz: you can usually rescue it by whizzing it, while it's still warm, in the blender. But remember not to fill your blender jar more than one-third full; hot liquids expand.

1 cup whole milk
2 cups heavy cream
¾ cup granulated sugar
Pinch of salt

6 large egg yolks
1 teaspoon vanilla extract
1½ teaspoons finely ground black
pepper, or more to taste

In a heavy medium saucepan, combine the milk, 1 cup of the cream, sugar, and salt. Warm over medium heat, stirring occasionally, until hot and steaming; it should be just barely too hot to touch. Do not boil.

Meanwhile, pour the remaining 1 cup cream into a large bowl. Set a mesh strainer across the top. In a medium bowl, whisk the egg yolks. Then prepare your ice bath: take out a large bowl—larger than the one you put the cream in—and fill it about a third full with ice cubes. Add about 1 cup cold water, so that the ice cubes float. (In a pinch, ice packs or bags of frozen peas work in place of the ice. You'll have to discard the peas afterward, or use them immediately.)

When the milk mixture is hot, remove it from the heat. Let it sit for about 30 seconds, then gradually, slowly, pour about half of it into the yolks, whisking constantly. Pour the warmed egg mixture back into the saucepan with the rest of the milk mixture. Cook over medium-low heat, stirring and scraping the bottom of the pan slowly and constantly with a heatproof spatula, until the custard thickens slightly, just enough to very lightly coat the spatula. If you draw a line up the spatula with the tip of your finger, the custard on either side of the line shouldn't run back together. On my stove, this takes 5 to 6 minutes.

Immediately pour the custard through the strainer, and stir well to combine it with the cream. Place the bowl carefully in the ice bath. Let cool, stirring occasionally. Then remove the bowl from the ice bath, cover it with plastic wrap, and chill it completely, preferably overnight, before churning.

When you're ready to churn the ice cream, stir in the vanilla and the black pepper. Taste it: Is there enough heat from the pepper? We find that 1½ teaspoons makes a good, balanced flavor, but you can add more, if you like.

Pour the custard into your ice cream maker, and freeze according to the manufacturer's instructions. Transfer the finished ice cream to a container with a lid and put in the freezer to harden for at least 2 hours before serving.

Yield: about 1 quart

PICKLING PLANT

To some people, a pickle is a pickle. I was one of those people until a couple of years ago. The pickle was the silent partner on the sandwich plate. It was a little green sidecar, the dinghy that floats alongside the ship. I usually pushed it out of the way. It was nothing to get excited about.

But then along came Brandon and, with him, a whole universe of things pickled and brined. Brandon craves acidic foods like people stranded in the desert crave water. His private world is filled, I like to imagine, with mirages in the shape of vinegar bottles and citrus fruits. When we met, he owned somewhere between twenty-four and thirty types of vinegar, a fact that he cited during our very first phone call, and with no small amount of pride. Today our collective kitchen has happily adopted most of them, except for the few stragglers that stayed behind with his old housemates in New York. The inventory runs from the simplest white wine vinegar to fancy aged balsamics, specimens made from Cabernet grapes, and others made from cherries, and, in most cases, a few brands and ages of each. Meeting him was like winning the lottery, only instead of a big check, my grand prize was a pantry full of vinegar.

Most of the time he uses them in measured quantities, but occasionally he will sip them from a spoon. For someone with a pretty precise palate, he takes a heavy hand to the acid on his plate. I need just enough salad dressing to coat the leaves, but one seat over, he's slurping at the jar. You think I'm exaggerating, but I'm not. I have watched him more than once reach for his water glass and get the vinaigrette instead. These were accidents, admittedly, but even as he raised the jar and the scent of vinegar hit his nostrils, he kept tilting it throatward. I watched in horror as the yellowish liquid slid into his mouth. He didn't even flinch.

When he's not consuming salad dressing, it's usually because he's moved onto pickles, another handy way of meeting his vinegar needs. Brandon has always had a thing for pickles, but until a few years ago, it was nothing particularly serious. Then he had what he calls his "pickle awakening." He was still living in New York at the time, but once when he came to see me in Seattle, I took him to Boat Street Café, one of my favorite restaurants, and he ordered the signature pickle plate. It came to the table looking like a painter's palette in shades of vinegar and salt: a stroke of green asparagus here, a splotch of peppers there, a splash of rosy onions and purplish prunes, spindly young carrots, even cauliflower tinted with turmeric. A heady cloud of vinegar hovered over the plate, and Brandon sniffed at it, looking genuinely moved. The word *pickled* feels too dinky to describe what had happened to those vegetables. Each was infused with a different spice: some sweet, some hot, some almost ticklish when they hit the tongue. These were not someone's soggy jarred spears; they were the kind that gets under your skin. Even I got into the spirit, stealing all of the prunes and most of the peppers.

When Brandon moved to Seattle, he applied for a job at Boat Street. That's where he was working when he met Olaiya and Sam. He even befriended the pickle makers themselves, chef-owners Renee Erickson and Susan Kaplan. With their guidance and a few old cookbooks, Brandon started pickling on his own. Our home kitchen often moonlights now as a small-scale pickling plant. Whenever we have a surplus of a particular fruit or vegetable, he commandeers the stove and cooks up a batch. The smell of hot brine can make you cough at first, but once you get accustomed, it's kind of intoxicating. On the right man, it makes a lovely cologne.

When Brandon and I started planning our wedding, it was pretty obvious that there would be pickles involved. Our rehearsal dinner was to be a picnic on the grounds of an old homestead, with a red barn and cows nearby, and everyone knows that a picnic is not a picnic, especially not on a farm, without pickles.

Our caterer offered to provide them, but we decided to do it ourselves. People thought we were out of our minds to want to do it, to take on yet *another* project in the midst of the wedding planning, the project to end all projects. Even my mother, Queen of Crazy Christmas Baking, tried to dissuade us. I'm glad we didn't listen. For all the heart and guts wrapped up in a wedding, planning it is essentially a cerebral exercise. Brining carrots and grapes and onions, on the other hand, is wholly, *heavenly* tangible. It's slow. It's messy. It's slippery and sticky. It made me feel like a real human being, which felt a lot better than being a capital-B Bride.

First on the list were pickled red onions, a regular in our refrigerator. Second in line were carrots doused in hot cider vinegar and scented with garlic and fresh thyme. They were spindly and sweet, as small and delicate as a lady's pinky and just the right height to stand, shoulder to shoulder, in a quart-sized Mason jar. It took all the strength we had not to eat every single one of them before the wedding. We also called into service a recipe from Boat Street for pickled grapes with mustard seeds and cinnamon. I would have never thought to pickle a grape, but they're completely delicious, crunchy, and sweet-tart. Based on a single taste, one of our rehearsal dinner guests offered to bankroll an entire pickling business, should we ever want to start one. So far, we don't plan to, but knowing Brandon, I wouldn't be surprised if we did.

SPICY PICKLED CARROTS WITH GARLIC AND THYME

2 cups apple cider vinegar, plus more
    for topping jars
2 cups water, plus more for topping jars
¼ cup granulated sugar
6 (5- to 6-inch) sprigs fresh thyme
5 large cloves garlic, thinly sliced
1½ teaspoons black peppercorns,
    cracked

1½ teaspoons red pepper flakes
Heaping 1½ teaspoons salt
Heaping 2 teaspoons brown mustard
    seeds
1½ pounds small (finger-sized)
    carrots, or standard-sized carrots,
    cut into sticks about ½ inch wide
    and 3 inches long

In a medium saucepan, combine 1½ cups apple cider vinegar, water, sugar, thyme, garlic, black peppercorns, red pepper flakes, salt, and mustard seeds. Bring to a boil over medium-high heat, then reduce to a simmer and cook, stirring occasionally, for 10 minutes. Remove the pan from the heat, and let cool for 5 minutes. Stir in the remaining ½ cup vinegar.

Put the carrots in a large, heatproof bowl, and pour the warm brine over them. Cool to room temperature.

While the carrots cool, wash 2 quart-sized canning jars and their lids in warm, soapy water.

When the carrots and brine are cool, distribute the carrots evenly among the jars, arranging them snugly. (Hands and fingers work best for this; tongs make a mess.) Using a ladle, divide the brine evenly among the jars. The carrots should be covered completely by brine. If they are not, add a mixture of 2 parts vinegar and 1 part water to cover.

Seal firmly and refrigerate for at least 3 days, or, preferably, a week; carrots are dense and take time to absorb the brine.

NOTE: Covered and refrigerated, pickled carrots will, in theory, last in-definitely, but we try to eat them within a month or two.

Yield: 2 quarts

PICKLED GRAPES WITH CINNAMON AND BLACK PEPPER
Adapted from Susan Kaplan

t hese may sound a little strange, but they're a crowd-pleaser. I like them best within the first four days after they're made, but some people like them even more after a week or two. Their pickled flavor gets stronger over time, and their skins will wrinkle slightly.

1 pound red or black grapes,
preferably seedless
1 cup white wine vinegar
1 cup granulated sugar

1½ teaspoons brown mustard seeds
1 teaspoon whole black peppercorns
1 (2½-inch) cinnamon stick
¼ teaspoon salt

Rinse and dry the grapes, and pull them carefully from their stems. Using a small, sharp knife, trim away the "belly button" at the stem end of the grape, exposing a bit of the flesh inside. Put the grapes into a medium bowl and set aside.

In a medium saucepan, combine the remaining ingredients. Bring to a boil over medium-high heat, then pour the mixture over the grapes. Stir to combine. Set aside to cool to room temperature.

While the grapes cool, wash 2 pint-sized canning jars and their lids in warm, soapy water. When the grapes are cool, ladle them into the jars. Chill for at least 8 hours or overnight.

Serve cold.

Yield: about 3 cups

SO EASY

Some nights, it's so easy. There's already soup in the refrigerator, and all it needs is warming. There's leftover chicken and a bag of green beans, and *ba daaaa!,* dinner is served. I love those nights. I try to live my whole life that way. Except for the nights when I'm making the soup, or roasting the chicken. That does have to happen sometime.

It helps, though, that I like mishmash meals, the kind where you reach into the refrigerator and pull out a few things that need attention—a neglected block of cheddar, let's say, and the end of a salami, and some cornichons and olives and a grapefruit—and that's dinner. I am a very lazy person, really, and I am also easily pleased. For as much as I love to cook, I love even more when cooking is unnecessary, and when all I have to do is eat.

To this end, Brandon is handy to have around. He can pull a meal from the seeming ether in five minutes flat. It's not guaranteed to be great, but it will almost always be good. When he was living in New York, he used to cook sometimes for his housemate Amie, and she has told me a few stories. Apparently, she once had a craving for hummus, but they had no chickpeas, tahini, or lemons, so Brandon pulled out a can of kidney beans, a clove of garlic, some olive oil and vinegar, and the Cuisinart. The results, Amie says cheerily, "were pretty good!"

Then there was the pancake episode. Because they had no eggs for the batter, Brandon threw in some extra oil instead. It goes without saying that this was much less successful than the kidney bean hummus, though the pancakes were edible, she tells me.

Like Amie, I have discovered that if you give Brandon a few ingredients, he will usually make good. He'll take the dregs of a bowl of homemade salsa, dump it into a pan with a can of black beans and half a tired onion, and ten minutes later, it's a very decent lunch. He'll take a few shallots left over from a recipe, peel them and toss them with oil and sherry vinegar, and roast them until they're soft and sticky. He can also take some arugula, a few pistachios, and a bar of chocolate and turn them into a salad. That's what he did a few days before our wedding, when my mother, who had flown in that morning, was coming to dinner.

It was a warm night, the kind when you throw open the windows and stand an oscillating fan next to the stove. While my mother and I set the table, Brandon assembled the salad. He washed some arugula. Then he chopped a fistful of pistachios and, on a whim, the corner of the block of chocolate that was sitting on the counter. Then he opened the refrigerator for a wedge of hard cheese and a jar of last night's vinaigrette. My mother had brought some figs, half-smashed in her carry-on, from the tree in her front yard, so he sliced them into quarters and piled them on one end of a serving platter. Next to them he laid a few thin slices of cheese. At the far end, opposite the figs and cheese, he made piles of pistachios and chocolate. Then he poured a glug of vinaigrette over the arugula, tossed it with one hand, and mounded it in the center.

It was almost too handsome to eat, but we did it anyway, with an old baguette that had been jolted to life in the oven and a bottle of champagne that, I'm pretty sure, was supposed to be saved for the wedding. It was delicious, a box of parts from different puzzles that somehow seemed to fit. My mother, a little suspicious at the start, scraped her plate appreciatively. But best of all, it was easy. Especially after planning an entire wedding. Of course, planning a wedding could make anything look easy—homemade puff pastry, hunting and butchering your own boar, making water from scratch—but really, it was.

We've now made that salad countless times, with or without the figs and cheese. Whenever we mention it to other people, they raise an eyebrow at the thought of arugula and chocolate, but when they taste it, they usually shut up. We've already had one of them declare it her favorite salad, which we took as a pretty good endorsement, since we hadn't even plied her with champagne. That's why I wanted to tell you about it. There's no time like the present to start eating chocolate with your greens.

Brandon likes to use Banyuls vinegar, a fairly esoteric type, in the vinaigrette for this salad, but when I wrote the recipe, I found myself worrying. I didn't want to suggest that someone go out and buy a bottle of expensive vinegar just for one salad. So I asked if he could suggest a more common substitute. He thought for a minute, and then he announced, "Sure! Tell them that if they don't have Banyuls, they can just use Cognac vinegar."

He's so warped. Which, of course, is why I married him.

ARUGULA SALAD WITH PISTACHIOS
AND CHOCOLATE

*B*anyuls vinegar is made from the Banyuls sweet wine of southwest France and aged in oak barrels. It has a caramelly, slightly nutty flavor, and goes incredibly well with arugula. But if you don't happen to have a bottle of it lying around, you can substitute sherry vinegar (or Cognac vinegar, *har har*), or you can buy some from Williams-Sonoma or Chef Shop.com.

FOR THE VINAIGRETTE

1 tablespoon Dijon mustard

3 tablespoons Banyuls vinegar

½ teaspoon salt

5 tablespoons olive oil, plus more to taste

FOR THE SALAD

About 8 ounces arugula

2 tablespoons finely chopped raw unsalted pistachios, for serving

2 tablespoons finely chopped bittersweet chocolate, for serving

---

First, make the vinaigrette. In a small bowl, combine the mustard, vinegar, and salt and whisk to blend. Add the olive oil and whisk vigorously to emulsify. Taste, and adjust as needed. Depending on your vinegar, you may need more oil. We often add 2 additional teaspoons, but it varies. This is a more acidic dressing than some, but it shouldn't hit you over the head with vinegar.

Put the arugula in a large bowl and add a modest spoonful or two of dressing. It's best to err on the side of underdressing at first: arugula is delicate, and it needs less dressing than other greens. Using two forks or, preferably, your hands, carefully toss the arugula, taking care to handle it as lightly as you can, since it bruises easily. Taste, and add dressing as needed.

Divide the dressed arugula among 4 plates. Serve with small bowls of chopped pistachios and chocolate on the side, allowing each eater to sprinkle his or her salad with a bit of each.

Yield: 4 first-course servings

I HAVE LEARNED NOT TO WORRY

Sometimes I still can't believe that I'm old enough to be some-one's wife. How on earth did that happen? It was only a few days ago, I could swear, that I was in the foyer of my parents' house, bumbling and biting my way through my first kiss. It couldn't have been more than a month ago, at most. Sometimes Brandon and I look at each other, shaking our heads, and say, "We're *married?* Get out!" It's a lot to wrap a head around.

Our wedding meant more than just the beginning of our marriage. It meant a new family, one that starts from just the two of us. For me, it also meant walking down the aisle without my father. I never thought I would have to do that.

I remember, in the weeks before our wedding, wondering what he would have said about all this. He would have liked to know Brandon. They would have holed up in his office upstairs, listening to Gene Krupa and talking about beer. It's strange, but sometimes when Bran-don laughs, he sounds exactly like Burg. Sometimes I could swear that he was still here, sitting right next to me. Wherever he is, I would like him to know that my mother gave me his wedding ring, and that we had Brandon's ring made from it, melted down and remolded. I know that he would have wanted that, to be a part of us in some way.

We had an Alice Walker quote printed on the back of our wedding program. "I have learned not to worry about love," it reads, "but to honor its coming with all my heart." It's hard not to worry, honestly, about making this sort of commitment to someone. But I want to honor Brandon. I want to honor what came before us. And I want to honor us.

Sometimes I forget how improbable our story is, and how uncertain it could have felt, because it didn't. I remember telling someone, shortly after I met him, that Brandon was like magic, that he could make things happen. He does, every day. He reminds me of something my mother once said about my father: that one of the things she loved about him was that she could learn so much from him. I know exactly what she means.

I used to think I had a good dowry. I can make a nice meatball and bake a fine chocolate cake. I can find my way without a map around Paris, Seattle, and Oklahoma City. I stand to someday inherit that stunningly ugly ceramic boar that sat on my father's bathroom counter. But Brandon brought with him more than I could have ever thought to want. He brought an eye for vintage champagne glasses, that Caetano Veloso song he always sings in the shower, the crease on top of his nose, and the stunning mess he makes on the kitchen counter. He brought his chana masala, his love for cabbage and chocolate, and his gentle questions about my father, whom he will never meet. He brought that mischievous look that he flashes when he asks if I want a chocolate malt, the radishes and the butter and the salt, and the way he asks me to marry him, grinning, over and over, almost every day. Sometimes when I see him across the room, I can hardly believe that I get to be his wife.

For our rehearsal dinner, we chose a clearing on the property of an old homestead next to a river about fifteen minutes north of Bellingham, with a dozen picnic tables and an old wooden water tower. Brandon's father strung tiny globe lights around the two white tents we rented, and we ran kraft paper down the tables. Then we topped them with small jars of homemade pickles and a larger jar for a centerpiece, filled with blue cornflowers, nigella, lavender, and thistle.

We were aiming for the kind of event where the bride could wear jeans and a ponytail, the kind of evening that goes well with a bottle of Hefeweizen and a game of Frisbee. We ate sandwiches of pulled chicken stuffed into soft rosemary buns. We ate Roma tomatoes roasted to a deep, opaque red, and roasted eggplant and squash and shiitake mushrooms, and cherry tomatoes cooked on the vine. We ate sliced heirloom tomatoes with fresh mozzarella and a fingerling potato salad with sweet onions, little green beans, and mustard vinaigrette. We ate tartlets filled with mascarpone and fat, purply gooseberries, and chocolate chip cookies made with oatmeal and coconut. We ate until dark, which comes late here in the summer, and then the mosquitoes came up from the river and chased us home.

The next day, at four o'clock on a cloudy afternoon, we got married. We stood in a park on the water, between two trees, under an enormous white tent with scalloped edges and open sides, and word has it that someone's dog ran around on the beach behind us for the better part of the ceremony. I also heard that a drunk bum wandered over, which I am grateful to have not noticed, though in retrospect, I like the idea.

I was a mess that day. I woke up feeling out of sorts, and when I sat down next to my mother at breakfast, I burst into tears. I hadn't expected it to feel so strange without my father. Every time I walked down the hallway of the hotel, I saw an aunt or an uncle or an old friend of his from Oklahoma. But he wasn't there. All morning, off and on, I kept catching myself starting to cry. After a while, I wasn't even sure why, which scared me half to death. There are pictures of me getting ready to come down the aisle, my eyes rimmed with red. I am sure that my bridesmaids were secretly devising an emergency plan, in case I should make a run for it.

But then the music started playing, and my mother looped her arm through mine. She walked me down the grassy aisle, both of us teetering in our heels, and she kissed me on each cheek, and then Brandon took my hand. Our friend Shauna was officiating, and it felt good to stand there next to her. My brothers David and Adam stood up and spoke about our family. Brandon's sister Courtney spoke about his family. Keaton talked about that night at the Alibi Room, the day after I first met Brandon. Sam spoke about his friendship with us. Brandon and I had written our own vows, and I sobbed only a little during mine, which at this point felt like a victory. When we kissed, he wrapped his arms around my waist and tipped me back, so that his curls fell onto my cheek. And when he righted me again, everyone clapped and cheered, and we ate potato chips and drank lemonade and walked to the reception with Sam and Brandon's childhood friend Steve carrying my long veil like the train of a dress, and we were married.

When you care about food, and when you're marrying someone who cares about food, and when you met this someone because of food, there is quite a bit of pressure to feed people well at your wedding. We gave it our best shot, and I think we did all right.

There were deviled eggs two ways: with crème fraîche and paddle-fish caviar, or with herbed aioli and capers. There were quartered apricots wrapped in prosciutto and grilled, served on thin toasts and dolloped with goat cheese. There were tiny corn cakes made up like open-faced BLTs, with basil mayonnaise and avocado, and there were toasted baguette slices with butter and radishes and salt. For dinner, there was smoked sockeye salmon with a salsa of nectarines and chiles. There was a fennel salad with shaved Parmesan, and baby beets with blue cheese and hazelnuts. There was a farro salad with feta and caramelized onions, carrots, and celery. And for dessert, there was cake, of course, which I'll tell you more about in a minute, and ice cream. And when my mother stood up and gave her toast, the minute she said my father's name, the sun came out. And then, for once, I wasn't the only one crying.

Our wedding was exactly what I hoped for, and still, when it happened, it felt like a surprise. In that way, it felt just like us. I don't know when I've ever been more proud of the two of us, and of what we love. I also don't know when I've ever been sorrier for not eating more deviled eggs. I'm telling you, and I learned the hard way, don't let socializing get between you and a platter of deviled eggs. And when you've had your fill, take the dance floor with your new husband, preferably to Ella Fitzgerald singing Cole Porter's "Night and Day," and when he dips you at the very end, when the horns are blaring, close your eyes tight and thank the heavens that the planning is through, and that the beer is cold, and that you can dance, dance, dance.

LITTLE CORN CAKES WITH BACON, TOMATO, AND AVOCADO

Adapted from Ciaò Thyme Catering and Doug Doolittle

In most circles, the words *wedding food* aren't exactly synonymous with *delicious food*. We wanted ours to be different. When we started planning, the caterer was one of the first elements we considered. In the end, when we decided to get married in Bellingham, we chose it not only because it was pretty and on the water and so on, but also because of the caterer we found there, Ciaò Thyme. When we asked them to make fingerling potato chips for after the ceremony, they clapped. When we said that we wanted deviled eggs during the cocktail hour, they grinned and started gushing about aioli and the hens at a farm nearby. And at the end of the night, they danced with us and kissed us both on the cheeks.

The recipe for these hors d'œuvres requires a little time and advance planning, but they're well worth the effort. For a vegetarian version, try replacing the bacon with thinly shaved Parmigiano-Reggiano cheese.

FOR THE ROASTED TOMATOES

½ pound cherry tomatoes (about 30 tomatoes), halved

2 teaspoons olive oil

FOR THE BACON

10 slices thin-cut bacon

FOR THE CORN CAKES

1 medium ear of corn

½ cup fine cornmeal

½ cup cake flour

2 teaspoons baking powder

¼ teaspoon baking soda

½ teaspoon kosher salt

½ cup whole milk (not low fat or nonfat)

¼ cup water

1 tablespoon canola oil, plus more for brushing the pan

1 tablespoon pure maple syrup

1¼ teaspoons apple cider vinegar

FOR SERVING

Good-tasting mayonnaise, such as Hellmann's

1 medium avocado, quartered from end to end and thinly sliced

A handful of fresh basil leaves, sliced thinly

Crunchy salt, such as Maldon salt or fleur de sel

First, prepare the tomatoes. Set an oven rack to the middle position, and preheat the oven to 325°F. Put the tomatoes on a rimmed baking sheet. Drizzle them with the oil, and use your hands to toss them gently, arranging them cut side up. Bake for 30 to 35 minutes, until they shrink slightly and their edges are gently shriveled. Set aside to cool. (Tomatoes may be roasted up to 3 days ahead. Refrigerate in an airtight container and bring to room temperature before serving.)

Next, prepare the bacon. Turn the oven temperature up to 400°F. Arrange the bacon slices in a single layer on a rimmed baking sheet. Bake until the fat begins to render, about 5 minutes. Rotate the pan, and continue to bake until the bacon is crisp and lightly browned, 5 to 6 minutes more. Transfer with tongs to a paper-towel-lined plate, and cool briefly. Using your fingers, snap each strip of bacon into 5 to 6 small "chips," each 1 to 1½ inches long.

Next, prepare the corn cakes. Put a small, heavy skillet (preferably cast iron) over medium-high heat. While it warms, use a sharp knife to cut the kernels from the ear of corn. Discard the cob. When the pan is hot, add the kernels and cook, shaking the pan occasionally, until the corn is browned in spots and fragrant, 30 seconds to 1 minute. Remove the pan from the heat, and scrape the kernels into the bowl of a food processor. Allow to cool.

While the corn cools, prepare the batter. In a medium bowl, combine the cornmeal, cake flour, baking powder, baking soda, and salt, and whisk to mix well.

In a Pyrex measuring cup, combine the milk, water, oil, and maple syrup, whisking or stirring with a fork to blend. (Do not add the vinegar yet.)

When the corn is cool, process it briefly in the food processor, until it is finely chopped. You want it to have some texture, but no big lumps. Add the corn to the dry ingredients, along with the wet ingredients and the vinegar, and whisk to just combine. The batter will foam a bit and thicken. Allow it to rest for 5 minutes.

Meanwhile, warm a nonstick pan or griddle over medium heat. When the pan is hot, brush it lightly with oil. Scoop the batter by the teaspoonful into the pan, forming round cakes about 1½ inches in diameter. Do not crowd the pan. Cook for about two minutes on the first side, until golden, then gently flip and continue cooking until the second side is cooked, another minute or less.

Transfer the finished cakes to a platter while you cook the rest of the batter, brushing the pan lightly with oil between each batch. (Corn cakes can be made up to 2 weeks ahead and stored in a ziplock freezer bag in the freezer. Thaw at room temperature, then revive their texture with a quick pass through a low oven or toaster oven.)

To finish, top each corn cake with a smear of mayonnaise. Place a slice of avocado on top of the mayonnaise, then a "chip" of bacon atop the avocado, and then a roasted tomato half, and finally a thin ribbon of basil. Sprinkle with a small pinch of salt. Serve immediately.

NOTE: These corn cakes, made a little bigger, would be good for breakfast, too. Just drop the tomatoes, avocado, mayonnaise, and basil, and serve instead with a fried egg and bacon.

Yield: about 4½ dozen corn cakes

WINNING HEARTS AND MINDS

E veryone needs a chocolate cake in her repertoire. Actually, if we're really going to get down to it, a good soup is also important, and a basic vinaigrette, and at least one type of cookie. But a chocolate cake is essential.

The dense, silky thing I call "my" chocolate cake was inspired by a recipe I found in a French cookbook a few years ago, a recipe for what is commonly, on that side of the Atlantic, called a *fondant au chocolat*. Derived from the verb *fondre*, or "to melt," its name translates roughly to "melting chocolate cake," which, I would argue, is what all chocolate cakes should be. It contains nearly half a pound of chocolate and an equal amount of butter, five eggs, about one cup of sugar, and a single tablespoon of flour. In the oven, it puffs like a bastardized soufflé, and when it cools, its crust crackles like the top of a brownie. When you slice it, it yields to the knife like soft fudge. I first made it only a handful of months before I met Brandon, and I don't think the timing was coincidental.

At the time, I was newly single and doing what felt, to me at least, like a lot of dating. I even asked out my cashier at the grocery store, however unsuccessfully. That fall, I made my chocolate cake for every man I dated, all two of them. I also made it once for my friend Kate, who requested the recipe immediately. Soon she had baked it for a guy she was seeing, and then again for an old flame who came to visit. She even called once from Jackson Hole, where she was skiing with friends for the weekend, to request an emergency reminder of the ingredient quantities, so that she could make it for a guy she'd just met. It was Kate who gave the *fondant au chocolat* the name by which it is now known: "The Winning Hearts and Minds Cake." Because, politics aside, that's what it does. It's not something you want to serve to someone you feel so-so about. It's what you serve when you want his undivided attention.

I would have made my chocolate cake for Brandon on his first visit to Seattle, had we had more than thirty-six hours together. I knew that I wanted him to stick around. I made it on his second visit, and his third, and his fourth.

When it came time to choose our wedding cake, we were adamant about one thing: it had to taste good. We didn't need a white cake, or frosting, for that matter, or multiple tiers, swags, or rosettes. We didn't even need to hire someone to make it. I wanted to do it myself. First I thought about banana cupcakes with a bittersweet ganache. I even tested a few recipes, one of which was pretty promising. But then, one night, I made the Winning Hearts and Minds Cake for a dinner party. Brandon walked into the kitchen as I was pouring the batter into the pan, and he took one look at it and said, "Why aren't we having *that* for our wedding cake?"

He knows a good thing when he sees it.

So I made twenty of them. It wasn't nearly as bad as it sounds. It was actually sort of therapeutic. The Winning Hearts and Minds Cake is a breeze to make, and it freezes beautifully. All I had to do was stir, bake, wrap, and freeze; stir, bake, wrap, and freeze; stir, bake, wrap, and freeze. The day before the wedding, our friends Ashley and Chris retrieved them from our freezer and delivered them to the caterer, each cake snug in its own 10-inch pizza box. It was the easiest wedding cake, or cakes, I can imagine. They weren't beauty queens, with their thick waists and crackly, crinkled skin, but I didn't care. The work-to-pleasure ratio was about 1:10, which is just the way I like it.

Our guests apparently liked it, too. I'd never seen so many empty, chocolate-smeared plates as I saw that night, scattered across tables and perched atop chairs. We had only three cakes left over, which we sent home with anyone who wanted them. My sister Lisa took one back to her hotel room. I later heard that the next morning, when she went to check out, she accidentally left it in the mini-bar refrigerator. By the time she got back upstairs to retrieve it, the housekeeper had come with her cart and its enormous trash can, on whose rim was now balanced, ever so precariously, the cake in its pizza box. Lisa was undeterred. She took it anyway. That's high praise for a wedding cake, I would say. The Winning Hearts and Minds Cake never fails.

The day after Brandon's first visit to Seattle, which now seems like pleasantly ancient history, I sent Kate an e-mail.

"He was *amazing*," I gushed. "So sweet. So funny. I drove him to the airport this morning and cried all the way home. I think this might be the best thing that's ever happened to me. And the hardest."

"I'm *so* excited for you," she gushed in reply. "You've been taking this on with your whole heart and that oversized mind of yours. Don't stop now. This is the bread and butter! This is what it's all about."

I burst into tears when I read that. I've never forgotten it. When I was making our wedding cakes, all those hours at the oven, all that stirring and baking, I kept saying it. *This is the bread and butter. This is what it's all about.*

It's going to sound silly, I know, but I think that what it all comes down to is winning hearts and minds. Underneath everything else, all the plans and goals and hopes, that's why we get up in the morning, why we believe, why we try, why we bake chocolate cakes. That's the best we can ever hope to do: to win hearts and minds, to love and be loved.

THE WINNING HEARTS AND MINDS CAKE
OR, OUR WEDDING CAKE

*t*his recipe is as simple as can be: all it takes is five ingredients, a bowl, a spoon, and a cake pan. Because it's all about chocolate, you'll want a good one whose flavor you love, with 60 to 70% cocoa solids. I like Scharffen Berger quite a bit, but in a pinch, I've also used Ghirardelli 60% chips. They have a nice flavor and are very inexpensive, and you don't even have to chop them, which saves a lot of time.

Also, note that this cake freezes surprisingly well. In fact, its texture and flavor are actually *improved* by freezing. Try to make it far enough in advance that you can freeze it for at least a day or so, and be sure to allow 24 hours for it to then return to room temperature before serving. It's worth the trouble.

---

7 ounces bittersweet chocolate, finely
  chopped
1¾ sticks (7 ounces) unsalted butter,
  cut into ½-inch cubes
1 cup plus 2 tablespoons granulated
  sugar

5 large eggs
1 tablespoon unbleached all-purpose
  flour
Lightly sweetened whipped cream,
  for serving

Preheat the oven to 375°F, and butter an 8-inch round cake pan. Line the bottom of the pan with a round of parchment paper, and butter the paper, too.

Put the chocolate and butter in a medium microwavable bowl. Microwave on high for 30 seconds at a time, stirring often, until just smooth. (Alternatively, you can melt the chocolate and butter in a double boiler or a heatproof bowl set over, but not touching, barely simmering water.) When the mixture is smooth, add the sugar, stirring well to incorporate. Set the batter aside to cool for 5 minutes. Then add the eggs one by one, stirring well after each addition. Add the flour and stir to mix well. The batter should be dark and silky.

Pour the batter into the prepared pan, and bake for about 25 minutes, or until the top is lightly crackled, the edges are puffed, and the center of the cake looks set. I usually set the timer for 20 minutes to start with, and then I check the cake every 2 minutes after that, until it's ready. At 20 minutes, the center of the cake is usually still quite jiggly; you'll know it's done when the center only jiggles *slightly*, if at all.

Remove the cake from the oven to a cooling rack, and let it cool in the pan for 15 minutes. Carefully turn it out of the pan and then flip it onto a serving plate, so that the crackly side faces up. Since the cake is fairly delicate, this can be tricky, but I've found that the easiest way is as follows.

Place a sheet of aluminum foil over the pan, and place a large, flat plate—*not* the serving plate—on top of the foil, facing down. (A small sheet pan would also work.) Hold the cake pan and plate firmly together and quickly, carefully, flip them. The pan should now be on top of the plate, with the foil between them. Remove the pan, revealing the cake, which is now upside-down. Remove the parchment paper. Place the serving plate gently atop the cake. Wedging your index fingers between the plates to keep from squishing the cake, flip them so that the cake is now right side up. Remove the foil.

Cool completely before serving, preferably with lightly sweetened whipped cream.

NOTE: This cake can be kept at room temperature, sealed in plastic wrap, for up to 3 days, or it can be refrigerated for up to 5 days. (Be sure to bring it to room temperature before serving.) To freeze it, wrap it tightly in plastic wrap and then foil, and it will keep for up to a month. Before serving, defrost at room temperature for 24 hours, still fully wrapped.

Yield: 6 to 8 servings

RECIPE INDEX

a

apples, *tarte tatin*, 108–9

apricots, honeyed, pistachio cake with, 278–79

arugula:
  bread salad with cherries, goat cheese and, 115–16
  salad with pistachios and chocolate, 296–97

Asian pear, fennel salad with Parmesan and, 238–39

avocado:
  little corn cakes with bacon, tomato and, 304–6
  sliced spring salad with feta and, 246–47

b

bacon, little corn cakes with tomato, avocado and, 304–6

banana bread with chocolate and crystallized ginger, 26–27

basil pesto, 273–74

beans, Ed Fretwell soup, 156–58

bittersweet glaze, chocolate cupcakes with, 44–45

black pepper:
  pickled grapes with cinnamon and, 291
  red cabbage salad with lemon and, 222
  –vanilla ice cream, 285–86

blueberry-raspberry pound cake, 20–21

bouchons au thon, 101

bread:
  banana, with chocolate and crystallized ginger, 26–27
  and chocolate, 64
  crumbs, 168
  salad with cherries, arugula, and goat cheese, 115–16

buckwheat pancakes, 68–69

Burg's French toast, 39–40

Burg's potato salad, 14–15

butter:
  microwaving, 68
  and radishes with fleur de sel, 216–17

buttermilk vanilla bean cake with glazed oranges and crème fraîche, 88–90

butternut soup with pear, cider, and vanilla bean, 226–27

c

cabbage:
  cream-braised green, 186–87
  red, salad with lemon and black
    pepper, 222
cakes:
  French-style yogurt, with lemon,
    204–5
  fresh ginger, with caramelized pears,
    75–76
  little corn, with bacon, tomato, and
    avocado, 304–6
  pistachio, with honeyed apricots,
    278–79
  pound, blueberry-raspberry, 20–21
  vanilla bean buttermilk, with glazed
    oranges and crème fraîche, 88–90
  wedding (winning hearts and minds),
    312–13
candy, espresso-walnut toffee, 82–83
caramelized cauliflower with salsa
    verde, 271–72
carrots, spicy pickled, with garlic and
    thyme, 290
cauliflower, caramelized, with salsa
    verde, 271–72
chana masala, 232–33
cherries:
  bread salad with arugula, goat cheese
    and, 115–16
  dried, cranberry chutney with
    crystallized ginger and, 210–11
chickpeas, chana masala, 232–33
chocolate:
  arugula salad with pistachios and,
    296–97
  banana bread with crystallized ginger
    and, 26–27
  bread and, 64
  cupcakes with bittersweet glaze,
    44–45

ganache, coconut macaroons with,
    94–95
Hoosier pie, 55–57
white, *cœur à la crème* with raspberry
    purée, 33–34
chutney, cranberry, with crystallized
    ginger and dried cherries, 210–11
cider:
  butternut soup with pear, vanilla bean
    and, 226–27
  -glazed salmon (*saumon gelée à la
    Louis XIV*), 181–82
citrus fruit:
  glazed, vanilla bean buttermilk cake
    with crème fraîche and, 88–90
  stewed prunes with cinnamon and,
    49
coconut macaroons with chocolate
    ganache, 94–95
cœur à la crème with raspberry purée,
    33–34
cookies:
  coconut macaroons with chocolate
    ganache, 94–95
  fruit-nut balls, 80–81
  pink, Jimmy's, 132–33
corn, little cakes with bacon, tomato,
    and avocado, 304–6
corn bread, custard-filled, 251–52
cranberry chutney with crystallized
    ginger and dried cherries,
    210–11
cream-braised green cabbage, 186–87
crème fraîche, vanilla bean buttermilk
    cake with glazed oranges and,
    88–90
cupcakes, chocolate, with bittersweet
    glaze, 44–45
custard-filled corn bread, 251–52

d

Doron's meatballs with pine nuts, cilantro, and golden raisins, 168–69
dried fruit pie, 147–49
Dutch baby pancakes with lemon and sugar, 131

e

Ed Fretwell soup, 156–58
eggplant, roasted, ratatouille, 124–25
eggs:
    ham, and mustard vinaigrette, frisée with, 264–65
    Italian grotto, 140
espresso-walnut toffee, 82–83

f

fennel(s):
    salad with Asian pear and Parmesan, 238–39
    two, tomato soup with, 256–57
feta, sliced spring salad with avocado and, 246–47
fleur de sel, radishes and butter with, 216–17
French-style yogurt cake with lemon, 204–5
French toast, Burg's, 39–40
fresh ginger cake with caramelized pears, 75–76
frisée with ham, eggs, and mustard vinaigrette, 264–65
frosting:
    for Jimmy's pink cookies, 132–33
    lemon icing, 204–5
fruit:
    dried, pie, 147–49
    -nut balls, 80–81

g

ginger:
    crystallized, banana bread with chocolate and, 26–27
    crystallized, cranberry chutney with dried cherries and, 210–11
    fresh, cake with caramelized pears, 75–76
    Scottish scones with lemon and, 174–75
glaze, bittersweet, 44–45
goat cheese:
    bread salad with cherries, arugula and, 115–16
    Italian grotto eggs, 140
    sliced spring salad with avocado and feta, 246–47
graham cracker crust, rum cream pie with, 150–51
grapes, pickled, with cinnamon and black pepper, 291

h

ham, eggs, and mustard vinaigrette, frisée with, 264–65
honeyed apricots, pistachio cake with, 278–79
Hoosier pie, 55–57

i

ice cream, vanilla–black pepper, 285–86
Italian grotto eggs, 140

j

Jimmy's pink cookies, 132–33

l

lemon:
  Dutch baby pancakes with sugar and, 131
  French-style yogurt cake with, 204–5
  icing, 204–5
  red cabbage salad with black pepper and, 222
  Scottish scones with ginger and, 174–75

m

macaroons, coconut, with chocolate ganache, 94–95
meatballs, Doron's, with pine nuts, cilantro, and golden raisins, 168–69
mustard vinaigrette, 264–65

n

noodles, zucchini with pesto, 273–74
nuts:
  arugula salad with pistachios and chocolate, 296–97
  espresso-walnut toffee, 82–83
  fruit-nut balls, 80–81
  Hoosier pie, 55–57
  pine, Doron's meatballs with cilantro, golden raisins and, 168–69
  pistachio cake with honeyed apricots, 278–79

o

oranges, glazed, vanilla bean buttermilk cake with crème fraîche and, 88–90

p

pancakes:
  buckwheat, 68–69
  Dutch baby, with lemon and sugar, 131
pears:
  Asian, fennel salad with Parmesan and, 238–39
  butternut soup with cider, vanilla bean and, 226–27
  caramelized, fresh ginger cake with, 75–76
pecans, Hoosier pie, 55–57
pesto, zucchini noodles with, 273–74
pickled carrots, spicy, with garlic and thyme, 290
pickled grapes with cinnamon and black pepper, 291
pies:
  dried fruit, 147–49
  Hoosier, 55–57
  rum cream, with graham cracker crust, 150–51
pine nuts, cilantro, and golden raisins, Doron's meatballs with, 168–69
pistachio(s):
  arugula salad with chocolate and, 296–97
  cake with honeyed apricots, 278–79
potato salad, Burg's, 14–15
pound cake, blueberry-raspberry, 20–21
prunes, stewed with citrus and cinnamon, 49
puff pastry, for *tarte tatin*, 108–9

r

radishes and butter with fleur de sel, 216–17
raisins, golden, Doron's meatballs with pine nuts, cilantro and, 168–69

ranch dressing, 14–15
raspberry:
  -blueberry pound cake, 20–21
  purée, *cœur à la crème* with, 33–34
ratatouille, roasted eggplant, 124–25
red cabbage salad with lemon and black
    pepper, 222
roasted eggplant ratatouille, 124–25
rum cream pie with graham cracker
    crust, 150–51

∫

salad dressings:
  mustard vinaigrette, 264–65
  ranch, 14–15
  vinaigrette, 246–47
salads:
  arugula, with pistachios and
    chocolate, 296–97
  bread, with cherries, arugula, and
    goat cheese, 115–16
  fennel, with Asian pear and
    Parmesan, 238–39
  frisée with ham, eggs, and mustard
    vinaigrette, 264–65
  potato, Burg's, 14–15
  red cabbage, with lemon and black
    pepper, 222
  sliced spring, with avocado and feta,
    246–47
salmon, cider-glazed (*saumon gelée à la
    Louis XIV*), 181–82
salsa verde, caramelized cauliflower
    with, 271–72
sauce, yogurt, 168–69
Scottish scones with lemon and ginger,
    174–75
sliced spring salad with avocado and
    feta, 246–47

slow-roasted tomatoes with coriander,
    192
soups:
  butternut, with pear, cider, and
    vanilla bean, 226–27
  Ed Fretwell, 156–58
  tomato, with two fennels, 256–57
spicy pickled carrots with garlic and
    thyme, 290
stewed prunes with citrus and
    cinnamon, 49

t

tarte tatin, 108–9
toffee, espresso-walnut, 82–83
tomatoes:
  chana masala, 232–33
  little corn cakes with bacon, avocado
    and, 304–6
  roasted, 304–5
  slow-roasted, with coriander, 192
  soup with two fennels, 256–57
tuna, *bouchons au thon*, 101

u

vanilla bean:
  buttermilk cake with glazed oranges
    and crème fraîche, 88–90
  butternut soup with pear, cider and,
    226–27
vanilla–black pepper ice cream, 285–86
vinaigrette, 246–47
  mustard, 264–65

w

walnut-espresso toffee, 82–83
wedding cake (winning hearts and
    minds), 312–13

Y

yogurt cake with lemon, French style,
204–5
yogurt sauce, 168–69

Z

zucchini:
noodles with pesto, 273–74
roasted eggplant ratatouille, 124–25

SIMON & SCHUSTER
READING GROUP GUIDE

A HOMEMADE LIFE

stories and recipes from my kitchen table

INTRODUCTION

A Homemade Life by Molly Wizenberg, freelance food writer and creator of the award-winning blog Orangette, is part touching personal memoir, part wonderful recipe collection. Molly recounts a life with food at its heart, where delicious recipes intertwine with the stories of her family, growing up, beginning a blog, even meeting and marrying her husband. Written in a lively, accessible style, *A Homemade Life* is as much at home on the bookshelf as it is in the kitchen.

DISCUSSION QUESTIONS

1. In her introduction, Molly describes her love for the intangible things about cooking. She explains, "When we fall in love with a certain dish, I think that's what we're often responding to: that something else behind the fork or the spoon, the familiar story that food tells" (p. 2). Are there any dishes that you associate with a particular story, person, time, or place? Describe those dishes and the intangible meaning they have for you.

2. Molly's father Burg was an important presence in her life. She describes him as "a real character, a very kind person, and even sort of a sap, but he could also be very difficult. He was not some mythic figure sent from on high" (p. 183). What do you think were Burg's strengths and weaknesses?

3. "When I was little, I thought my mother came from the most perfect family." (p. 51). Later in the book Molly explains that she was closer to her mother than her father, but she spends more of *A Homemade Life* describing Burg and his outsized personality. Why do you think this is?

4. Based on her description of her parents, what traits do you think Molly inherited from each of them? How do you think those traits affect her life?

5. People often associate food with celebrations and holidays. In the chapter "Italian Grotto Eggs" (p. 135), however, Molly describes a dish she made for Burg as he was dying of cancer. How did the egg dish provide relief for Burg? How did it provide relief for Molly? Do you associate any recipes with a sad or tragic memory?

6. Molly describes meeting her future husband online in the chapter "Baby Steps" (p. 195). Does making a romantic connection online hold any connotations for you? If a friend told you she was going to meet someone who emailed her blog, what would you think?

7. In the chapter "Summer of Change," Molly admits, "Whenever I don't know what to do, Paris is where I've gone" (p. 162), and she has spent a significant amount of time there. What does Paris mean to Molly? What does it provide her?

8. What does the concept "whatever you love, you are" (p. 153) mean to Molly? How did she use it to better understand her father?

9. Throughout the book, Molly mentions that she has difficulty embracing change, that she likes the concept of routines—almost to the point of being boring. What are the aspects, both positive and negative, of this character trait?

10. Molly defines happiness as "a pan of slow-roasted tomatoes" (p. 189). Can something specific and tangible define happiness? If so, what defines happiness for you?

11. When her father was near death, Molly states, "I know it's awful to say it, but I was so relieved that morning, when I saw the splotches. I didn't want to stop him. I was terrified of stopping him. I pulled my hand away from his face. I stood up, ran my fin-

gers down his forearm to smooth the hair, and stepped back. Then I left the room, and I don't remember what I did" (p. 144). The sentences leading up to the last are descriptively vivid. Why do you think Molly doesn't remember after that point?

12. In the chapter "The Hardball Stage" (p. 72), Molly shares the story she wrote as a teenager about, as she puts it, "how one wordy teenager found her way into the kitchen." What does the essay reveal about her relationship to her family? about her relationship to food? Optional exercise: Write a personal food-related story to share with the group.

13. What do you think *A Homemade Life* means to Molly? What does it mean to you?

ENHANCE YOUR BOOK CLUB

Check out Molly's award-winning blog: www.Orangette.blogspot.com. Using Molly's blog photos as inspiration, have your book club members take photos of some of their favorite foods. Bring them to the book club discussion to display.

For your book club discussion, bring a box of orangettes. They can be ordered from online retailers like www.ChocolatDuMonde.com or make them yourself (www.About.com offers a recipe). Or select one of the recipes in the book to make and share at the meeting.

Make your own cookbook. Each member of the group can contribute a favorite recipe (or recipes) and brief stories that explain them. Use photos if you have them—and be sure to include a photo of the members of the group! Organize all the materials in a booklet and share copies with the group.

A Conversation with
Molly Wizenberg

Can you tell us a bit about your life since publishing A Homemade Life? *Have there been any special projects, meals, or recipes? Does Seattle still feel like home for both you and Brandon?*

It's been busy around here, to say the least! In August of 2009, Brandon and I opened a restaurant. It's called Delancey, and it's in the Ballard neighborhood of Seattle. It's a Brooklyn-style wood-fired pizzeria, inspired by all the great pies that Brandon grew up eating in New York and New Jersey. A restaurant is probably the last thing that anyone expected of us, given that Brandon is a musician by training, and that I've written quite a bit about how much I dislike (!) working in a restaurant kitchen, but what can you do? He makes a killer pizza. I'm so proud of him.

Do you still enjoy writing your blog, Orangette? *Has it changed since you began it in 2004?*

I love writing for the blog. Probably more than ever, actually. The blog is where I can be the most spontaneous in my writing, where I can really play. It's also an incredible community. I'm continually blown away by the conversations that crop up in comments, by the people that I've met, by the way it has completely reshaped my life over the past six years. It sounds cheesy, but I mean every word.

At your book events or through your blog, do readers ever share their own food stories with you? Does one of these stand out in particular?

Absolutely. Talking with readers and hearing their stories has been my favorite part of book events. When I write, I feel as though I'm having a conversation with my readers—only, the thing is, I never actually get to see their faces or hear their voices. Book events give me that chance, and I'm so grateful for it. The fact that food gives us a common ground to meet on, that it gives us something to share—that's what it's all about. Now I'm really sounding cheesy.

Does Paris continue to be a special place for you? Have you been back since the publication of your book?

Paris will always be a special place for me. I haven't been back since the book came out—this year was so busy!—but Brandon and I are hoping to steal away for a trip sometime in 2010. I miss it.

List three items that are in your refrigerator right now, and what significance they have for you.

Peanut butter—it's not glamorous, but I could eat it every day. I'm pretty sure my body is at least 75 percent peanut butter.

Maple syrup—this particular jug of syrup was given to me by one of my readers. It came from her trees in upstate New York, and it's fantastic. I don't think there could possibly be a better present than maple syrup from your very own trees.

Apples from the farmers' market—one of the best parts of living in Washington! There's one stand in particular that has lots of heirloom apples, and they have the best names. Right now, I've got a couple of Black Twigs, one Gold Rush, and a couple of Waltanas.

In A Homemade Life *you write about both of your parents, but there seem to be more stories about your father and his outsized personality. Is there a reason for this?*

I needed to write about my father. There were so many details and moments and stories that made up who he was to me, and I didn't want to forget. I needed to write about him to assure myself that I would remember. But I also needed to write about him so that I could start to let go of some of the harder moments of his illness and his death. In putting them down on paper, I got to take them out of my head and store them somewhere else. I didn't know it until I was deep into the book, but I still had a lot of grieving to do, and writing helped me to do it.

Has your relationship with your mother changed in the years since the death of your father?
We were always close, and we still are. But we've become more intentional about spending time together. It's not easy, since we live far apart, but every year, the two of us go away together, just for a few days, and do lots of eating and drinking and catching up.

From potato salad to Christmas cookies to Hoosier Pie, in the book you describe many recipes that are traditions in your family. Have you and Brandon created any new traditional recipes?
We're still pretty fixated on Hoosier Pie, to tell you the truth! Old traditions die hard—or however the saying goes. But we're making new ones, too. Slowly but surely I've taken to making the same chocolate layer cake for our birthdays every year, and I get irrationally excited about it. I'm still working on the frosting, though. Maybe this will be my lucky year.

What is your opinion of the slow food movement in this country? Do you believe it is on the rise? How do you think the current economy has or will affect it?
Anything that encourages people to eat more real food and less processed food, to find pleasure in cooking and sharing food, is a great thing.

What are you working on now? Do you have plans to write another book?
Well, I'm into my third year of writing a monthly column for *Bon Appétit* and my sixth year at Orangette, both of which keep me busy!

I'm also the de facto manager / wineglass polisher / baseboard scrubber / errand runner / CFO of Delancey, and that keeps me even busier. (Or crazier, depending on your point of view.) But I do want to write another book, and getting a start on that is my goal for 2010. Fingers crossed.

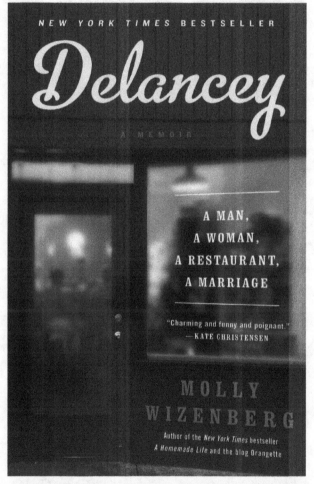